Managing Technical People

INNOVATION, TEAMWORK, AND
THE SOFTWARE PROCESS

Watts S. Humphrey
Carnegie Mellon University

 **ADDISON-WESLEY**

An imprint of Addison Wesley Longman, Inc.

Reading, Massachusetts • Harlow, England • Menlo Park, California
Berkeley, California • Don Mills, Ontario • Sydney
Bonn • Amsterdam • Tokyo • Mexico City

 **Software Engineering Institute**

The SEI Series in Software Engineering

The cover art is reproduced courtesy of SuperStock, Inc.

Portions of this book were previously published by Prentice-Hall.

Library of Congress Cataloging-in-Publication Data

Humphrey, Watts S., 1927–
    Managing technical people : innovation, teamwork, and the software process / Watts S. Humphrey.
        p.   cm. — (The SEI series in software engineering)
    Includes bibliographical references and index.
    ISBN 0-201-54597-7
    1. Computer software—Development—Management.   2. Industrial project management.   I. Title.   II. Series.
    QA76.76.D47H86   1997
    005.1'068'3—DC20   96-41109
                                                                          CIP

Access the latest information about Addison-Wesley books from our World Wide Web page: http://www.aw.com/cseng

1 2 3 4 5 6 7 8 9 10-MA-00 99 98 97 96

In memory of Al Pietrasanta,
a fine engineer and a good friend

Preface

Have you ever noticed how one project will succeed and another fail? On my first management job, I was assigned to a partially completed project. A small crew of inexperienced engineers was developing a complex cryptographic communications system for the U.S. Army Signal Corps. Even though none of them had previous development experience, they completed the work on time and met all the government's specifications. From the very beginning, I could sense that this was a winning team. They were energetic, enthusiastic, and excited about their work. What causes some teams to have this winning quality, and how can managers help their teams to achieve it?

This book has grown from my years in technical management. It captures my experiences as well as lessons I have learned from the many fine people I have worked with in nearly 50 years as an engineer, manager, and executive. During my 27 years with IBM, I was involved in developing the enormously successful IBM 360 and 370 systems. I also managed much of IBM's commercial software development for both the 360 and 370 systems and spent several years in IBM corporate finance. I was also Director of IBM's Glendale Development Laboratory and the 2000 engineers who developed IBM's intermediate-range computing systems, printers, banking products, and software systems.

Since retiring from IBM, I have worked for another 10 years at the Software Engineering Institute (SEI) at Carnegie Mellon University. Here, I founded and led the Process Program and have been named an SEI Fellow. During this time, I have been fortunate to participate in many innovative hardware and software projects and have been exposed to both successful and unsuccessful projects at many development organizations throughout the world.

Although some of the experiences described in this book happened many years ago, their lessons are as true today as they were then. History is a marvelous teacher as long as we are willing to learn. In this book, I have captured some of the lessons that I have found most helpful. I hope you will find them helpful as well.

The Importance of Commitment

It has long been recognized that the dedication which produces superior performance is best obtained through deep personal commitment. Truly outstanding achievements generally result from a dedicated drive to meet defined goals. The foundation for such a commitment is belief in the goal and a strong desire to achieve it. When people want to accomplish something so deeply that they put everything else aside, they often perform at their very best. In fact, they occasionally go far beyond what they thought possible. That is the kind of dedication that breaks the four-minute mile, invents the electric light bulb, or deciphers the structure of the DNA molecule. Such deeds are not done casually or by people who don't care. They come from hard work and from the dedication of people who are deeply and personally committed. Commitment is the first step in achieving superior performance. This is as true for modern technology as it is in any other field.

Suppose, for example, you needed a new computer program. You would want the programmers to give this work high priority and to dedicate their energies to its success. Although no simple procedure can ensure they do this, there are some methods that usually work. Many managers can achieve such dedicated performance occasionally, and some managers seem to do it almost at will. The key is to understand and respect the employees and to follow sound management principles. This knowledge and these principles are the subjects of this book.

The Manager's Role in Innovation

Among the many factors that can improve professional performance are self-confidence, skill, and respect. Negatives that can block creativity include boredom, resentment, or simple misunderstandings. Some conditions are constant, while others are positive at one moment and negative at another. Some teams perform well at one time but later, when faced with seemingly identical circumstances, are not productive at all. The complexity of professional performance comes from the inherent complexity of the professionals themselves—that is, from human nature. Every professional has talents, desires, and fears, and these are the variables the manager must work with to obtain the dedication that produces superior performance.

There is no single formula for achieving superior results. This is a people problem, and people are all different. The best you, the manager, can hope for is to know and care about the people who work for you and to understand what has succeeded in similar situations in the past. Then apply this history with a healthy sprinkling of common sense.

In striving for superior performance, you need to combine many elements:

- A challenging and worthy goal

- Talented, motivated, and capable people

- The training and support to enable the work to be properly done

- A manager with the drive and vision to make it happen

- A leader who understands and cares about his or her followers

Although each of these elements may vary in type and degree, they must all be present. This book talks about these elements and some of the steps managers can take to supply them.

The Book's Structure

Employee commitment can be obtained only by leadership. Leaders must establish the goals and convince their subordinates to accept them as their own. Part One deals with the elements of leadership and those leadership standards that sustain dedication and enthusiasm. The manager's leadership largely determines the organization's performance. Starting with leadership principles in Chapter 1, the key standards of commitment, professionalism, and respect for individuals are treated in Chapters 2, 3, and 4.

Without motivated and capable employees, no technical organization can prosper. Part 2 discusses motivating and developing individual professionals. The goals of engineers and scientists are the subject of Chapter 5, Chapter 6 describes the way professionals' attitudes change throughout their careers, and Chapter 7 outlines the application of situational leadership to the management of technical and professional people. Chapter 8 focuses on the professionals' responsibility to learn the technical methods of their chosen fields and to apply them with discipline.

Efforts spent in identifying and developing the careers of future leaders of the organization are the most important investment any management can make. Part 3 addresses the identification of the technical and managerial professionals who will lead the organization: Identifying talented people is described in Chapter 9, while Chapters 10 and 11 discuss the development of high-potential technical professionals and future executives.

To be successful, most organizations must innovate. Part 4 describes the innovation process and techniques for ensuring its effectiveness. Innovation is a structured process involving creative professionals, resources, and opportunity management. The key, however, is the skill and competence with which management combines these elements into an overall effective process. Chapter 12 discusses the importance of innovation in modern technology, and Chapter 13 describes the innovation process as well as the roles of inventor, champion, and sponsor.

Since much of the work in high technology is too massive to be handled by individuals, the basic working unit is the technical team. Part 5 examines technical teams: Chapter 14 describes their structure and behavior, Chapter 15 outlines some useful principles for managing teams, Chapter 16 summarizes the key environmental needs of innovative teams, and Chapter 17 discusses reward and recognition programs. Chapter 18 outlines the special characteristics of the most important team in the organization: the management team.

Major technical projects can involve hundreds or even thousands of professionals working in many separate teams. Such work is generally supported by administrative staffs and organizational support systems. If these systems are properly designed, they will assist the manager in controlling the work, but inappropriate structures will be a serious impediment. Part 6 deals with organizational structures: Chapter 19 summarizes the principles for structuring technical organizations and the need for integration mechanisms. Chapter 20 discusses the changes in management style as organizations grow and the impact of these changes on innovation. Chapter 21 reviews the political nature of the technical manager's job and the relationship between power and bureaucratic behavior.

The technical manager's job is to introduce new products, develop better processes, and solve new problems. While this invariably involves change, each change in advancing technology is progressively more difficult. The most effective way to handle this growing complexity is to build the organization itself so it can handle the more challenging problems of the future. Part 7 deals with this vital dimension of modern technical management. When organizational problems are structural, they can be addressed through organizational change, as described in Chapter 22. When, as described in Chapter 23, the change involves the working processes, however, it must be handled more carefully. Often, organizations face fundamental problems, and a more formal change process is required to address the attitudes and practices of the managers and professionals. This assessment process is outlined in Chapter 24.

Part 8 addresses the management strategy for introducing and managing change. A management strategy is particularly important because managers must lead and guide their people as they work to change and improve the organization. Chapter 25 describes the principles of process maturity, why they are important, and how they are used. Chapter 26 then outlines a process maturity-based strategy for improving the organization's resource management. This covers the improvement priority for the people-development and support actions. Chapter 27 describes a management strategy for process improvement and the manager's responsibilities at each step of the improvement process. Chapter 28 concludes the book with suggestions on how to make it all happen.

Relationship to Prior Work

If you have read my earlier book, *Managing for Innovation: Leading Technical People*, you will likely notice some similarities with the material in many of these chapters. When I began writing what was to be a second edition of that work, it was soon clear that I needed to add a substantial amount of new material. Much has happened in the ten years since I wrote the earlier book. For completeness, I therefore decided to add three chapters to deal with maturity models and one on disciplined personal processes. Chapters 8, 25, 26, and 27 are thus entirely new. I have also made substantial additions to Chapters 15, 16, 18, 19, and 24 and added an entirely new last chapter. Because the remaining material in the prior book was still as pertinent today as when first published, I have included it with only modest revisions.

Acknowledgments

Over the years, I have had the good fortune to participate in many challenging projects and to work with many talented people. I particularly remember the early help and guidance of Dr. Gerhardt Groetzinger at the University of Chicago and Dr. George Cohn at the Illinois Institute of Technology. Fred Anderson and George Sokol at Sylvania Electric Products were both good friends and fine managers. At IBM I worked with and for many capable and impressive people. Among the most memorable were T. Vincent Learson, Jerrier Haddad, Bob Evans, John Opal, and George Kennard. I am especially indebted to Dr. Arthur Anderson for the opportunity to work with him in assessing the technological effectiveness of IBM's Data Processing Product Group.

I am also indebted to Jack Kuehler who, as IBM president, asked me to return to software for my last four years before retirement. After several years in IBM Corporate Headquarters, my work as the IBM Director of Software Quality and Process provided the foundation for my second career at the Software Engineering Institute (SEI) at Carnegie Mellon University.

At the SEI, I have also been fortunate to have many stimulating and supportive associates. Although I cannot possibly name them all, I particularly acknowledge the support of Bill Curtis, Bill Peterson, and Ron Radice. I also want to especially thank Larry Druffel, Director of the SEI, for his invaluable help and support over the years.

I also again thank the friends and associates who generously took the time to review and comment on the earlier version of this book. They were Dick Case, Ted Lux, Janet Perna, Bill Timlake, and Bill Weimer. Professor Dave Rodgers of the New York University Graduate School of Business was also very helpful in guiding me through the body of relevant management literature and suggesting references to put this work in proper perspective. In completing this new book, I am particularly indebted to Bill Curtis, Howie Dow, Suzie Garcia, Bill Hefley, Julia Mullaney, and Mark Paulk for their invaluable comments and suggestions.

Two others who have provided invaluable help over the years are Karola Yourison and Sheila Rosenthal of the Software Engineering Institute library. Every time I asked for a reference or article, they somehow magically produced it, often in practically no time. To them, I give special thanks. Also, my secretary, Marlene MacDonald, has been a great help with the many copies, revisions, and reviews for the manuscript of this book. My heartfelt thanks to her as well.

A word of very special appreciation is also due my family. My brother Phillip, a professor and a scientist, has offered many invaluable comments, and my daughters Sarah and Katharine provided helpful suggestions on style and format. My wife Barbara also deserves recognition for her patience and understanding during the many months of writing and rewriting and rewriting.

Finally, I dedicate this book to the memory of Al Pietrasanta. Al was a good friend and a marvelous engineer. After a successful development career, he joined the headquarters of my IBM software group to design, develop, and introduce a management training course. Al was responsible for training over 1000 of IBM's software managers on how to better plan and manage their work. As a result of his course, IBM's commercial software development groups soon learned to deliver software products on schedule and at planned cost. They have been doing it ever since. Al did a marvelous job and I learned a great deal from him during our long association, both at IBM and later.

Watts S. Humphrey   *Sarasota, Florida*

Contents

Chapter 10 Developing Technical Talent   105

Chapter 11 Developing Managerial Talent   117

PART 4   Innovation   135

Chapter 12 The Importance of Innovation   137

Chapter 13 The Innovators   145

PART

1

The Manager
as Leader

1

Technical
Leadership

W hen John Keffer took over as manager of the printer group in IBM's Endicott laboratory, the group's main products were old and increasingly exposed to competition. He knew his team needed technical stimulation, so he purchased several of the leading competitors' products and installed them in his laboratory. He then challenged the engineers to find all the ways these machines were superior to the IBM products.

In the next six months, his people took the competitors' machines apart, estimated their costs, and learned their strengths and weaknesses. They soon saw how to make even better machines of their own, and they eagerly proposed plans for several attractive new products. They now faced a challenge they could really understand and were raring to tackle it.

By presenting the problem to his engineers in this way, John made them understand and accept the vital importance of his goals. Imaginative leadership of this kind is a key aspect of successful technical management.

THE LEADER'S GOALS

The technical leader's most important role is to set goals and drive unswervingly to meet them. One of the best examples of such leadership is the way Bob Evans handled the introduction of IBM's 370 computers. After Bob directed the development of the earlier IBM 360 machines, he was sent to Washington to head IBM's military products division. He returned to computer development some five years later when the time had come to replace the 360 systems. Competition was increasing, and new technical improvements made it likely that even better machines would soon be available. To meet this threat, a new IBM system had been under development for several years and the time for announcement was drawing near.

During the same period a new concept called virtual memory had excited the interest of university experts and leading computer users. Machines incorporating the new concept would have the advantage of seeming to have more memory than was actually there. Because virtual memory would greatly simplify the customer's programming task, many designers argued that the new 370 machines should have this capability. An opposing faction, however, argued that virtual memory was inefficient and that rapidly declining memory costs would allow the same result to be achieved more economically with larger memories. Their argument did not convince the virtual memory advocates, however, so the debate raged on. The issue was complicated by the high cost of the needed changes to the 370 design and the resulting one year's delay in announcing the new system.

Bob Evans saw that virtual memory was important and realized that a decision must be made. The marketing people and the leading engineers, programmers, and scientists were all asked for their views. There was, unfortunately, no hard evidence to support either side, so Bob had to rely upon his intuition. As the debates raged, however, he became increasingly convinced that this new direction, though unproven, was the way of the future. Therefore, within a few months of taking over IBM's systems development, he stopped several years of work, redirected thousands of engineers and programmers, and launched the virtual memory IBM 370 systems. This act of technical leadership not only changed the IBM product line, but it set a new direction for the data processing industry.

Bob Evans's 370 decision was an act of leadership because he used technical judgment when the stakes were high and there were no clear answers. The natural course would have been to wait and see if the situation would clear up by itself, but in this case delay would have made the decision by default. The prior design would have been completed and the 370 systems would not have included virtual memory. Instead, Evans faced the issues, took risks, and made a complex decision rather than simply letting events unfold. After the fact, such acts of leadership seem so right that the uncertainty and contention are forgotten. But at the time, the right course was not obvious, and the leader's role was decisive.

THE LEADER'S CONVICTION

In addition to setting the direction, the leader must have the courage to stick with it. James MacGregor Burns points out that "Leadership...is grounded in the seedbed of conflict."[1] Once leaders make decisions, they must drive to overcome all obstacles, and when their people are ready to give up, they must rally them for another try. This is the way General David Sarnoff of RCA acted when he shaped the future of color television.[2] In 1950 RCA and CBS disagreed over the way color television should be broadcast in the United States. The RCA design used an advanced, three-color picture tube that was under development. CBS advocated a mechanical system using a readily available technology that spun colored disks in front of the picture, much like the synchronized shutters on a movie projector. Although the CBS system seemed complex, it was thought by many to be less risky than the unknown RCA tube.

In 1950 the Federal Communications Commission approved the CBS proposal. At the time, Sarnoff said, "We may have lost the battle, but we'll win the war." He was convinced that the RCA system was superior, and he accelerated development of the tricolor tube. On December 17, 1953, after RCA had demonstrated its system, the FCC recognized the tricolor system's technical advantages and reversed itself, thus making the RCA design the industry standard.

With all the resources of RCA at his command, Sarnoff originally had not been able to convince the FCC. They had the final authority, and they had spoken; consequently everyone but Sarnoff thought the tricolor system was dead. Sarnoff, however, kept his people working on the tube, and when they succeeded, the television industry was revolutionized. The engineers did a remarkable job, but it was Sarnoff's conviction that carried the day.

LEADERS AND THEIR FOLLOWERS

The leader's drive and spirit provides the focus and energy for an organization, but the leader must first attract followers to the cause. Without them no leader has the power to perform. A leader's power thus stems from the ability to attract willing followers, while a management's directives limit freedom of choice. The power to control is not the same as the power to lead, for leadership is a mutual relationship, and as Burns says, "All leaders are actual or potential power holders, but not all power holders are leaders."[3] Fred Brooks put it best when he said, "Even the most rabid revolutionary must have a few loyal troops."[4]

Leaders must also care about their followers. Caring is more than just practicing what the personnel manual preaches; it is thinking about the people, their needs, and their aspirations. Caring is demonstrated when a Napoleon knows the names of his gunners or a Tom Watson remembers the wives and children of his factory employees. This is why, for example, great generals refuse to expose their troops to risks they themselves would not personally face. When leaders feel this way, their troops sense it and will follow them anywhere.

TRANSFORMATIONAL LEADERSHIP

One way to excite people's imagination is to build on their dreams and ambitions. Most engineers and scientists aspire to greatness and long to participate in the excitement of some grand venture. Tracy Kidder captures this attitude in his description of Tom West's team building for his Eagle computer project at Data General. Dismissing the rumor that his team was building a "kludge" or a patched-up machine, he portrayed his project as an effort "to try to build the unattainable, the perfect computer."[5] West talked for weeks to engineers about his plans and how important they were to Data General. He described the competition, the problems in the marketplace, and the exciting kind of new machine he planned to build. West put together a dedicated technical team that worked incredibly long hours to design the best computer they could imagine. They were in a tough competitive race with another Data General project, and their tremendous effort paid off with a successful new Data General machine.

By convincing their followers to dedicate themselves to their goal, leaders are practicing what Burns calls "transformational leadership."[6] Such leadership is rewarding for everybody involved. The engineers and programmers gain enormous personal satisfaction, and the company gets a superior product. This excitement is typical of such projects as the RCA tricolor tube or the IBM 370 computers. Not all technical projects have this character, however, and none of them can be this rewarding all the time. Every engineer faces months of routine for every day of excitement, and the typical scientist spends years of preparation for each discovery. The mundane preparatory work must be done well, however, or it will not build the solid foundation required. As Henry Kissinger once said, leadership comes from "the subtle accumulation of nuances, a hundred things done a little better."[7]

TRANSACTIONAL LEADERSHIP

Every manager has what is called legitimate power. It is the official power of a manager's position, and he or she assumes it instantly upon taking office. It includes such key rewards as salary increases, job assignments, and promotions. Managers have wide latitude in deciding who works on what project, who is recognized, and who is promoted. Employees know that their manager's opinion is important, and they work hard to earn and to keep their manager's favor. Although managers rarely use this reward-and-punishment power overtly, it lurks behind everything they do.

Leadership based on legitimate power is called transactional leadership.[8] It can motivate action, but it also has limitations. For example, employees with worries about their salaries or the next promotion are more likely to focus on what the boss wants rather than on what the job needs. They are thus unlikely to be as creative or to hotly debate a controversial technical issue.

Because engineers and scientists have professional pride, most are anxious to do a good job even if it is not exciting. One example of this is the way a product manager saved an important printer project. The engineers had proposed a new printer to replace an earlier machine. The older printers were so profitable, however, that the financial staff questioned the need for a replacement project. The engineers struggled with these business issues but soon gave up and went to the product manager to get his agreement to cancel the program. To their surprise, he was not sympathetic. He told them their job was to get this better technical product out the door, and if the financial people weren't convinced, they must convince them. He expected them to succeed. The engineers went back to work and ultimately showed the financial staff how their machine's technical advantages made business sense as well. The program was completed and the result was a very successful new product.

Although the product manager clearly provided leadership, it was not the traditional kind. He did not threaten, offer a reward, or assert authority. He did not even appeal to his employees' loyalty or suggest a better way to do the job. What he did was to point out that they had not tried as hard as they might. By giving up before exhausting all possibilities, they had not measured up to their own standards. Dedicated professionals feel ashamed when it is clear they have failed to perform as they know they should, and a challenge to try again can be a great stimulus.

One wonders why these engineers didn't do the job right in the first place. Why did the product manager have to give them a lecture and send them back to try again? The reason is that most people need periodic encouragement to do their best. They need to be charged up and reminded that the goal is important and achievable. In technology, there are many failures for every success, and it is easy to become discouraged. Engineers and scientists are constantly struggling against adversity: The first cost estimates are always too high, initial schedules are generally missed, and market projections are invariably too low. Developers who give up too easily will never complete a product, and their manager must sense this and urge them to try harder. Managers should guide, support, and help, but above all, they must not let their people quit too soon.

LEADING FROM BELOW

It is tempting to view leadership as something that "someone up there" does, but every manager can behave like a leader, whether running a corporation or a two-person department. The stakes, of course, are dramatically different in the small organization, but that does not reduce the importance of leadership. In fact, no technical organization can do superior work unless its junior managers take charge of their jobs and energize their people. Even the most dynamic corporate executives can accomplish little unless they inspire subordinate managers to also act as leaders.

In principle, there is little difference in the leader's role, whether he or she is at the top of the organization or somewhere down in its bowels. In practice, however, there is one enormous difference. The senior executive typically recognizes the need to take action, while the junior manager is often immersed in a sea of bureaucratic attitudes and routine responsibilities.

The way Peggy handled her job is a good example of subordinate leadership. After carrying out several assignments very well, she was considered ready for a management promotion. The three plant stockrooms were being consolidated under a single new department, but several candidates had already turned the job down. When they offered it to Peggy, she saw it as an opportunity and jumped at the chance.

Peggy resolved to do her management assignment the very best way she could. She took pains to learn the details of each of her operations and then started looking around to see how the firm's other plants operated their stockrooms. She soon found that no one had any good measures of stockroom performance and that the established procedures had generally been in place for many years. She also found that her stockrooms did not share inventory with each other and that there were no backup procedures.

With this background, she met with her staff and asked them what they thought. They all believed that the procedures were outmoded and could be greatly improved. After reviewing her plans with her manager, she organized her own people into a series of study teams for analyzing operations and proposing new methods. Her enthusiasm excited her team, and they willingly did this work in addition to their regular jobs. After several months' work, they produced a streamlined procedure and a proposal to consolidate the three stockrooms into two. The result was both an inventory cost reduction and better stockroom service.

By leading her people, Peggy ended up leading the entire organization. Her work was soon recognized as an example by all the plants. By attacking a routine job in a creative way, she both helped her organization and gained the visibility needed for further promotion.

THE LEADER'S VISION

Perhaps the most vital single characteristic of the leader is vision. Tom Watson, Jr., in the 1950s, saw that the computer was key to IBM's future and, over his father's strenuous objections, literally drove International Business Machines into the computer business. The early leaders of AT&T showed this same vision when they built the long lines telephone business, often at the expense of the more lucrative local phone operations. The lack of an animating and guiding vision is, in fact, the single most significant reason for IBM's failure to maintain its leadership position in information processing. When Tom Watson, Jr., relinquished the reigns of IBM in 1970, a series of new chief executives took over. Their visions were principally of financial growth rather than IBM's role in the society of the future. While they may have had strong personal views on the company's future, only their financial views were clear to the organization. These were extraordinarily capable executives, but they did not provide the animating principles the company desperately needed. Such a lack of vision often leads to fatal mistakes and missed opportunities.

The tragedy of IBM's declining fortunes is that this lack of vision was solely an executive problem. IBM's technical people had strong views on what the company should do. One letter to the IBM senior vice president and group executive, Spike Beitzel, in November 1970 in fact, argued that IBM should establish operational compatibility as its key strategic objective. The letter went on to say:

> interconnected systems, as well as interconnected networks of systems will be of growing importance in the 1970s and a major factor in the 1980s.[9]

This vision anticipated by over 20 years the networked systems of today. It foresaw that people would move work dynamically across networks and among systems of many types. Had IBM listened to and heeded the vision of its technologists, it likely would have seen the overriding importance of programming and computer networks. The tragedy was that senior IBM management didn't listen to these voices. Top management was too preoccupied with setting growth targets and expanding into new businesses like satellite communications, educational publishing, and telephone switching.

It is interesting to examine the common preoccupation with corporate growth from a different perspective. Suppose, for example, a corporate executive learned that the principal goal of a subordinate was to get a bigger department. This would be viewed as empire building and severely criticized. Such executives, however, see nothing wrong with a corporate strategy of simply getting bigger. They do not see goals of 15% growth or increased market share as empire building on a larger scale. Without an integrating purpose, increased size is destructive. A bigger organization may satisfy the executive's ego, but if it is just another empire, it will sooner or later collapse.

LEADING TECHNICAL PROFESSIONALS

Since no organization can consistently outperform its leadership, the leader carries an enormous responsibility. There are, however, few simple formulas to guide leaders. Lee Iacocca suggests, "When you're in a crisis, there's no time to run a study. You've got to put down on a piece of paper the ten things that you absolutely have to do. That's what you concentrate on. Everything else—forget it. The specter of dying has a way of focusing your attention in a big hurry."[10] This, of course, states the need for clearly understood goals that the entire organization knows and accepts.

Leaders also set the pace for their organization; quoting Iacocca again: "The speed of the boss is the speed of the team."[11] You can't give every project a breakneck pace, but when the boss is relaxed about a day or two's delay, the organization will go to sleep. As Fred Brooks has said, "Schedules slip a day at a time."[12] The boss must insist on meeting commitments and hold his people to them, even if it means working late or through a weekend.

Finally, no important success ever comes easy. Charles Kettering once said that if you "keep going...the chances are you will stumble on something, perhaps when you are least expecting it. I never heard of anyone stumbling on something sitting down."[13]

When people are discouraged and ready to quit, there are usually some avenues they haven't explored. The leader needs to ask, What untried alternatives are there, and has anyone else faced this problem before? Who are the leading experts and have they been contacted? It is surprising how often technical people find a creative answer after the boss has urged them to try one more time. Championship fighter James J. Corbett expressed this idea in a most compelling way:

> Fight one more round. When your feet are so tired that you have to shuffle back to the center of the ring, fight one more round. When your arms are so tired that you can hardly lift your hands to come on guard, fight one more round. When your nose is bleeding and your eyes are black and you are so tired you wish your opponent would crack you one in the jaw and put you to sleep, fight one more round—remembering that the man who always fights one more round is never whipped."[14]

NOTES

1. James MacGregor Burns, *Leadership* (New York: Harper & Row, 1978), p. 38.

2. <u>RCA Executive Biography: David Sarnoff</u> (New York: RCA Corporation, 1970).

3. Burns, *Leadership*, p. 18.

4. F.P. Brooks, private communication.

5. Tracy Kidder, *The Soul of a New Machine* (Boston: Little, Brown, 1981), p. 67.

6. Burns, *Leadership*, p. 425.

7. Thomas J. Peters and Robert H. Waterman, Jr., *In Search of Excellence: Lessons from America's Best-Run Companies* (New York: Harper & Row, 1982), p. 82.

8. Burns, *Leadership*, p. 425.

9. Richard Thomas DeLamarter, *Big Blue, IBM's Use and Abuse of Power* (New York: Dodd, Mead, 1986) p. 361–362.

10. Lee Iacocca and William Novak, *Iacocca: An Autobiography* (New York: Bantam Books, 1984), p. 186.

11. Ibid., p. 95.

12. F.P. Brooks, *The Mythical Man-Month* (Reading, MA: Addison-Wesley, 1995), p. 154.

13. Michael LeBoeuf, *Imagineering: How to Profit from Your Creative Powers* (New York: McGraw-Hill, 1980), p. 238.

14. Ibid.

CHAPTER

2

The
Commitment
Ethic

I learned a lesson the day I first carried a hardware product through to final announcement. The machine was almost completely developed and, without question, it would work. We had detailed parts lists, and the manufacturing, testing, and service plans were fully documented. The cost estimates and schedules had also been completed and signed off by everyone involved. I expected the approval for manufacturing release and announcement to be a formality and was surprised to have the review meeting drag on interminably. The questions were so detailed that it seemed everyone was looking for reasons to object.

By the afternoon of the first day of the review, my annoyance must have shown, for one of the older and more experienced engineers pulled me aside and asked if I had ever been through one of these reviews before. I had not, of course, so he explained that these people weren't just nit-picking; they were getting ready to make a commitment. "And when they do," he said, "they will move heaven and earth to do what they say. Give them time to get comfortable; it will pay off in the long run." It did.

The discipline of commitment is hard to live with, but it can be a great comfort. When technical groups must coordinate their efforts to produce a coherent result, schedules are needed and must be based on mutual agreements or commitments. Unfortunately, people rarely make accurate estimates, and something unexpected always comes up that causes delay. Then everyone has to scramble to meet the schedule. But why does everyone scramble instead of accepting the delay and blaming bad luck? The difference is the attitude of commitment.

THE ELEMENTS OF COMMITMENT

When one person makes a pact with another and they both expect it to be kept, that is a commitment. Gerald Salancik defines commitment as the way to "sustain action in the face of difficulties."[1] In technical work there is rarely the comfort of familiar ground. Just about everything engineers and scientists do is a first of some kind. When people work together in this surprise environment, they must support each other; and this support must be based on a commitment discipline.

Consider the case of a programming project that was threatened by a change in engineering schedule. The programmers were completing the control program for a special purpose machine when the engineering manager called to say the first test machine would be delayed by two months. Since they were about to start testing, the programmers were in a panic. Because the programming manager had been an engineer, however, he knew what to do. He phoned the engineering manager and told him that the programming schedule was totally dependent on delivery of the test machine, and that if it didn't arrive on time, he would call an immediate meeting with the president to tell him the cause of the delay.

In the turmoil that followed, the engineers found they could keep the date for the test machine after all. They had needed an additional machine for the service department and thought they could divert the programming machine to solve the problem. When forced to take responsibility for the delay, they found another answer. Engineering had committed the current schedule to the president and they were proud of always meeting their commitments.

The motivation to meet commitments is largely the result of the way the commitments are made. First, the commitment must be freely assumed. Although in the practical laboratory or manufacturing environments the degree of commitment flexibility is often limited, the person or persons who have to deliver should feel they had some choice. Even if they are only given a brief opportunity to speak up, to object, or to propose changes, they will feel bound by the promise only if they feel they undertook it willingly.

Commitment visibility is equally important, for only when the commitment is public is the professional's credibility at stake. As Gerald Salancik points out, "Acts that are in secret or unobserved lack the force to commit because an act that has not been seen cannot be linked clearly to an individual."[2] This link—accountability—is of course the key. Personally making the commitment puts the professional's credibility on the line. Credibility is essential, for without it professionals are on their own. Lee Iacocca summed it up when he said, "Credibility is something you can earn only over time. And if you haven't earned it, you can't use it."[3]

Another programming example shows what can happen when these conditions are not met. The development project was seriously behind schedule, and it was clear that the original delivery date could no longer be made. Marketing was very concerned and threatened to escalate the issue to corporate headquarters if the schedule slipped any further. The project manager knew something had to be done, so he negotiated with the marketing managers and finally got their agreement to a schedule slip of three months. Even though this was the best he could do without a big corporate investigation, the programmers were not at all happy when they heard about it. As one of them said: "That's his date; I wish him luck."

The project manager had honestly tried to do his best, but he should not have acted entirely on his own. Since none of the programmers were involved in setting the new schedule, they did not feel personally committed to it, and not surprisingly, the postponed deadline was missed as well. Although the corporate escalation had been delayed, the manager had a tough time explaining why the schedule had slipped twice in three months.

MAKING RESPONSIBLE COMMITMENTS

Another requirement for responsible commitments is preparation. The commitment must first be explicitly defined and estimated. If several people are involved, they should all participate, and their views should be carefully considered. It takes time to make everyone familiar with the job and what they are expected to do, but this is the only way to establish a solid foundation for the commitment.

Next comes the actual agreement. In the simplest case, two people are involved: one who wants the work done and another who is expected to do it. Both want prompt and economical performance, but their interests are opposed. One wants an aggressive commitment to ensure the fastest possible completion, and the other wants a comfortable buffer to allow for unexpected problems. The result is a negotiation where the skill and relative power of the two parties determines the outcome.

The third commitment step is performance. When all goes according to plan, there is no problem—but this is rarely the case. There are always surprises, and an unwritten law of technology says that all surprises involve more work. With experience, technical people learn to allow for this, but their plans can never be entirely accurate. A final crash effort is thus invariably needed to meet the agreed deadline.

When the smoke has cleared, the work should be reassessed to understand what went wrong and how to make a better commitment next time. The estimates should be reviewed to see what was overlooked, and the contingencies should be revised to include the new experiences. By comparing actual performance with the estimates, the professionals learn to make better estimates. This is why the people who will do the work should make their own plans: to learn how to make commitments they can meet.

COMMITMENTS OR CRUSADES?

Although the commitment attitude is vital, it can be carried too far. In one case a low-cost printer was needed for a banking machine, and the plan was to use a special print-wheel mechanism. A small rotating plastic wheel was to be embossed with the print characters, and when the right character was in position, it would be hit by a hammer and driven into the ribbon to print the character on the paper. The first models were simple and inexpensive and worked quite well, so the concept seemed promising.

As development progressed, however, problems came up one after another, and the project was soon in serious trouble. First, the print-wheel plastic was too soft to make a clear impression, so small metal type slugs were inserted. Next, because the plastic held the type slugs too tightly together, adjacent characters smeared on the paper. This was fixed by using metal fingers to hold the slugs, but the fingers soon started to break. Spring steel was substituted next, but the springs vibrated and sometimes made multiple characters. This final problem was solved by using a compound spring that damped the oscillations. While the end result was a working printer, the original simple concept had become so complex and expensive that the design was no longer practical.

The engineers had become so dedicated to solving each problem that they lost sight of the original goal. Not only did the changes increase costs, but they gradually destroyed the original simple concept. As the problems compounded, the engineers should have called for an overall reassessment or asked for expert assistance. While their dedication was laudable, they lost their perspective in a blind drive to meet the original commitment.

Commitment hypnosis is a relatively common problem. Festinger, Riecken, and Schacter point out that people convince themselves that what they want to happen must happen.[4] For example, when shown undeniable evidence that their design won't work, engineers frequently redouble their efforts. They seem convinced that a little more time and one more attempt will solve this last problem.

OVERCOMMITMENT

One trick of the optimist is to get management so committed to the project that it can't be canceled. Development engineers, for example, often rush to get their product announced in the belief they will then be ensured against a change of plans. An extreme case came up early in the development of the Concorde supersonic aircraft.[5] In the negotiations between Britain and France, a clause was inserted to the effect that a partner who withdrew would have to pay the entire costs of both parties up to that point. This clause made it impractical for either side to back out, regardless of the subsequent problems, since the costs of withdrawing escalated as the program progressed. Few organizations can afford such technological crusades. Internal commitments are essential, but management should suspect a development team that urges them to make an irrevocable commitment. Often, the engineers smell a problem and are trying to ensure their project against cancellation.

Usually it makes sense to drive relentlessly through every obstacle, but sometimes these crash efforts only add to the costs of a hopeless venture. Not all technical projects can succeed, and the engineers most intimately involved are generally the last ones to face reality. This is when more senior managers can be most helpful. By remaining objective, they can sense when new problems are portents of failure and can call for a technical review, get research help, or hire a leading consultant. Independent advice is often needed to balance the enthusiasts, for a technical team that has gotten itself into trouble will rarely get itself out without help.

MANAGING COMMITMENTS

One special equipment proposal illustrates a common commitment problem. In 1963, I was manager of IBM's proposal for the FAA Enroute Air Traffic Control Computers. The design engineers had worked hard to come up with a superior technical proposal, but their development schedules and manufacturing cost estimates were not competitive. The customer had called for a nine-month delivery, and the sales department insisted that several competitors would meet this schedule at a price of $65 million. IBM's engineers tried everything they could think of to reduce the cost and price. Even with every financial trick imaginable, the price still came in at almost $100 million and the best possible schedule was twelve months, and even that was risky.

Debate on this important proposal reached the top of the business. The sales manager was convinced the schedule and price would lose the order, while we hoped the customer would recognize the quality of the technical proposal. After much discussion, Tom Watson backed the engineering position and a discouraged marketing team was told to do their best to sell the proposal. To everyone's surprise the FAA was so impressed with the IBM design that they chose it in spite of its longer schedule and higher price.

There is always the fear that a competitor will have a lower price or a better schedule. Management's drive to beat the competition accounts for much of the pressure on engineers and programmers. Schedules are always too long and costs invariably too high. The higher the stakes, the greater the pressure to cut and to take a greater risk.

In these circumstances, it is hard for managers to know how hard to push their people. This is when a commitment discipline is crucial. Responsible professionals will search for every way they can think of to improve the program, but when they run out of improvement ideas, they can only commit to what they think they can do. If management wants to gamble on something better, the professionals will do their best, but they cannot commit. First class technical executives support their people when they reach this point.

CHANGING COMMITMENTS

The other side of this coin is the problem of deciding when to change an existing plan. Every plan is a commitment, but it must also be a basis for managing the work. With a realistic plan the engineers can coordinate with their co-workers, but when the plan is unrealistic, coordination is practically impossible. People will make extraordinary efforts to meet a plan they believe in, but when the schedule is ridiculous, motivation is lost and performance suffers.

Managers must sense when a tight commitment ceases to motivate their people. There are no infallible signals, but it is usually easy to tell when they lose heart and begin to slack off. Progress reviews become nervous affairs where nobody wants to speak first. Status is suddenly hard to define, and none of the checkpoints seem very crisp. The reason is that everybody knows the project is in trouble, but nobody wants to be the first to say so and risk being blamed. This is when the manager must call for a comprehensive review to find out just where things stand. Without a clear understanding of the current situation, there is no point in making a new plan.

DOING A THOROUGH JOB

Judy, a development manager, did everything right, but her project ran into unexpected problems. She then met with all her people to review status and to understand exactly where things stood. Everyone was given a chance to speak up, to voice concerns, and to make suggestions. She next met with her three first-line managers to agree on a new schedule, and then she went to the laboratory director and vice president to get agreement. When she told them about the new schedule, they were not pleased, but they recognized the problems and agreed that it was probably the best she could do.

Within a week, one of the first-line managers shamefacedly came to Judy to tell her that one critical function had been overlooked and that more time would be needed than the new schedule allowed. She was staggered because the function was clearly called for, and the additional work would certainly require a schedule change. Rather than go forward immediately, however, she called her managers together and told them to inventory every key project function to ensure that nothing else was overlooked. In the process, they found two more items and the schedule was adjusted accordingly. When she took this story to the senior managers, they were highly critical of this new change, but when she explained the problem and what she had done, they agreed she had taken the proper action.

BUILDING THE COMMITMENT ETHIC

A commitment is a mutual agreement between two or more people who trust each other to perform. Ken Haughton, who was then manager of the "Winchester" file development program in the IBM laboratory in San Jose, California, found that his managers were not working together as effectively as he felt they should. The problem, he believed, was one of mutual trust, so he asked the department heads to define and document their mutual commitments. Weekly meetings followed to discuss these and any new interdependencies. The entire management team thus developed a thorough understanding of their working relationships and were better able to communicate. This built the trust needed for an effective commitment discipline.

Ken had realized that an effective management team must communicate openly and freely. Without such frequent contact, small disagreements inevitably fester, and mistrust soon develops. These interdepartmental agreements opened up management communications, and after they served this purpose, the formal agreements were no longer needed.

COMMITMENT OWNERSHIP

The person making a commitment should feel responsible to meet it. The case of one staff department shows how this works. This group was responsible for issuing periodic quality reports. The data they needed was distributed over many files, which had to be manually assembled and analyzed each month. Frequent special studies were called for, and every one turned into a crash effort to laboriously rework this same material by hand. Because the tasks were so repetitive, the group members were discouraged and morale was almost nonexistent.

The group manager knew that a computerized data base would be more efficient, so he had the group work out a proposal. Since no additional staff resources were available, they planned to defer some of their regular work and fit the rest into their tight work load. When they took their plan to the director, the job was expected to take a full year. The director, however, needed a new operating plan the following summer and knew this data base system would be enormously helpful. Unfortunately, summer was only nine months away, and he was reluctant to direct this overworked team to arbitrarily shorten their schedule. He told them why he needed this system in nine months and asked them to do their best.

The entire department worked hard for the next several months, and after much searching, they figured out a way to do the job much faster. They found an existing program that did much of the job. This saved three months' work. The entire department came to the next status review meeting. They were proud to meet the director's request and wanted him to know it.

This is a fine example of commitment. The director made sure his people understood the problem, and he asked them to do their utmost to solve it. Had he insisted that they do the job in nine months, it would have been his date and not theirs. By outlining the need and asking for their help, however, he put them in control. They thus felt personally committed to do their best.

NOTES

1. Michael Tushman and William Moore have included an article by Gerald R. Salancik in their book *Readings in the Management of Innovation* (Marshfield, MA: Pitman, 1982). On page 208, Salancik discusses the commitment process and why it is important in innovative work.

2. Jeffrey Pfeffer, in his book *Organizations and Organization Theory* (Marshfield, MA: Pitman, 1982), quotes Gerald Salancik on page 291.

3. Lee Iacocca, and William Novak, *Iacocca: An Autobiography* (New York: Bantam Books, 1984), p. 267.

4. Pfeffer, in *Organizations*, quotes Festinger, Riecken, and Schacter on page 294.

5. Gerald Salancik discusses this subject on page 210 in Tushman and Moore, *Management of Innovation.*

3

The Importance of Professionalism

arlan Mills was one of the great thinkers and innovators in software engineering. He had been an IBM Fellow and a professor of computer science at the University of Maryland, where he used to tell his students that his standard was perfection. He concluded that with the right knowledge and discipline, error-free programs could be written by almost any competent professional. He therefore insisted that for their class project they each produce a program that was defect-free the very first time it was run on a computer.

In Harlan's view many programmers simply did not understand the importance of doing perfect work well enough to make the necessary effort. Learning to write perfect programs, however, is not easy. Special techniques are needed, so Harlan showed his students how programs should be structured and what tools, languages, and practices to use. He believed, however, that the key requirement is the personal commitment to do error-free work. The techniques are important, but Harlan was convinced that perfect results could be produced only by programmers who were dedicated to excellence.

This was a tough lesson. The students were initially staggered by the discipline of writing a simple defect-free program. They struggled through, however, and soon found that they could do it. What was more, they discovered that working this way was actually more rewarding and easier. Instead of starting with a general idea of what the program should do and immediately plunging into writing the code as they had done before, they now thought through the design completely before starting. When the design was done, they would write the code, and then rigorously inspect it before doing any testing. Changes used to be a serious problem, but now they were practically eliminated, and the saving in time and effort more than compensated for the added work of design and inspection.

Harlan's technique was more than just a classroom exercise. Paul Friday, one of his students, took a job with the U.S. Bureau of the Census, and his assignment was to write a complex real-time program to control a nationwide network of 20 computers. He completed the 25,000 instruction program on time, and it was used in processing the entire 1980 U.S. census without making a single error! This achievement was so important that Paul was given a gold medal, the highest award of the U.S. Department of Commerce.

This is an example of professionalism at its best. Professor Mills's students had to learn the best technical methods, and they had to develop the discipline to rigorously use them. Harlan, as their leader, taught them how, and he spent many hours building their dedication to excellence. He exemplifies the kind of professional commitment that produces superior performance.

THE ELEMENTS OF PROFESSIONALISM

The two key elements of professionalism are the knowledge of what to do and the discipline to do it. Technical knowledge is the true mark of professionals, for it sets them above their less learned fellows. In historic terms, however, it is only recently that humankind has learned to pass this knowledge from one generation to the next. Early word-of-mouth communication was totally inadequate for technical material, and it was not until Gutenberg developed his printing press in A.D. 1440 that volume communication of technical material was practical.

In the century after Gutenberg, scientific development began in earnest. Leonardo da Vinci, Nicolaus Copernicus, Sir Francis Bacon, Galileo Galilei, and Johannes Kepler were all born in this period. The reason for this remarkable explosion of talent was best explained by Sir Isaac Newton when he said, "If I have seen farther it is by standing on the shoulders of giants."[1] This is the most fundamental principle of professionalism: the knowledge of what others have learned and the discipline to build upon it.

REINVENTING THE WHEEL

William Norris, the chairman of Control Data Corporation, has said that "the technological wheel is being wastefully reinvented every day."[2] Technical blindness has many costs, but one of the most important is legal.

When a product is improperly designed or constructed, there is a risk that somebody will get hurt. With the increasing uses of technology this risk has now grown to where just about every engineer and scientist should be concerned. James Henderson estimates that 25% of all new-product litigation alleges engineering negligence, and Frank Fowler points out that most technical negligence is due to the designer's failure to use readily available information.[3] He cites the example of a mechanical engineer who did not consider the fatigue properties of steel in designing an automobile bumper. Since bumpers are frequently stressed, even an uninformed jury would likely view such an oversight as negligence.

With the continuing rapid advance of technology, product development grows more complex. As the design problems increase, these products are also being used in newer and more demanding applications. Computers on board the Boeing 777 jet airliner, for example, contain over 2 million lines of code.[4] Modern television sets contain hundreds of thousands of microprogram instructions, and the operation of the newest automobiles is controlled by networks of interconnected computers and software. Design mistakes in such products can easily lead to costly manufacturing changes, embarrassing product recalls, product development delays, or even physical damage. The potential risks of poor quality technical work are increasing every day.

Products get used in many ways, and each new application creates added liabilities. To be reasonably safe, professionals should be aware of the latest advances in their fields and use this knowledge in their work. If they don't, their work, when viewed in hindsight, may be deemed incompetent, and that could be very expensive. It is both safer and cheaper to know the subject and use this knowledge than to face the indefinite risk of product liability.

THE BENEFITS OF AWARENESS

Besides legal protection, technical awareness also has important benefits. Dick Daugherty, the manager of a manufacturing plant in Raleigh, North Carolina, faced a major expansion program to handle the growing volume of orders for a family of new communications products. In a few months, manufacturing capacity had to double, and then volume would continue to increase for several more years. Such problems as handling waste paper reached crisis proportions, and materials handling, inspection, shipping, and packing were all under intense pressure. Dick and his employees solved each problem as it came up, but these enormous volumes were a new experience, and they had trouble anticipating the next crisis.

During a review with the company vice president, Dick was asked what he planned to do about the problem. The executive was satisfied with his answer that he was getting help from some company experts, but the question started Dick thinking about other sources of experience. In the next six months he and his team met with production experts from several parts of the United States and Japan, and they found many ideas they could use. Although these companies were in different industries and had different problems, the interchange of information stimulated their thinking and helped steer them from several blind alleys. Some time later, Dick estimated that more than half the new ideas introduced in his plant during this period were traceable to these outside meetings.

The cost of technical blindness can be severe. If engineers or scientists are not aware of current technology, the products they design will likely not be competitive. New concepts generally appear almost simultaneously in several places, and alert professionals will quickly pick them up. Robert K. Merton says, "Great ideas are in the air, and several scholars simultaneously wave their nets."[5] If one new idea can replace or improve a key product, it is essential to learn about it before the competition does. Professionals who keep themselves informed provide the only practical protection against this risk.

MANAGING AWARENESS

Awareness is so obviously important that it seems unnecessary to spend much time on it. Unfortunately, most professionals make little effort to stay technically current. They don't read the technical literature, go to conferences, or take available technical courses. IBM ran a survey of nearly 200 programmers to find out what they were doing to stay up to date. The key findings were as follows:[6]

1. Seventy-two percent read trade magazines, but less than 19% read technical journals on a regular basis.

2. Forty-two percent had attended company-sponsored symposia, workshops, or seminars, but only 8% had been to external professional conferences.

3. Seventy-one percent spent five hours or less per month of personal or job time in keeping informed of the latest technical events in their fields.

4. Eighty-seven percent had never published any external (to IBM) paper.

Even though most of these professionals had college degrees and had worked an average of more than 10 years, they were obviously not keeping up with their professional fields. Technical currency is, however, not just a problem for programmers.

Keeping current used to be an almost impossible job, and the doubling of the volume of technical information every 10 years has rendered manual search methods totally inadequate. The general availability of computerized libraries, abstracting services, searching systems, and the World Wide Web now provide ready access to enormous volumes of material. Reference librarians can help find almost any kind of information in a few moments.

Reading is the most effective way to stay current, but technical meetings are also helpful. The formal papers are one source of input, but the informal exchange of ideas with the other attendees is often even more valuable. One study asked a group of engineers and programmers their views about internal technical conferences, and their responses are shown in Table 3.1.[7] Clearly, 75% felt they gained useful information from the meetings, and one in five felt they had learned something important to their current work.

Managers can help the people who report to them by emphasizing the value of technical awareness. Do they know who is doing the best work in the field? Have they retained the leading experts as technical consultants? What do they know about competition? Are they aware of pertinent work at the local university? And what relevant technical articles or books have they read? When professionals are frequently asked such questions, they make a greater effort to stay technically aware.

Table 3.1 Survey of 85 Attendees at IBM Conferences

	Percent
Had a good time	8
Stimulating discussion	17
Got valuable general information	36
Got specific information for my project	15
Got very important information for my project	6
Got specific information for a colleague's project	18

KNOWLEDGE: ONLY THE BEGINNING

All the knowledge in the world, however, is useless without the will to use it. There is a story about a county agent who called on an old farmer. "Lem," he said, "How would you like to farm twice as well as you do today?" "Shucks," said Lem, "I only farm half as good as I know how already."

Few people do their jobs as well as they know they could. Abraham Lincoln expressed the proper attitude when he said:

> I do the very best I know how—the very best I can; and I mean to keep doing so until the end. If the end brings me out all right, what is said against me won't amount to anything. If the end brings me out wrong, ten angels swearing I was right would make no difference.[8]

Engineers and programmers almost always have good ideas about how their jobs could be improved, but when asked why they don't do the jobs that way, they invariably make excuses: They are too busy; management won't support them; the current project is too far along to change. They insist they will do the job better the next time—but unfortunately these next times rarely happen.

DOING THE JOB THE RIGHT WAY

Some years ago, I was put in charge of IBM's commercial programming development laboratories—a group of nearly 4000 engineers in 15 laboratories in 6 countries. This was a time of crisis because the IBM 360 systems had been announced and hardware was being delivered. The 360 programming systems, however, had not been completed. The original promised delivery date had been postponed several times over the past year and nobody believed the current dates.

I first visited each laboratory to meet the managers and see how the work was going. At each stop, I asked to see the development schedules and plans. While some groups had scratched up notes, nobody had sound engineering plans. I then asked the management team to describe the best way they could think of to develop software. They all started with an estimate and a plan. When asked why they didn't work this way, they said they didn't have time.

This was clearly nonsense. No one had time to do the job right, but they could always make time to fix the problems later. As long as I let them develop and ship products without estimates and plans, they would continue to do so. Such crisis management, however, would never solve our delivery problems.

Since 360 programming was so critical, I needed management support. Frank Cary was then senior vice president for IBM product development and manufacturing, so I went to see him. With his support, I issued a directive to all the programming managers. Henceforth, until I had a documented development plan on my desk, no programming product would be funded, announced, or shipped. Every group was told to produce plans for their current work and to get these plans agreed to by all involved groups.

This directive caused a crisis in all the laboratories. But it had the desired effect: The development groups completed their initial plans in about 90 days. This IBM programming organization, which had never before delivered a product on time, didn't miss a date for the next two and a half years.

While this action was simple in concept, few of the engineers knew how to make good plans. They needed help from the hardware estimating groups and guidance on how and when to develop plans. Searching for the best engineer to lead this work, we found Al Pietrasanta, who worked in the Federal Systems Division. He had successfully led several projects, and was an experienced teacher. He joined the software headquarters group to develop and introduce a software managers' course to train engineers on how to estimate and plan programming work. He developed an excellent course and over the next several years he and his people trained over 1000 software managers.

While directive management is rarely appropriate, it is sometimes necessary. When the people know how to do good work but aren't doing it, management must set standards and insist they be met. Here, the programmers soon found that the project plans helped them do better work. They had previously missed every schedule, and costs were always out of control. Now they were meeting commitments. Their new-found credibility and the aura of success were exhilarating.

Good work has many benefits. When the professionals thoughtfully decide on the best way to do a job, it is probably the easiest, fastest, and most economical way as well. Few people think through the best way to do a job, and fewer still do the job the way they know they should. True professionals, however, have the competence to find the best way to do a job and the discipline to do it just that way.

THE DISCIPLINE OF VISIBILITY

It is hard to do superior work, and it is almost impossible to do it in secret. When a professional's work will not be publicly exposed, he or she faces a terrible temptation to cut corners. It is not often that one sees the dedication of the ancient cathedral craftsmen who carefully carved the backs of the angels' heads. Even though they knew no human would admire their work, they firmly believed the Almighty would. The technician on my first engineering project, Pete Sabatini, had this attitude. Once, we had to delve deep into the system's innards to correct a problem we had hit in system test. We found carefully color-coded wiring that was squared off and neatly wrapped, and we recognized Pete's handiwork. Sure enough, *his* work was OK.

Visibility gives a professional an extra motivation to do thorough work. He thinks more logically about the alternatives and makes an extra effort to find the key references. One example of the effect of visibility came up at the IBM Systems Research Institute (SRI).[9] At the time, SRI taught IBM engineers and programmers the latest system concepts. When the SRI advisory board suggested that they teach a course on distributed processing, which was just emerging as an important new systems idea, the faculty said the field was too ill structured to teach. Upon questioning, however, they agreed that someone would have to structure the material for the first time and that they could probably do it.

The three faculty members who were selected to develop and teach this course investigated all the available IBM and competitive products, talked to several university professors, and read all the relevant technical papers. They were surprised at how much material was available and how quickly they reached the limits of available knowledge. When the course was offered, it was an immediate success.

This example shows the power of visibility. These instructors knew their students would be experienced engineers and programmers and that some of them would be working on distributed systems. If the material were superficial, they could expect loud criticism. They were thus highly motivated to learn the subject completely and to present it logically.

THE HARD WORK OF VISIBILITY

When people don't want to write papers or give talks, there are always plenty of excuses. The best work is often proprietary, and management is understandably reluctant to publish an article that will help the competition. Confidentiality, however, is not an insoluble problem. There are often nonconfidential ways to describe important work, and no security classification lasts forever.

When talented technical professionals publish, the competition learns their names and may try to recruit them. This is also a serious concern, but it makes no sense to try to conceal outstanding people. Engineers or programmers who seek visibility will distrust managers who try to hide them. It is better to treat them well enough so they want to stay, and then ensure that they get the technical credit they deserve.

Writing a paper, presenting a talk, or teaching a course takes a lot of work. Engineers, scientists, and programmers generally are very busy. Once they get past the excuse stage, however, they must give this work sufficient priority. For something to get done, it must get to the top of the priority list and stay there long enough to be completed. Busy people seldom get to their lowest priority tasks. Many professionals, however, write publications on their own time, and it is surprising how many will make this extra effort when asked.

One example is the IBM System 38. When it was announced, the project manager felt that some technical papers should be published on the machine's key features. Announcement was clearly the best time to publish, but everybody was very busy resolving the many final engineering and programming details. Because of these pressures Brian Utley didn't expect many responses, but he decided to ask for volunteers anyway. The response surprised him. Project members wanted to publish their work, and they were willing to put in the needed extra time. A total of 29 papers were bound together and published in the book *IBM System/38 Technical Developments*.[10]

In retrospect, this response is not surprising. Everyone likes to be recognized, and people who have published know the thrill of seeing their names in print. Many first-time authors seriously doubt they could produce a publishable paper, and simply asking them is a compliment. They are flattered to be recognized as having something to say that is worth publication. When faced with a real opportunity to publish, they will generally find the time to do the work.

PRIDE OF AUTHORSHIP

Another example came up shortly before I retired from IBM. Two engineers, Bill Beregi and Gene Hoffnagle, had been working on the architecture for a new software development support environment. We had planned a special issue of the *IBM Systems Journal* on the software process and Bill and Gene had agreed to write a paper on their work. They were very busy, however, and could never find the time to start to work. As the deadline approached, I made the ultimate threat: Either they write the paper in the next week or I would. Horrified at the prospect of their manager writing a paper on their work, they completed the paper on time.[11]

THE BENEFITS OF VISIBILITY

One advantage of a professionally visible organization is the pride and self-confidence it generates. Self-confident people are more willing to fight for their beliefs and to take the risks of creative work. It takes conviction and self-reliance to defend a new idea or propose a change. As John W. Gardner has said, "Excellence is not an achievement of demoralized or hopeless individuals."[12]

A professionally well-known group is also more attractive as a place to work. The best candidates want to join a leadership team, and the employees are more inclined to stay. A reputation for excellent work is also a help in the marketplace. Customers feel more comfortable when dealing with a recognized leader.

When Jack Kuehler ran IBM's technology division, the semiconductor operation in Burlington, Vermont, had been doing excellent technical work but was not recognized as an industry leader. Jack decided to do something about this. The semiconductor industry was then in volume production on 64K memory chips, and development was just beginning on 256K chips. The Burlington laboratory, however, already had a 288,000-bit chip in pilot production. This 288K chip was four times larger than the best units then in volume production.

When Jack was invited to talk to an electronics show in Boston, his staff told the press that he would make an important announcement. The publicity attracted a lot of attention, and when Jack described the new 288K units, IBM Burlington made the front page of the *Wall Street Journal*. This was more than just an exercise in public relations, however, for it helped to build the pride and spirit of the Burlington team. For the next several years, they were the first in the industry to announce almost every new computer memory advance.

PROFESSIONALISM AND PERFORMANCE

IEEE Spectrum ran a survey to find out how managers and professionals felt about professionalism. An astounding 81% of respondents felt that it was either "essential" or "strongly helpful" for engineers to keep technically up to date.[13]

Some years ago, an RCA study compared the job performance of 200 engineers from four RCA laboratories with their professional behavior.[14] The study selected nonmanagers between 30 and 60 years of age and ranked according to their managers' judgments of their job performance. The engineer subjects were then asked to fill out a questionnaire on their professional activities. The results showed a strong correlation between job performance and professional activity in presentations, patents, awards, and technical currency. The study's authors attributed the lack of correlation in publications to the fact that most of the participants were too busy to write papers for publication. Since at least some engineers who publish do so because they are not very busy, the value of such work is hard to demonstrate statistically.

A study by Robert Crook also shows a significant correlation between professional activity and job performance.[15] He studied eight technical teams of between 20 and 60 professionals in two development and two manufacturing locations. To determine the performance of each team, he interviewed five senior managers and averaged their ratings. In sum, he found that more members of the high-performing teams belonged to technical societies and that they spent more than twice as much time in technical reading. They also attended more conferences, published twice as many papers, and had more than twice the patent activity.

THE MANAGER'S ROLE IN PROFESSIONALISM

There are many things managers can do to set a professional example in their departments. Engineers and scientists who have never searched the literature or written papers don't appreciate the benefits of such work, and since they invariably have more to do than they can handle, they won't make the effort unless encouraged. If they are asked the right questions, however, they are more likely to give professional activities the priority they deserve. Some steps for building and maintaining a professional attitude are the following:

1. When reviewing a project, ask the engineers what they know about the work of other groups in their technical specialty. If someone has a better product, why is it better, who is doing the leading work in the field, and what experts have they contacted?

2. Read technical journals and send copies of interesting articles to project members with comments and questions.

3. At promotion reviews, explore the professional histories of the candidates. Have they given talks, published papers, filed patents, or taught courses?

4. In promotional announcements, highlight such professional accomplishments as talks, articles, and patents.

5. Celebrate outstanding contributors at a recognition dinner or other special event.

6. Invite key people to give occasional talks or papers at technical society meetings, and give them special recognition when they do.

7. Above all, managers set the professional tone for the organization. If they behave professionally, their people are more likely to do so as well.

NOTES

1. Stephen Jay Gould, The Panda's Thumb (New York: Norton, 1980), p. 47.

2. Ernest J. Breton, "Reinventing the Wheel," *Mechanical Engineering*, March 1981, p. 54.

3. Ibid.

4. Karl Sabbagh, *21st-Century Jet* (New York: Scribner, 1996), pp. 264–266.

5. Gould, *The Panda's Thumb*, p. 47.

6. These data came from a survey of 163 IBM programmers from several development laboratories. The survey concentrated on experienced programmers, although some recently hired computer science graduates were included. While the sample was small, little or no correlation was found between experience, degree level, educational specialty, and professional behavior.

7. This information came from a survey of 150 IBM professionals who attended interdivisional technical liaison conferences. They were asked what benefits they had gained from such meetings in the previous three years. Eighty-five of the 150 attendees provided complete responses.

8. Michael LeBoeuf, *Imagineering: How to Profit from Your Creative Powers* (New York: McGraw-Hill, 1980), p. 170.

9. From 1960 to 1990, the IBM Systems Research Institute (SRI) provided advanced systems education to technical employees.

10. *IBM System/38 Technical Developments* (Armonk, NY: IBM Corporation, 1978).

11. Gene F. Hoffnagle and William E. Beregi, "Automating the Software Development Process," *IBM Systems Journal*, vol. 24 no. 2 (1985).

12. John W. Gardner, *Excellence* (New York: Harper & Row, 1961), p. 104.

13. John Adams, "Survey Finds Different Views Held by Managers, EEs, on Education," *The Institute*, vol. 8, no. 10 (October 1984).

14. W.J. Underwood and M.A. Keating, "RCA Study Links Professional Success with Job Performance," *The Institute*, vol. 8, no. 10 (October 1984).

15. Robert Anthony Crook, "Factors Affecting Technical Productivity and Creativity of Engineers," unpublished Master of Science Thesis in Management of Technology, Massachusetts Institute of Technology, May 1984.

CHAPTER

4

Respect for the Individual

I nformed and motivated professionals do the best work. Take the case of Fred, an experienced engineer who was looking into the problem of circuit card damage during shipment. Such damage was not a new problem, and the previous investigations had always stopped when losses were found to be within estimates. This time, however, Fred looked more deeply and found that major cost savings were possible. The current shipping packages, for example, gave only limited physical protection and no protection from electrostatic damage. The delicate circuit boards were very expensive, and it was apparent that a special shipping case would more than pay for itself. It took months to get approval to build some sample packing boxes and get them tested. Agreement for a larger pilot test took even more time. After these tests were successful, the OK for full-scale production came more quickly.

Although this change was ultimately accepted, there were many times when Fred could easily have given up. Often, he seemed to be the only person trying to solve the problem. Engineering, for example, spent weeks debating the costs and how they should be covered; manufacturing didn't want to change their shipping and inventory procedures, and service objected to grounding the case before opening it. Since electrostatic damage was the major issue, this grounding step was an essential part of the cost justification; so Fred stuck to his guns. The full-scale field test proved him right.

Professionals often must choose between the easy answer and a much more difficult thorough analysis. Invariably some superficial solution permits unmotivated professionals to get by, but this rarely solves the tough problems. Major advances are made by people who are motivated to do a thorough job and don't give up under pressure. As H.L. Mencken once said, "For every complex question there is a simple answer, and it is wrong."[1]

THE STANDARD OF RESPECT

To do such dedicated work, professionals must be interested in their jobs, motivated to succeed, and confident of their role in the organization. If they are not, they will likely wonder about their next assignment, complain about not getting a raise, or worry about the boss's opinion. Professionals with serious job or personal concerns cannot deal objectively with their management or think creatively about their assignments.

Employees' attitudes are affected by many factors unrelated to their work. The single most important work-related factor is the manager's behavior, however. There are several things managers should do to enhance their employees' attitudes, but the essential first step is to respect their need for personal value. John Gardner defines happiness as striving for meaningful goals,[2] and unhappy professionals rarely do their best work. This means that workers should have clearly defined goals and a manager who respects their role in achieving them.

If managers do not demonstrably respect their people, these people will not trust their managers. Without respect and trust even the most challenging work becomes a chore. To strive to meet the organization's goals, the employees must feel their interests parallel those of their managers. When this mutually trusting relationship is coupled with challenging work, then jobs are truly exciting. Motivational studies show that both the employees' work and a trusting relationship with their managers are paramount. If either is lacking, nothing else can compensate.

The Elements of Respect

Respect for the individual rests on an attitude of fairness. Each person must be valued as an individual and treated according to his or her personal wants and needs. Merit salary scales and job evaluation programs help ensure that those doing the best work earn the greatest rewards. Of necessity, promotions must be infrequent, and they should be granted according to performance. Clearly, some will be unhappy when they are passed over, but even they will grudgingly respect a fair and objective program.

William A. Cohen describes what happens when the people don't trust their management.

> Several years ago during the recession, an engineering organization in a California division of a company went from twenty engineers to just seven in less than three weeks due to a rumor. What happened was this: A major contract was lost. One engineer overheard the president of the company tell the director of engineering to wind up the

in-house work that was being done, and he heard the president say, "That's the last time we'll have to bid one like that." The engineer spread the word that in-house work would cease and that he had heard the president say they were getting out of this area of business. He added that no doubt they would all be laid off. This word got around the engineering group but was not fully believed until a written communication came down ordering all in-house projects to be closed out. That was all that was needed to start a panic and a mass exodus. What the engineers didn't know was that another division in the company, also in California, had taken on a major project that would last for an indefinite period. Even before hearing of the contract loss, top management had been planning to close down the in-house programs and put all twenty engineers on this other project.[3]

Cohen's conclusion from this is an excellent prescription for the respectful environment:

The best answers to rumor are open communications with your subordinates and timely truthfulness. By timely truthfulness I mean that you should keep your subordinates informed on a regular basis and be frank and honest when dealing with them. If you keep communication channels with your people open...a situation like the one described above cannot happen to you. You'll get to the members of your organization first, before rumors can get started. And if a rumor or two does slip by, your people will go where they should for the truth—to you—and you will be trusted and believed.

A Spectrum–Lou Harris survey of 4000 engineers reinforces this view:

When asked what factors contribute to productivity and satisfaction in the work place, those surveyed indicated human relations above all other factors. These included getting more and better information from their managers about decisions that affect engineers, having more to say in decisions that affect them, and having a greater chance for recognition and promotion.[4]

These depend on the managers' conviction that their people are the organization's most important asset.

THE OPEN DOOR POLICY

Although the standard of respect necessarily starts at the top of the organization, it will not be generally followed unless there is some kind of independent appeal process. When managers are not fair to their people, the employees need some way to get help. Skip-level interviews and speak-up programs can be valuable, but they do not usually have the discipline required. An open door policy, as practiced by several leading corporations, ensures every employee the right to communicate with senior management through a channel that is independent of the immediate supervisor. Although this sounds counter to the need for a close and respecting relationship between the manager and each employee, its purpose is not to circumvent the good managers but to provide a safety valve to protect against occasional management mistakes or incompetence. Further, when managers know that each of their actions can be appealed, they will take greater pains in their dealings with their subordinates.

Open door policies typically allow employees to appeal to any person of greater authority at any time about any issue the company can help with, even to the chairman of the board. Of Delta's program, Peters says, "What makes it work is that something happens when the Open Door is used."[5] Every single complaint is viewed as important, and a rigorous administrative process is established to ensure rapid and objective handling.

During my years at IBM, the company had an Open Door Policy with the following guidelines:

1. Individual employees who have a problem are encouraged to first resolve it with their (respective) immediate managers. If they cannot do so to their satisfaction or if they do not want to discuss it with their managers, they may go to higher management. If they are still not satisfied or if they choose not to use any of these intermediate avenues, they can appeal to the personnel department or go all the way to the chairman of the board.

2. In the case of appeals to senior executives, an impartial investigator is promptly assigned who is a relatively senior manager and is organizationally separated from the employee. This investigator should have no prior awareness of the case and no prior or current relationship with any of the parties involved.

3. The investigator contacts the employee within 24 hours of being assigned and meets with the employee before talking with anyone else. This ensures that the investigator starts with an open mind. The investigator then does the fact gathering as the employee's advocate.

4. At the initial employee meeting, the investigator explains the Open Door process, listens to the employee's concerns, and asks questions about the issues and the people involved. The investigator then personally interviews everyone who has an important bearing on the case.

5. The investigation is kept confidential and strictly confined to the issues raised. If, however, the investigator finds other topics that should be addressed, he or she can expand the investigation at his or her discretion or initiate a separate investigation.

6. At the conclusion, the investigator prepares a final report, then reviews his or her findings, including the recommendations, with the employee.

7. The investigator reviews this report with the executive who received the original complaint. The executive makes the final decision and writes a letter to the employee thanking him or her for using the Open Door and summarizing the conclusions.

8. Management must never take any action that could appear as retaliation for an employee's Open Door appeal, and all records of the appeal are kept in a separate file that is not available to line management. This file is retained for a maximum of three years. In no case is any mention of the Open Door or any material relating to it put in the employee's personnel file.[6]

Open Door Experience

Although the IBM Open Door Program was expensive and time consuming, it was remarkably effective. During my years with IBM, I was the investigator for a number of open door appeals to the chairman's office. Each appeal took a great deal of time, but the review process was very effective in clarifying and resolving the issues. In one case, for example, an employee complained that he had not gotten a promised promotion. The review found that the current and several previous managers had not done a proper job of counseling this employee. His performance had been adequate but had not warranted a promotion. Nobody, however, had clearly told him that or why.

With few exceptions, employee problems result from poor management communication. Either the managers are reluctant to be honest with their employees or they don't communicate at all. Open door programs provide an effective way to identify and fix such problems. IBM management training programs, for example, stressed the importance of such communications.

PEER REVIEW PROGRAMS

Control Data Corporation established a peer review program to achieve much the same objectives as the open door process.[7] Here, employees talk first to their respective managers, then, if necessary, to the personnel department.

Personnel will then assist them in raising the issue to the right executive level for prompt decision. If still dissatisfied, employees can call for a peer review, and the case is referred to the Employee Advisory Resource Ombudsman, who assists them. A three-member committee is formed with one executive and two peer members, who then hear the case and reach a majority decision.

In the first CDC case, a lower-level department manager in a manufacturing plant had a personality clash with his plant manager. He felt he was being unfairly blamed for cost overruns and other problems, so he refused to sign his next performance plan. The plant manager took this as further evidence of his uncooperative attitude and fired him. On appeal, line management supported the plant manager, but the peer review board reversed the decision and ordered the junior manager reinstated.

Of the first 11 peer review cases, only 4 were decided in favor of the grievant, in 2 the peer members outvoted the executive, and 8 of the 11 decisions were unanimous. CDC found that management had accepted this process and that local managers were doing more aggressive problem solving. They reported that the employees felt an increased sense of fairness and more protection against arbitrary management decisions.

Peer review programs directly affect employee attitudes both by providing them personal safety and by improving management behavior. When employees trust their management to be fair with them, they think more constructively about their jobs, are more willing to take risks, and are far more inclined to fight for what they believe in.

ESTABLISHING A RESPECTFUL ENVIRONMENT

When I was director of the IBM Laboratory in Endicott, New York, I made a practice of seeing anyone who asked for an appointment. My secretary was instructed to interrupt me whenever someone not on my immediate staff asked if I was available. One day a veteran machine shop employee stopped by to see if I would see him for a few minutes. Although he said it wasn't important, my secretary called me out of a meeting, and within two minutes, we were talking in my office. The machinist soon got over the shock of meeting with the laboratory director and started to tell his story.

It seems the machine shop had a lot of long-term company men who proudly arrived on time every morning and frequently worked well past quitting time. Tardiness was greeted with a loud rapping of hand tools, so few had the temerity to arrive late. A young design engineer had recently started to hang his coat on the machine shop rack so that he could sneak into his department without his lateness being noticed. He left every day promptly at quitting time.

After a few occasions of this, the machine shop was in an uproar, and the veteran felt he had to do something. He hadn't really expected me to see him, but he felt obliged to make a token effort. If I hadn't seen him right then, he would probably not have had the nerve to make an appointment, and the problem might have continued to fester. The shop crew never forgot this, and when I later left the lab for a job in corporate headquarters, they made me a special memento. When you respect your people, they will generally respect you.

Nothing can be more disruptive than to have some people in the organization openly getting away with something. Lee Iacocca calls this equality of sacrifice: "If everybody is suffering equally, you can move a mountain. But the first time you find someone goofing off or not carrying his share of the load, the whole thing can come unraveled."[8] Some of the steps that help establish such an evenhanded and respectful environment are the following:

1. Every decision should be carefully explained so the people involved can see why it is fair and reasonable.

2. Senior managers should demonstrate interest in their employees' concerns and publicly urge people to come to them or the personnel department for help.

3. Several ways should be provided for the people to voice their concerns to senior management.

4. The open door principles should be used in handling appeals, and the employees should be thanked for speaking out.

Although such attitudes should be reflected at the division and corporate level, all managers can follow these principles in their own departments.

NOTES

1. *Business Week,* April 21, 1980, p. 25.

2. John W. Gardner, *Excellence* (New York: Harper & Row, 1961), p. 103.

3. Reprinted, by permission of the author, from *Principles of Technical Management,* by William A. Cohen, pp. 198–199 (©) 1980, AMACOM, a division of American Management Association, New York. All rights reserved.

4. Fred Guterl, "Spectrum/Harris Poll—The Job," *IEEE Spectrum,* vol. 21, no. 6 (June 1984), p. 38.

5. Thomas J. Peters and Robert H. Waterman, Jr., *In Search of Excellence: Lessons from America's Best-Run Companies* (New York: Harper & Row, 1982), p. 253.

6. This is a paraphrase of the material IBM provides to all its managers on the Open Door Policy.

7. Fred C. Olson, "How Peer Review Works at Control Data," *Harvard Business Review,* November-December 1984, p. 7.

8. Lee Iacocca and William Novak, *Iacocca: An Autobiography* (New York: Bantam Books, 1984), p. 230.

PART

2

Managing Technical and Professional People

5

The Goals of Engineers and Scientists

The great scientist Helmholtz once said, "Scientists with an inner drive to knowledge acquire a higher understanding of their relation to humanity. They experience the whole world of thought as a developing entity, which is infinite in comparison with the brief life of a scientist."[1] Scientists strive for knowledge and personal meaning. They see themselves as discoverers searching for hidden order and simplicity behind nature's apparent complexity. The Wurzburg physics professor Wilhelm Wien once compared theoretical physics to mountain climbing:

> When I was a young physicist, I took on problems because they interested me. I didn't solve many, gave them up, didn't care. As when I climbed in these mountains, in physics I climbed quickly with no thought to the route, and I couldn't reach the top. I often remember my teacher, Helmholtz, who likened himself to a mountain climber who doesn't know the way, who climbs slowly, who reverses frequently and has to find another way up, and who sees the best way to the top only too late. Like Helmholtz, I no longer expect to find the royal road at once. I don't hurry but spend most of my time choosing problems that I and my students can solve. It pays off in physics, I've learned, and it pays off in the mountains too.[2]

Scientists search for the meanings and relationships in nature, but engineers seek to create their own monuments. George Eastman pointed out a common thread between engineers and scientists when he said that "with an ideal, the journey's end is never reached; there is always the experiment—the hazard of going beyond where anyone else has gone."[3] Charles Eames, designer of the chair named for him and other beautifully functional products, expressed the designer's attitude when he said, "We need to design for ourselves, but deeply for ourselves. Then we're likely to discover that the result satisfies other people."

Engineers and scientists share a basic drive to accomplish something they can point to as their own unique achievement. Tracy Kidder captures this attitude in the words of Ed Rasala, one of the Data General engineers who helped to design and build the Eagle computer:

> "I was looking for"—he ticked the items off on his fingers—"opportunity, responsibility, visibility."
> What did those words mean to him though?
> Rasala shrugged his shoulders. "I wanted to see what I was worth," he explained.[4]

The best engineers and scientists don't work for a company, a university, or a laboratory; they really work for themselves.

WORK ASSIGNMENT

Because of the professional's need for unique achievement, managers need to carefully match people with their work assignments. This involves more than technical issues, however, for the individual's interpersonal skills and abilities are often just as relevant. In research and advanced development, for example, the objective, in W.O. Baker's words, is "a compact, highly motivated community of scholars who interact with one another."[5] Baker was chairman of the Bell Telephone Laboratories, where he produced a highly creative environment by mixing talented people from many disciplines in an integrated community where they could stimulate one another.

In manufacturing and product development the objectives are more pragmatic: develop a machine or improve a production process. Here, success is measured not only in technical terms but in schedules and dollars. Most large projects start with a highly technical design phase, but the work gradually shifts to such business questions as manufacturing scale-up, parts costs, and change control. Interested only in advanced technology, some engineers view these later phases as pure drudgery. This work, however, is essential in the final phase of every product development. On the Eagle computer, for example, each machine had to be rewired after every test session:

> Making the changes was slow, routine labor, but it required great concentration, for a careless mistake in rewiring could cost them precious time and was the more maddening because it was unnecessary. Figuring that the debuggers were likely to be more careful than technicians with no emotional stake in Eagle, Rasala insisted that his Hardy Boys [engineers] do the rewiring themselves.[6]

All development projects have occasional highs, moments of excitement, but these are separated by days or even months of dogged hard work. The engineer who resents this routine should consider the example of the Leakeys, who have devoted two generations to archaeological research. Another example is Dr. Jonas Salk, who dedicated many years to preparation and clinical testing before he could introduce his polio vaccine. Thomas A. Edison once described genius as "one percent inspiration and ninety-nine percent perspiration."[7]

Part of the satisfaction of development work is the thrill of seeing the working result. The development team's excitement grows as it surmounts obstacle after obstacle to get the product out the door. In the final crash effort, senior designers check program listings, technical managers oversee the daily builds, and everybody watches the test results. No one complains about drudgery or thinks about quitting time. This is the thrill they have worked for, and wild horses couldn't drag them away.

Some people like to solve technical puzzles, but others seek team excitement. The lone scientist is at one extreme, the engineering team member at the other. Most professionals intuitively understand their own talents and seek work that best suits them. Managers who can sense this match can generally make the best job assignments, but even they should always get people to "sign up." Success in matching talents to assignments can depend on convincing the engineers to voluntarily enlist to do the job.

HIERARCHY OF NEEDS

The professional's technical skills and native abilities are important, but even more important is his or her state of mind. The late psychologist Abraham Maslow's five-level hierarchy of human needs can help managers understand employees' emotional status.[8] The most fundamental needs are for food and shelter, closely followed by the need for personal safety. These are rarely at stake in the working professional world, but just about everyone needs level 3, the support of friends and the reinforcement of membership in a social group. After a person has gained the security of membership, his or her needs then escalate to the fourth level: the desire for recognition and status. Finally, the apex of Maslow's hierarchy is self-actualization, where the individual seeks the personal satisfaction of accomplishing a difficult task. It is this highest need that is satisfied when a professional singlehandedly overcomes all obstacles to achieve a creative success. This is the motivation level that all technical managers seek for their people, and it is only possible after all of the lower level needs have been satisfied.

Hygiene Factors

Dr. Frederick Herzberg has combined Maslow's hierarchy with a priority structure that divides motivational factors into two classes.[9] The first class, the motivators, provide a positive drive for accomplishment; the second are "dissatisfiers," which "demotivate" by their absence. If, for example, someone has achieved membership in a group, his or her next concern is with esteem and recognition. Now that the need for membership is satisfied, however, further memberships will provide little additional drive. Similarly, salary satisfies a basic need for food and shelter and provides very important motivation up to a point. Beyond this, however, it is called a hygiene factor; it merely preserves motivation but its value as a further incentive declines.

Engineers and scientists spend many years building their knowledge and skills, and they naturally seek an opportunity to apply these talents. This motivation can be very selective, however. A software engineer who wants to design a communication control program will often have no interest in designing an accounting application. Similarly, circuit design may be interesting at one point in an engineer's career but hold no attraction at a later time. Needs change with experience, and when engineers have proven to themselves that they can do something, further performance of that same task is of little interest. Personal factors are also important, for working with one team or one particular manager may be exciting, but membership in another group with another manager may be totally uninteresting.

Individual needs can change very quickly. The most effective managers appreciate the unique circumstances of each of their employees and intuitively sense the challenges that will most effectively motivate them.

LOCALS VERSUS COSMOPOLITANS

Professor R. Richard Ritti, of New York University, has studied engineers and scientists in large organizations, and he finds an important difference in their attitudes.[10] He applies the term "locals" to those with traditional engineering attitudes, and he calls the scientists "cosmopolitans." Locals' careers are a succession of assignments where they dedicate themselves to solving the organization's problems. In a sense, they are model employees, for they seek satisfaction through achieving the objectives of the organization that employs them. Rasala, for example, expressed this local attitude when he said,

> I guess the reason I do it fundamentally is that there's a certain satisfaction in building a machine like this, which is important to the company, which is on its way to becoming a billion-dollar company. There aren't that many opportunities in this world to be where the action is, making an impact.[11]

Scientists, on the other hand, measure their success in terms of the boundaries of science and often become so engrossed that they ignore the practical world around them. Russell McCormmach captures this attitude in his description of a chance meeting on a walk in Heidelberg, where

> Kirchhoff asked Helmholtz if he had noticed the peculiar light reflected from a rough sea at sunset, and then for half an hour the two physicists stood thinking about that while Helmholtz's wife stood thinking about those peculiar creatures, physicists, all three standing for half an hour in soaking rain.[12]

Scientists want to learn, to understand, and to teach. They seek the company of their peers in seminars, technical meetings, and conferences, and their loyalties extend beyond the confines of job and organization. The focus for the scientist's career is his or her special field of interest; the current job is merely a convenience that permits the individual to pursue it.

Ritti found that these seemingly opposed attitudes of engineers and scientists are not so much products of their education and background as of their working environment. Engineers who work in research laboratories, for example, behave much like scientists, publishing papers and attending conferences. Similarly, scientists in product development laboratories are much more conscious of cost and schedule.

Maslow's hierarchy explains this seeming contradiction in terms of the needs for membership and recognition. These needs can best be satisfied by the organization where the professionals work, and they must conform to its values to be fully rewarded. Research laboratories thus breed cosmopolitans because they value cosmopolitan behavior, but engineering environments reinforce the more pragmatic local attitudes. The organization and its management can thus have a profound effect on the behavior of its members.

THE NEED FOR INFLUENCE

In spite of the great pressure to conform, people have differing interests and abilities. They want work that appeals to them and fits their unique talents. Unfortunately, many professionals find they have little influence over the selection of their assignments. The junior scientist has to set up experiments, gather data, clean equipment, or calibrate instruments. In product development, the more junior engineers end up building breadboard models, expediting parts, or maintaining test records. Similarly, young software engineers frequently start in maintenance or in system test and release. On their very first assignments, these young engineers and scientists are often saddled with seemingly routine chores while their more influential co-workers get the more interesting jobs. They soon realize that influence is an important part of job selection. Most professionals thus seek job advancement so that they can have a greater say in what they will do.

Another reason people seek advancement is self-protection. Engineers and scientists quickly find that if they do not manage their own work, somebody else will. In an interview with *IEEE Spectrum*, Dr. Parker, an MIT scientist, described what happens then: "If you don't take responsibility for supervising others or for going after the money, doing all the things that you could care less about," he argues, "then somebody else will do it, and you will be directed by that person."[13]

This pursuit of influence is generally motivated by professionals' desire to work on projects that appeal to them. As Peter Drucker has said, "The focus has to be on the job....The job is not everything, but it comes first....If a job itself is not achieving, nothing else will provide achievement."[14]

Although few professionals can expect a steady diet of exciting and stimulating work, they all want their fair share. When they are assigned work that does not use their technical skills, they don't feel productive, even though they may be very busy. Ritti found that "if his work assignment is blocking performance, blocking goal achievement, the engineer will feel both underutilized and relatively powerless to do anything about it."[15] These feelings lead to dissatisfaction with the job. Rensis Likert has said that satisfaction goes with challenge, and "for professional work, there is a positive relationship between job satisfaction and performance."[16]

Engineers and other professional people want to be productive; therefore they seek the satisfaction of accomplishment and recognition. These rewards, however, come with only some of the jobs, and professionals quickly discover that they must get the right assignments in order to make progress. This one fact explains why so many engineers and scientists move into management: to have more control over their own destiny.

NOTES

1. Russell McCormmach, *Night Thoughts of a Classical Physicist* (Cambridge, MA: Harvard University Press, 1982), p. 138.

2. Ibid., p. 120.

3. This George Eastman quotation is engraved on a plaque in the lobby of Eastman Kodak's headquarters building in Rochester, New York.

4. Tracy Kidder, *The Soul of a New Machine* (Boston: Little, Brown, 1981), p. 143.

5. Michael Wolf, "Managing Large Egos," *Research Management,* July 1982, p. 7.

6. Tracy Kidder, "The Microkids and the Hardy Boys," *IEEE Spectrum,* vol. 18, no. 9 (September 1981), p. 48.

7. Bergen Evans, *Dictionary of Quotations* (New York: Bonanza Books, 1966), p. 266: 17.

8. Abraham Maslow, *Motivation and Personality* (New York: Harper & Row, 1954).

9. Frederick Herzberg, B. Mausner, and Barbara Snyderman, *The Motivation to Work,* 2nd ed. (New York: Wiley, 1959).

10. R. Richard Ritti, *The Engineer in the Industrial Corporation* (New York: Columbia University Press, 1971).

11. Kidder, "Microkids," p. 52.

12. McCormmach, *Night Thoughts,* p. 12.

13. Gadi Kaplan, "We Look at Ourselves: The Researcher," *IEEE Spectrum,* vol. 18, no. 8 (August 1981), p. 46.

14. Peter F. Drucker, *Management, Tasks, Responsibilities, Practices* (New York: Harper & Row, 1974), p. 266.

15. Ritti, *The Engineer,* p. 124.

16. Rensis Likert, *New Patterns of Management* (New York: McGraw-Hill, 1961), p. 15.

CHAPTER

6

The Changing
Professional
Career

As people mature, they gain a better understanding of themselves and learn to appreciate their own strengths and weaknesses. They can then set more realistic goals than they could when they were younger, and can adjust career objectives to better fit their potentialities.

The case of Dan, a talented young scientist who worked for me when I first joined IBM, is a good example of the way professionals' attitudes change during their careers. Early in his career, Dan was enormously concerned about status and job titles and made a big fuss about the size of his office and the style of its furniture. At the time, office space was extremely tight, and my entire department was moved to temporary quarters in a nearby shopping center. The entrance was at the back of the building by the trash cans, and only one of the offices had a window. My office didn't have a carpet, my furniture was scratched and dented, and no one's office even had a door. Dan saw this as a personal affront, and although I tried to convince him that these conditions were only temporary, he soon quit to join another company. In spite of this early immaturity, however, Dan was highly competent and soon gained considerable fame in his specialty. In fact, he later was the principal inventor of an important new computer architecture. Years later, he was entirely happy with a cluttered office in a university department and felt no concern about the lack of carpets or expensive furniture.

EVOLVING PROFESSIONAL GOALS

Throughout their careers, professionals learn from their successes and failures. Successes build self-confidence, and defeats often provide graphic evidence of shortcomings and limitations. As they debug their programs, software engineers constantly face the consequences of their own fallibility. When engineers learn to realistically accept themselves, they are better able to establish rewarding career goals.

Every professional is different, of course. Some mature quickly while others struggle with the problems of recognition and membership. Any generalizations must be misleading in detail, but it is useful to think of career stages in terms of decades in a professional's life.

While professionals in their 20s and early 30s frequently dream of great achievements, they often lack the skills or dedication to accomplish them. Time seems limitless, and they rarely recognize the enormous effort required to overcome limitations in their training or experience. It takes time to build skills, and they are frequently disappointed when the first job provides little in the way of new technical skills or knowledge. It usually takes some time before young engineers realize that the toughest problems aren't technical at all. They need to understand professional work, perfect interpersonal skills, build a foundation of self-confidence, and learn the value of personal discipline. Although knowledge, skills, confidence, and discipline will all generally come with experience, young professionals can be greatly helped by supportive managers and senior associates. At this stage, their greatest need is sufficient self-confidence to try things on their own. The manager can help in this regard by recognizing and encouraging good work.

Professionals who have turned 30 have few doubts about their own ability, but they also begin to realize that a working lifetime is not so long after all. Thirty is halfway to 60, and this distant milestone suddenly seems uncomfortably close. The 30-year-old professional has generally gained a realistic appreciation of his or her abilities and thrives on difficult and challenging work. Those who have not yet faced reverses, however, are often too cocky to seek help. An understanding manager can suggest they take more care and help them temper their optimism. Although few realize it, the 30s are the make-or-break years. This is the stage when those destined for success will reach full stride. The greatest risk is some disaster that may tarnish a budding engineer's reputation.

By the end of their 30s the most successful engineers and scientists need little management guidance. The less fortunate, however, face new problems. Many talented and ambitious professionals somehow lack the luck, skill, or support to achieve the success they had dreamed of. For them, time is now running out, and they often feel compelled to make a last frantic drive for the promotion they are convinced they deserve. At this point, the greatest need is for a sympathetic and helpful manager who can assist them to reassess their own ambitions. For some, it is wise to break out of the current job rut and make a new start, while others should come to terms with their limited potential. Professionals must make this call for themselves, but an understanding manager can be an enormous help.

By their late 40s most professionals have a realistic view of their prospects, but their need for personal reinforcement is probably greatest. It is easy for young engineers or scientists on their way up to feel self-confident, but those who have passed their peak often face serious problems. It is with these more mature workers that the manager should take the greatest pains to assign challenging work and to be generous in recognizing superior performance.

The late career extends from the late 40s through the 50s and beyond. In this stage, professionals have generally accepted their fate and dismissed their dreams for what they were. While they may still think fondly of what might have been, they find comfort in their position as respected elders. They like to help their younger colleagues and are no longer so concerned with the boss's favor. They will generally speak their minds, and managers should learn to listen and use their experience. This highly rewarding career phase is the one *Passages* author Gail Sheehy entitles "no more bullshit."[1]

AGE AND CREATIVITY

Enrico Fermi, while a professor in the physics department at the University of Chicago, created quite a stir among the graduate students when he said that those who had not made a significant scientific contribution by the age of 21 never would. He never stated the basis for his opinion, but it worried a lot of promising young scientists. According to popular myth, productivity declines with age, but despite this myth and Fermi's opinion, an increasing body of evidence points the other way.

In 1951 Donald Pelz of the Survey Research Center at the University of Michigan started a multiyear study of the attitudes, environmental circumstances, and performance of the scientists and engineers at the National Institutes of Health. The study was ultimately expanded to encompass some 1500 engineers and scientists at a number of university, corporate, and government laboratories. The survey researchers did find that performance peaked at an early age, but they also found that it declined very slightly thereafter. The precise point at which peak performance occurred depended on the technical field: It was earlier in the more abstract fields of mathematics and theoretical physics and later in such pragmatic specialties as biology and geology. The initial peak generally occurred in the mid 30s, but a late peak occurred in the mid to late 50s. The double-peak phenomenon occurred in all the groups of engineers and scientists studied, and the dip between the two peaks was not very significant.[2]

A 1979 UNESCO study of several European research institutions also identified a late peak of productivity. Although the study found that the productivity of academic scientists declined toward the end of their careers, there was a late peak after about 30 working years. Surprisingly, the scientists in industry showed a less severe decline throughout their careers than the academics and they had an earlier late-life peak after about 25 years of industrial experience.[3]

Although there is little data on the effect of age on the creativity of engineers and scientists, Donal Henahan has studied the late-life creativity of such artists as Rossini, Sibelius, Ives, Elgar, and Copland, who gave up composing at the height of their careers. He also notes that some artists, like Verdi and Milton, remained creative well into old age, but that Copland and Stravinsky stopped composing and continued in new careers as conductors of their own music well past their 80s.[4]

Harry Levinson cites several examples of late-life creativity. Santayana and Sandburg composed major works in their 70s, and Sigmund Freud remained active into his 80s. Benjamin Franklin invented bifocal lenses when he was 78. Sophocles wrote *Oedipus Rex* at 75 and *Oedipus at Colonus* at 89. Pablo Casals was still music's greatest cellist at 90. And Titian completed a major masterpiece at 95 and started another at 97![5]

Age does, unquestionably, have an impact on creativity. Gail Sheehy talks about the "unanticipated crucible" that occurs around the age of 40.[6] At this most stressful age, creative people undergo an important change. Sheehy cites the examples of Beethoven, Goethe, Ibsen, and Voltaire, who had important crises in their mid to late 30s. One of the best known midlife crises was that of Gauguin, who left his wife at 35 and ran off to Tahiti, where he was to create his famous paintings. For such artists as Chopin, Mozart, Raphael, Rimbaud, Purcell, Baudelaire, and Watteau, the crisis at this point in their lives was fatal. London psychoanalyst Elliot Jaques studied the life histories of a random selection of 310 outstanding artists and found that the death rate took a sudden jump between the ages of 35 and 39 and then fell below normal shortly after the early 40s.[7]

The midlife crises of highly creative artists are well documented. One suspects that the age effect on the creativity of technical people is similar, though this has not been verified. While its nature and degree can be highly personal, it is clear that, for creative people, the late 30s and early 40s is a highly stressful period. Once they pass this hurdle, however, many engineers and scientists continue their creative work for many years. Alexander Graham Bell, for example, invented the telephone when he was 27, but he continued to invent for another 45 years. Albert Einstein was working energetically on modifications and extensions to his Unified Field Theory well into his 70s, and many of Thomas Edison's 1100 inventions were produced late in his 84-year life.

AGE AND PERFORMANCE

In spite of the encouraging data on the continued creativity of older people, age undoubtedly does affect performance. In 1980 Richard L. Sprott edited a series of studies on this subject that provide clear evidence of declining ability with advancing years.[8] This decline was largely related to performance speed, however, and not to intellectual ability. One of these papers gives the results of the Wechsler Adult Intelligence Test Scores (WAIS) for a series of people in different age groups. Six untimed verbal tests and five nonverbal performance tests were administered.[9] As shown in Table 6.1, verbal performance remained essentially flat, while timed performance declined. Most of the declines were less than the standard test deviation of 3, however.

An interesting counterexample is described by Szafran, who tested a large number of airplane pilots between the ages of 20 and 60.[10] His findings indicate "no age-associated differences in performance even under very demanding overload conditions." Although there are many possible explanations for this surprising finding, Szafran himself concluded that this was a highly practiced sample from which the poor performers had been eliminated by natural selection. It appears, therefore, that not everyone's performance declines with age and that health, practice, and occupation can play an important role.

Table 6.1   Means of WAIS Scores by Age During Middle Adulthood

Test	Age Range				
	20–24	*25–34*	*35–44*	*45–54*	*55–64*
Verbal					
Information	9.8	10.3	10.3	9.9	9.9
Comprehension	10.0	10.2	10.2	9.9	9.6
Arithmetic	10.0	10.1	10.2	9.8	9.4
Similarities	10.2	10.1	9.2	9.0	8.4
Digit span	9.9	10.0	9.6	9.0	8.4
Vocabulary	9.6	10.3	10.4	10.1	10.1
Performance					
Digit symbol	10.1	9.9	8.5	7.5	6.3
Picture completion	10.1	10.0	9.8	8.6	8.0
Block design	9.9	10.0	9.4	8.5	7.7
Picture arrangement	10.5	9.7	9.1	8.0	7.3
Object assembly	10.1	10.0	9.3	8.5	7.8

Source: Excerpted from *Measurement and Appraisal of Adult Intelligence* by David Wechsler. Copyright © 1972. Reprinted by permission of Oxford University Press, Inc.

A further series of tests addressed the effect of age on reasoning ability.[11] A large number of men were tested on intellectual performance in two series of tests six years apart. While the proportion of men who solved the problems declined with age, there was no deterioration in reasoning ability for any of the groups under the age of 70. Again, a natural selection process screened out those men who could not solve the problems twice, but the intellectual performance of the remainder did not decline in the six-year interval between tests except for this oldest group.

More recent studies by the MacArthur Foundation and others have shown that the intellectual capacities of many people can actually improve with age.[12] When they separated out the effects of illness, the experimenters found that for many people the ability to handle intellectual tasks continued to improve, even into the late eighties. While older people tended to be somewhat slower than their younger peers, the quality of their results was not only not impaired but actually improved.

Many complex factors determine the effect of age on performance. Health, generational differences, intelligence, and continued activity all have a role. For those who remain physically and mentally competent, however, there is no statistically significant evidence of a decline in intellectual performance until well after the normal working years. Speed of performance, however, does generally deteriorate, but not to any disabling degree before the age of 65 or 70.

AGE AND MOTIVATION

AT&T made a 20-year study of the changing attitudes of managers in order to better identify future leaders.[13] The researchers found a high correlation between job attitudes and career progress and they identified the single most important difference to be the high priority the future executives placed on their work: Their jobs were increasingly important to them as they advanced. Conversely, those managers who limited their efforts to the traditional 40 hours did not advance as fast or as far. Career success clearly depended on the manager's willingness to do more than the minimum required by the job.

Priorities understandably change with age, and one's willingness to strive for a promotion is always balanced against the demands of private life. Most employees intuitively sense their potential and limit their efforts accordingly. Although the most ambitious may choose career over home, few people are willing to make the personal sacrifices that senior executive positions require. For the rest, the heavy personal investment is not balanced by the questionable odds of continued advancement. With age and experience, this career tradeoff gradually but steadily swings toward the home.

The management pyramid inexorably narrows at the top, and promotional progress is increasingly competitive. Since every promotion has only one winner and many losers, most employees regularly face vivid reminders of their approaching career limits. This reality can be highly traumatic, as demonstrated by the frequency of such midlife problems as alcoholism, divorce, heart attack, and ulcers. Many topped-out employees are still ambitious, and can preserve their health and sanity only by withdrawing from active job involvement.

BURNOUT

The phenomenon of job withdrawal is called burnout. A study by the University of Chicago found that burnout is generally caused by an employee's feeling helplessly trapped in a meaningless job.[14] It is not caused by age, overwork, or exhaustion but is more a defense against the loss of self-esteem caused by an apparent lack of personal value.

As an IBM experience demonstrates, receiving a meaningful assignment can reenergize even burned-out employees. A major IBM project had gotten into trouble, necessitating a crash effort. A new manager was named, and he started looking for a half dozen engineers. The only people available were some older hands who had been out of the mainstream for many years. The manager reluctantly selected them because he had no alternative. Jerrier A. Haddad, a retired IBM vice president, said of this project that

> these six...did a crackerjack job. Somewhere along the line in their careers they had been allowed to drift. Younger people had been given the newer, more challenging assignments, and these six just went along as before. But when someone offered them a challenge, they leaped at it.[15]

When a person is out of action for a long time, his or her reputation suffers. Routine jobs with little challenge evoke reduced performance; one dull job inexorably follows another. All departments have top and bottom performers, and those labeled as losers rarely are able to climb out of their deepening rut. If managers assign all the stimulating work to the stars, they will shine brighter while those at the bottom dim.

This vicious circle was made clear to a manager who told his vice president he could get rid of the bottom 15% of his department and still get his department's job done. The boss surprised him by demanding the names of these people so he could reassign them. After several weeks, the manager admitted that he could not come up with a list. All members of his department were performing useful work, although some were less effective than others. By examining their performance more closely, he had found that the poor performers had been given the dull work, and no matter how hard they tried, they could not perform up to his expectations. Looking for people to get rid of had forced him to focus on the poorer performers, which led to his discovery that they were all capable of better work.

The way a routine assignment affects an employee is illustrated by the case of Craig, an experienced programmer. After he had worked for the data processing department for several years, Craig was given a semiclerical task as a filler between assignments. The job of keeping track of computer usage and producing the weekly reports was so dull, however, that he lost all interest in his work. He only did the bare minimum needed to get by, and his performance rapidly deteriorated to the point where he was considered incapable of a more challenging job.

At this point, the manager was asked to provide a new data processing service, and since no one else was available, he reluctantly asked Craig to handle the task until he could find someone else. To everyone's surprise, Craig took the job and got right to work. He quickly identified and ordered the needed equipment, arranged for new space, and worked out introduction plans for all the departments. He started arriving at work early and often stayed well past quitting time. When the service was installed on schedule, it had few problems and everyone was so impressed that Craig soon had several offers of a next assignment.

THE MANAGEMENT–EMPLOYEE PARTNERSHIP

Some employees use dull assignments as an excuse for poor performance, rationalizing that if they had challenging jobs, they could excel. They thus blame management for their "burned-out" attitudes, accusing their managers of not challenging them. A second and perhaps more insidious risk for managers is the propensity to underestimate employees, stimulating the best performers while ignoring the rest.

No commandment or bill of rights guarantees every employee an interesting and challenging job. In fact, the reality of the workplace is often just the reverse. But with the right attitude, almost any job can become rewarding. Challenges are largely self-made, and most jobs contain some kernel of opportunity that can be developed into an exciting task.

Consider again the case of Craig's dull assignment. He could have used the routine nature of his reports to his advantage. By reexamining the way the computer work was accounted for, he could have devised a system for automatically recording usage. This would have led to automating the reports, while providing a personal challenge for him and a service to his department.

To be fully effective, managers and their people should form a partnership. By striving to do their jobs in the best way, professionals help their organization while they stimulate themselves. Managers can encourage this process by assigning meaningful work to each of their employees and helping them discover a creative approach to the tasks that must be done.

The Cuckoo's Egg is a book that describes a fine example of the creative opportunities in routine work. Reviewing the time records for computer usage at his laboratory, Clifford Stoll noticed a minor usage discrepancy. It was only a minute in a large amount of time, so most people would have ignored it, but Stoll was curious. His curiosity, coupled with his dogged determination to understand what turned out to be an enormously complex situation, was responsible for apprehending a computer hacker in Germany who had been penetrating U.S. government computers. Based on his creative approach to a routine task, this discovery led Clifford Stoll to publish a book about it and gain international recognition.[16]

CAREER RISKS AND AGE

As engineers and scientists age, they have fewer career options and less time to recover from mistakes. Unfortunately, an employee's defects are often remembered more vividly than the successes. With the passing years fewer doors are open to professionals with mixed histories. They eventually realize that they are no longer considered when new assignments open and that their current jobs are all that is left to them. With such limited options, they lose self-confidence and increasingly play it safe so as not to risk this one remaining assignment.

Superior technical work, however, entails risk, and technical people who play it safe rarely excel. An example of the problems this can cause was the evaluation done of a new testing method proposed by a research department. The proposal was highly controversial because costly new test equipment had recently been installed that the new methods would not use. The laboratory manager had been outspoken in his push to control budgets, so the engineer doing the evaluation suspected that the lab manager wanted the proposal rejected. The evaluator was so nervous about the likely reaction that he focused only on the proposal's problems, overlooking its many advantages. When he recommended no change, the lab manager was pleased, but the research department appealed to higher management, insisting on a more thorough study. When the second evaluation concluded in research's favor, it was clear that the first evaluator's attempt to play it safe had caused a six-month delay and an increase in total project costs.

MANAGING THE OLDER PROFESSIONAL

As Helmholtz said on his seventieth birthday, "The first seventy years are the best."[17] Age is relative, and most older employees couple experience and wisdom with surprising vigor. Old age, however, can also accentuate attitudes and habits. When some people have lived with issues for a long time, they see them as immutable facts. Harry Levinson has said,

> Too many people accept what is for what will be. They most often say, "I can't do anything about it." What they really mean is that they won't do anything....There are indeed alternatives in most situations. Our traps are largely self-made.[18]

In these cases, however, age is rarely the problem. With few exceptions, healthy employees, regardless of their age, are capable of imaginative and energetic work. Job tenure, however, is a different matter. Employees who have been in the same job for extended periods tend to think in constrained patterns and to see fewer options and alternatives. Although long-term employees are often the older people, the manager should recognize that age is not the problem and insist on stimulating them with a move to a new assignment.

NOTES

1. Gail Sheehy, *Passages* (New York: Dutton, 1976), p. 46.

2. Donald C. Pelz and Frank M. Andrews, *Scientists in Organizations: Productive Climates for Research and Development* (New York: Wiley, 1966), p. 177

3. Richard Stankiewicz, "The Size and Age of Swedish Academic Research Groups and Their Scientific Performance," in *Scientific Productivity: The Effectiveness of Research Groups in Six Countries,* ed. Frank M. Andrews (Cambridge: Cambridge University Press, 1979).

4. Donal Henahan, "The Mystery of the Dropout Composer," *New York Times,* March 14, 1982.

5. Harry Levinson, "On Being a Middle-aged Manager," *Harvard Business Review,* July/August 1969, p. 82

6. Sheehy, *Passages,* p. 36.

7. Ibid.

8. Richard L. Sprott, *Age, Learning Ability, and Intelligence* (New York: Van Nostrand Reinhold, 1980), p. 51.

9. Ibid., p. 55.

10. Ibid., p. 104.

11. Ibid., p. 146.

12. Several long-term studies of the Medicare population and others were reported in the *New York Times* issues of February 26, 27, and 28, 1996.

13. Ann Howard and Douglass W. Bray, *New York Times,* March 21, 1982, sec. 3, p. 2.

14. Patricia Brooks, "Burnout," *Think,* vol. 48, no. 1 (Armonk, NY: IBM Corporation, January/February 1982), p. 26.

15. Ibid., p. 26.

16. Clifford Stoll, *The Cuckoo's Egg* (Garden City, NY: Doubleday, 1989).

17. Russell McCormmach, *Night Thoughts of a Classical Physicist* (Cambridge, MA: Harvard University Press, 1982), p. 139.

18. Levinson, "Middle-aged Manager," p. 89.

CHAPTER

7

Motivating Technical and Professional People

As Lee Iacocca once said, "When it comes to making the place run, motivation is everything."[1] Motivation, obviously, makes the place run because it makes the people run. Highly motivated people drive themselves to overachieve, while many of their brighter and more capable associates accomplish far less. The basic reason is the difference in their motivation.

Some people are so motivated that they overcome great personal disadvantages to achieve impressive success. Dave Schwartzkopf is both an outstanding example of what a motivated person can accomplish and one of the most impressive people I have ever met. Dave has been nearly blind since birth and suffers from a speech impediment that caused him to be treated as mentally retarded until he was nearly 16 years old. Luckily, one of his teachers then recognized his exceptional talents and had him moved to a more appropriate school. This completely changed Dave's life, and he rapidly worked through school and college to become an engineer. He then joined IBM, and when I met him, he had progressed through several technical assignments to become manager of a technical education group. His enormous drive and motivation have earned him both a successful technical career and the respect of all who have known him.

Motivation is what makes people persist when they run into serious roadblocks. Success in almost any field is governed by both knowledge and perseverance, and those who give up too easily rarely succeed. In modern technology ideas are cheap; the crucial factor is the ability to couple ideas with the right combination of skill and perseverance. It is not as important to have the right ideas as it is to have the drive and motivation to make your ideas right.

David C. McClelland has studied the characteristics of achievement-motivated people and found that they share certain traits: "the capacity to set high but obtainable goals, the concern for personal achievement rather than the rewards of success, and the desire for task-oriented feedback (how well am I doing?) rather than for attitudinal feedback (how well do you like me?)."[2] Motivated employees set their own goals and are their own toughest taskmasters. At the highest level of motivation, people seek challenges and strive to overcome obstacles, not because they want any external reward or benefit, but because they find satisfaction in their own achievements. As A. Ray McCord, the executive vice president of Texas Instruments, once said, "The employees will set tougher goals for themselves than any manager would dare to set alone."[3]

THE POWER OF MOTIVATION

One remarkable example of the power of motivation was the work of George Judson, an IBM engineer who was working in the Endicott laboratory when he learned his son had leukemia. This was at a time when leukemia was generally considered fatal. Deeply concerned, George spent much of his time at the hospital talking to the doctors and trying to understand what they could do to cure his son's disease. He learned there was an urgent need to separate the blood into its major components, or fractions, for treatment while it was circulating in the patient's body. Since many of the component cells of human blood are extremely fragile, however, building a machine to do this was quite a challenge.

Pondering this problem, George began trying out some of his ideas in the laboratory. He soon put together some parts and began to see how such a machine could be made to work. He then got permission to build an experimental blood cell separator and arranged for cooperative clinical testing with the National Cancer Institute. Within a year, the completed unit worked so well that the institute contracted with IBM for further development work on machine improvements. Interest in the device grew so quickly in the cancer research community in the United States and Europe that a small production line had to be set up to meet the demand. Although his son did not live to benefit from his work, George went on to make many contributions to medical instrumentation, and the company recognized his achievements by making him an IBM Fellow.

MOTIVATION AND TECHNICAL COMPETENCE

It is commonly felt that technical talent applies only within a narrow field of specialty but that motivation is universally useful. While this is true to some degree, it is far too simplistic a view. Technical competence generally grows throughout a professional's career and is a constantly expanding asset. It is also more widely applicable than generally realized, for a professional with skills in one field can generally contribute in another.

The advantages of experience were demonstrated by the compiler expert who reworked the reader interpreter for the first release of IBM's OS/360 control program. A trainee had written the initial reader interpreter, and it was so slow that the fastest IBM computer at that time could not keep up with a card reader. Because of his compiler experience, however, the experienced engineer was able to redesign the program over one weekend to get a 1000 times performance improvement!

In both hardware and software, technical skills are widely applicable. Since the basic concepts of science and engineering apply to all technology, the knowledge and intuition gained in one area generally help in many others.

Motivation, however, is a different story. As professionals gain competence, they do not necessarily gain motivation. Often, in fact, employees' motivation declines as they gain experience. This is because a creative engineer or scientist who has learned how to accomplish something has little interest in doing it again. This explains why engineers may be fascinated by a particular problem and reject all other opportunities in order to work in this one area. Once they have satisfied their curiosity, however, they may abruptly lose interest and seek an immediate change.

Motivation is fragile. It depends on the person, the task, the environment, and the professional's immediate associates. The technical factors are important, but so are feelings and associations. The key point, however, is that almost all the nontechnical elements of employee motivation are directly controllable by the professional's immediate manager.

THE EVOLUTION OF MANAGEMENT

A dramatic change in management thinking started at the beginning of the twentieth century. Early management methods were based on Frederick Winslow Taylor's *Principles of Scientific Management*.[4] Published in 1911, this pioneering work proposed that employees be treated essentially like machines. Work was to be subdivided into well-structured elements and each worker assigned to a single repetitive task. Since they were assumed to have no feelings, unique abilities, or motivations, workers were told precisely how to do their jobs and paid on a piece-work basis. Taylor's mechanistic approach to management has been called "Theory X."[5]

Although Theory X takes an essentially negative view of employees, it was generally accepted until Elton Mayo of Harvard University started his famous productivity studies at Western Electric's Hawthorne, Illinois, plant in 1924.[6] These studies were intended to find the mix of lighting and other conditions that produced the highest worker productivity. By the end of the studies nearly ten years later, they had started a revolution in management thinking that continues to this day.

In the first three of his studies, Mayo adjusted the lighting and other conditions in the Western Electric factory to see how the work environment affected worker productivity. These studies divided the employees into control and test groups, the former continuing to work under normal conditions, while the work conditions for the latter were changed. Much as expected, Mayo found that the productivity of the test group improved with improvements in working conditions. Unexpectedly, however, he found that removing these changes did not return productivity to its former values. To understand what was happening, Mayo conducted an extended series of studies that showed that many factors contributed to worker productivity. Then and since, the popular interpretation of these results has been that the improvement in productivity resulted principally from the attention the workers received during the experiment.

A more recent interpretation of Mayo's data has shown that his results are quite consistent with current findings: Worker productivity is influenced by many factors, including pay provisions, worker attitudes, physical conditions, and management behavior.[7] An important factor in his studies that Mayo did not recognize at the time was workers' feedback on their performance. Data feedback has subsequently been found to have a profound effect on workers' performance. It is, in fact, the principal focus of recent work in improving the performance of software engineers.[8] In the Hawthorne experiments, the study group had ready access to data on their work and the control group did not. Also, the study group had frequent meetings with management to discuss their progress and the study results. While this is more or less consistent with the view that study conditions influenced worker behavior, the modern interpretation is that data feedback and improved management communications produce positive results, even without a study.

Mayo's results were the first to demonstrate that the way workers were treated was a crucial factor in determining their performance. These ideas ultimately attracted broad support. In 1960 Douglass McGregor characterized the new approach as "Theory Y."[9] Its basic premise is that people are psychologically motivated to work, and management should help and support them rather than coerce them. This is the basic concept behind much of modern management thinking.

Theory X and Theory Y are diametrically opposed. While Theory X assumes the worst about the employees, Theory Y assumes the best. Not surprisingly, the truth generally falls somewhere in between. If managers always treat all of their people the same way, they will be wrong at least some of the time. This is because only some people are highly motivated, and no one, not even the highly motivated, is *uniformly* energetic and hardworking. A more balanced management strategy, which recognizes the highly individual nature of "people management," is called situational leadership.[10] It states that managers should change their approach depending on the situation and the current needs of each of their people.

Situational leadership can be very helpful in improving the motivation of professional employees. With skill and understanding, managers can decide when to direct their people and when to delegate to them. New employees, for example, may need detailed instructions, while more experienced professionals can be given more leeway. They must naturally be told what is wanted, but they need not be instructed on how to do it. Ultimately, as employees' ability and initiative increase, managers can delegate increasing amounts of decision making to them. The proper use of such flexible management styles will steadily improve professionals' motivation and result in their doing correspondingly better work.

BUILDING TASK MATURITY

As shown in Figure 7.1, situational leadership concerns two different dimensions of employee performance: task maturity and relationship maturity. Task maturity deals with technical competence, while relationship maturity considers employees' attitudes toward their jobs and their management. Task maturity is built throughout an employee's education and working career, and as it develops, the manager should progressively increase the complexity and challenge of the person's assignments. The professional's abilities are thus continually taxed, thereby developing and improving his or her technical competence and task maturity.

The advantages of such an approach were demonstrated by a sales training experiment run by a large insurance company shortly after the World War II. New sales recruits were divided into three groups, each to receive a different kind of training. One group received comprehensive instruction on how to sell insurance, including specific guidance on how to act and what to say in every anticipated situation. The second group was given minimal

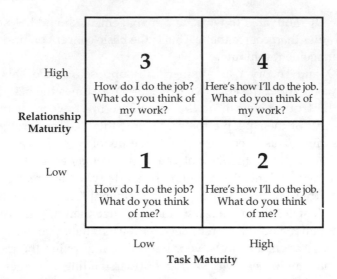

Figure 7.1   Task and Relationship Maturity

training and then assigned to work with an experienced salesperson who acted as an on-the-job tutor. After accompanying their tutors on sales calls for several months, this second set of trainees was then sent out on their own. The third group was given minimal training and then immediately sent out to make solo sales calls. After several months of selling, they were brought back to headquarters for comprehensive instruction.

The long-term performance of these three groups varied considerably. Not only did the first group have the worst initial sales record, but their performance lagged the others for the duration of the study. Secretly observing the first group, the experimenters found that these salespeople were not thinking for themselves. Most of their efforts were devoted to remembering their canned sales pitches; they were lost in unexpected situations. Although the second group did better, the third group performed best, both initially and throughout their entire sales careers. The latter trainees clearly learned most effectively from a training program that directly related to the experience they had gained by flying solo. Although they had made mistakes when they first made sales calls on their own, they also had quickly learned how to rely on their own judgment. This experience then provided them a vivid appreciation of the selling process and the best possible foundation for their later training program.[11]

Learning is most effective when the trainees can see its direct relevance to their needs. Whether in the laboratory or in the classroom, real problems provide a motivation that is hard to duplicate. The same principle applies to new engineers and scientists. They should be given challenging problems and just enough guidance to get them started and keep them out of serious trouble. While some will need more help than others, the general principle is the same as the salesperson's solo flight: Get them on their own as soon as possible. They should be encouraged to come back for help whenever they need it, but they will learn best by trying to solve their own problems and learning from their own mistakes.

BUILDING RELATIONSHIP MATURITY

When professionals have developed a reasonable level of task maturity, they should be able to work on their own. Whether they actually can, however, depends on their relationship maturity. The fact that people are technically capable of doing a job does not necessarily mean that they can, or will, do it. They may lack self-confidence, resent some management action, or have some severe personal problem. There are as many varieties of relationship problems as there are people, and just about any personal problem can severely limit employee performance. The following examples illustrate the wide variety of issues involved.

A young engineer had worked for several months before being given a project to do by himself. His progress was good, and it seemed he would finish on schedule and within budget; but then he went to the personnel department to complain about his salary and lack of promotion. On investigation, the personnel manager found no real salary or promotion problem and concluded that this engineer was really troubled by lack of attention from management. As a new employee he felt lost and unsure without the reinforcement of frequent management contact. The manager had given him too much independence before he was ready. Although he belonged in box 1 of Figure 7.1, this engineer was being managed as if he were in box 4.

Another case concerns an experienced programmer. Given a new application program to design, he worked for several months with frequent management interaction but didn't make much progress. When his performance was reviewed, he seriously disagreed with his poor rating and complained that his direction was so specific that he felt like a flunky. He was confident he could do the job but felt he had not been given the chance. Since he was entirely capable of doing the work, his manager should have told him what was wanted and given him the independence to do it on his own. This engineer was being managed in box 3 of Figure 7.1 when he really belonged in box 2.

A third situation involves an experienced engineer who was temporarily assigned to the headquarters staff. His manager asked him to develop a new training program for the entire division. He was apprehensive, however, and told his manager that he didn't know any of the headquarters people and had no idea where to start. The manager took several hours to tell him what he had in mind and why the job was important, but he insisted that the engineer make his own contacts and work out the program specifics by himself. The engineer soon found several people who made some very good suggestions, and he quickly put together the outline of the program. His manager agreed to the outline, and in less than a year the engineer had a pilot program underway. He had found his own way around headquarters, had become familiar with the other staffs, and had made many presentations to senior managers and executives. Thrown into the deep end, he had quickly found that he could swim. This engineer was properly managed, as in box 4 of Figure 7.1.

In a fourth case, I was given the job of running a small circuit design department. We had several new college graduates and Ed, an experienced engineer with a master's degree from MIT. As I gave design assignments to the young engineers, I would suggest various circuit approaches for them to try. I insisted, however, that they do the design work themselves. In several cases, when I checked back a day or two later, I found that the engineers had made no progress. In each case, they had talked to Ed, who had used his theoretical knowledge to prove that none of the suggested approaches would work. Since these were not difficult circuit problems, I decided to give Ed a circuit to design by himself. Even though this was a simple problem, he soon came back to me with an extensive analysis to show that it couldn't be done. I knew he was wrong, however, since I had already built the circuit myself. I found, however, that Ed could not produce work of his own; he could only criticize what others proposed. Once we removed Ed, the junior engineers quickly completed all the circuit designs. Ed was in box 2 and his relationship problem was disabling.

Another example involves a newly hired professional with a degree in computer science. Because the department manager did not have an immediate project available, he asked the newcomer to coordinate departmental test activity temporarily. His shift supervisor was an old hand in the testing business who had not completed college, and Bill resented having him as boss. This upset him so much, in fact, that he did not even do his simple coordination job very well. The department manager soon realized there was a problem and discussed the situation with the shift supervisor. They both agreed that Bill was technically very capable but that his attitude was a serious problem. The manager then talked to Bill, who complained that his education was so much better than his supervisor's that *he* should be leading the group. The manager agreed he had the training to do more challenging work but pointed out that his current performance was so poor no manager would give him a better assignment. Bill was both smart and ambitious, and he realized that if he couldn't do a competent job of test coordination, he could not get promoted, regardless of his education. He buckled down, did a first-class job, and soon was given a new and better assignment. This engineer was in box 2 of Figure 7.1 and, with proper management, was helped to move to box 4.

As these examples show, relationship maturity is a complex combination of many factors. For professionals to do superior work, they must be capable of working at the self-actualizing level. This is extremely difficult for anyone, and the more severe their personal problems, the harder it is. Managers should examine each of their employees and look for symptoms of relationship immaturity. If employees perform below expectations, are hard to deal with, complain about lack of advancement, or constantly seek support, they likely have such concerns. Managers should then talk with them to see if they can identify the problems that lie behind this behavior. They can then either provide the support themselves or get professional help.

BUILDING MOTIVATION

The process of building employee motivation is different from enhancing their competence. Once employees have learned a skill, they will retain it almost indefinitely. Motivation, however, is slower to develop and can be destroyed in an instant. Highly motivated employees can be antagonized or discouraged by a manager who overlooks their achievements, assigns them uninteresting work, or unintentionally offends them. Managers should realize that, as James MacGregor Burns has said, "People need appreciation, recognition and a feeling of accomplishment, and the confidence that people who are important to them believe in them."[12]

This, of course, requires a sustained and relatively intimate level of interaction between managers and each of their employees. Pelz's studies showed that the most productive scientists were those whom management gave a moderate degree of freedom.[13] Those at either end of the freedom spectrum were less productive. At one extreme, those with the greatest freedom tended to work by themselves and lacked the stimulation of frequent management interaction and the resulting challenge of short-term goals. Tightly managed scientists, at the other extreme, were invariably well motivated, but Pelz found they were too constrained by their manager's style and thus not very creative. He found that when the manager's style was not directive, there was a strong positive correlation between professionals' performance and their frequency of management contact. Rensis Likert similarly found that total independence is rarely as productive as a reasonable level of sustained interaction.[14] In several studies he has shown that young scientists who saw their superiors at least daily performed significantly better than those left to operate independently.

In the final analysis, professionals are potentially their own best managers, and they will be most effective when their own personal standard is superior performance. Managers can build this attitude by showing frequent interest in the work of each of their employees, involving them in the decisions that affect them, recognizing and respecting each as an individual, and giving individuals reasonable control over how they do their jobs.

MOTIVATING TECHNICAL PROFESSIONALS

Although no simple formulas can assure employee motivation, the following guidelines are generally helpful in motivating technical people. The manager should do the following:

1. After professionals have gained a minimal level of experience, focus on the output that is wanted, giving the professionals progressively more discretion on how to produce it.

2. Hold frequent informal meetings with each of the professional employees and ask questions about their technical approach, whom they have talked to, and what they know about others' work in the field.

3. Probe the goals and standards the professionals have set for themselves. If they are not seeking excellence and pursuing aggressive goals, be supportive of what they have done, but challenge them to be more aggressive.

4. When professionals seek advice, suggest avenues to explore rather than give specific direction. Managers should certainly discuss their own ideas, but employees should have the freedom to accept them and be expected to justify their own final conclusions.

5. Be enthusiastic about good work and make sure that employees know it.

6. Involve the most productive people in at least some nonproject activities. Since an exclusive project focus limits creativity, they should occasionally participate in relevant studies, task forces, or committees.

7. Ask the most promising professionals to present their work to senior managers, customers, or outside professional groups. This both builds their self-confidence and motivates them to structure their work more logically.

8. Finally, require professionals to make the plans and estimates for their own work. If they are too conservative, ask tough questions and probe for contingencies and soft spots. A relaxed management will rarely get the best performance, for good people thrive on hard work, especially when their managers demand it.

An example of how well these guidelines for motivation can work is a course I have taught to graduate software engineers[15] on the subject I call the Personal Software Process (PSP). The course shows software engineers how to apply process management principles to their personal work. Students in the course write a total of 10 programming exercises and gather data on their work. The engineers are challenged to find every defect in their programs before they do the first compile. At the beginning, most engineers question the need to do this, but by the end of the course they see that an early emphasis on quality produces better programs faster than before. They also find that when they have a lot of defects in compiling they will invariably have trouble in test. Data on over 100 students who have completed this course show that with this approach test defects are reduced by an average of five times while average productivity increases 30%.[16]

THE MANAGER'S STYLE

Many managers see a conflict between the need for strong leadership and the need for more employee participation in decision making. There is, however, no real conflict. Professionals want to do important work and they want to do it their way. The strong leader reinforces the urgency and importance of the goal, while the participative manager recognizes success and provides the freedom and support his or her people need. A good manager must be capable of both leading and supporting.

Engineers and scientists quickly become uneasy when their managers leave them alone. They wonder if their assignment is still important or if they have fallen into disfavor. They may suspect some unknown change in plans or a secret reorganization. The brighter they are, the more likely they are to dream up imagined problems to distract them and limit their creativity. The best insurance against this problem is daily management contact and the challenge of crisp and important goals.

Participation does not mean relaxation. Important work calls for urgency, with aggressive schedules and a challenging pace. If the department members seem too comfortable and relaxed, tighter deadlines are needed.

If the job is to take a week, schedule a meeting for the day seven days from the starting date and don't accept a delay without an explanation. The manager's style should be honest and participative, but it should also be demanding.

NOTES

1. Lee Iacocca and William Novak, *Iacocca: An Autobiography* (New York: Bantam Books, 1984), p. 56.

2. David C. McClelland's research is briefly summarized by Hersey and Blanchard in *Management of Organizational Behavior*, 3rd ed. (Englewood Cliffs, NJ: Prentice-Hall, 1977). The references they list are David C. McClelland, J.W. Atkinson, R.A. Clark, and E.L. Lowell, *The Achievement Motive* (New York: Appleton-Century-Crofts, 1953) and *The Achieving Society* (Princeton, NJ: International Thompson Organization, Van Nostrand, Reinhold, 1961).

3. A. Ray McCord, "Improving Productivity—A Way of Life at TI," *Assembly Engineering*, January 1980, p. 52.

4. Frederick Winslow Taylor, *The Principles of Scientific Management* (New York: Harper & Row, 1911).

5. Douglass McGregor originally coined the term "Theory X" in his book, *The Human Side of Enterprise* (New York: McGraw-Hill, 1960). Paul Hersey and Kenneth Blanchard have provided an excellent discussion of early management thinking starting on page 90 in *Management of Organizational Behavior*, 3rd ed. (Englewood Cliffs, NJ: Prentice-Hall, 1977).

6. Hersey and Blanchard, in *Management*, describe the Hawthorne studies starting on page 51. The basic references for this work are F.J. Roethlisberger and W.J. Dickson, *Management and the Worker* (Cambridge, MA: Harvard University Press, 1939); T.N. Whitehead, *The Industrial Worker*, vols. 1 and 2 (Cambridge, MA: Harvard University Press, 1938); and Elton Mayo, *The Human Problems of an Industrial Civilization* (New York: Macmillan, 1933).

7. H.M. Parsons, What Happened at Hawthorne? *Science*, vol. 183, March 8, 1974, pp. 922–932.

8. Watts S. Humphrey, *A Discipline for Software Engineering* (Reading, MA: Addison-Wesley, 1995).

9. McGregor, *The Human Side of Enterprise*.

10. Hersey and Blanchard provide a comprehensive treatment of situational leadership in Chapter 7 of *Management*.

11. The late professor Bud Kilpatrick, of the Universities of Delaware and Ohio State, specialized in transactional psychology. He described this insurance company example at an IBM management class in 1968, but there is no record of its publication.

12. James MacGregor Burns, *Leadership* (New York: Harper & Row, 1978), p. 374.

13. Donald C. Pelz and Frank M. Andrews, *Scientists in Organizations: Productive Climates for Research and Development* (New York: Wiley, 1966), p. 51.

14. Rensis Likert, *New Patterns of Management* (New York: McGraw-Hill, 1961), p. 24.

15. Watts S. Humphrey, *A Discipline for Software Engineering* (Reading, MA: Addison-Wesley, 1995).

16. W.S. Humphrey, "Using a Defined and Measured Personal Software Process," *IEEE Software*, May 1996.

8

Professional Discipline

The word *discipline* often connotes punishment or regimentation. The dictionary, however, has these definitions:[1]

Training to act in accordance with rules, drill

An activity, exercise, or a regimen that develops or improves skill

Punishment inflicted by way of correction and training

Although one of these definitions does relate to punishment, it is only the third after two that deal with training and skill development. Here, we use the second definition, discipline as a way to develop or improve skill. The disciplined behavior of professionals is thus a way for them to improve their ability to practice their professions. Note also, however, that this refers to intelligent behavior. Thus suitably skilled and practiced professionals must understand the methods they use and know when they should be applied or where they should be adjusted or replaced.

THE NEED FOR DISCIPLINE

In this increasingly complex modern society, the public is almost totally dependent on the capability of many skilled professionals. Professional pilots fly the airplanes people travel in, and skilled doctors care for their health. Many commonly used products are designed to meet rigorous operational and safety criteria. In short, many people's comforts and even their lives are almost constantly in the hands of the many professionals who design, manufacture, and operate sophisticated modern products.

As technology pervades modern life, the quality of everyday products becomes increasingly important. In transportation, farming, manufacturing, and financial work, products must operate properly. When these systems fail, people's lives are disrupted, inconvenienced, and possibly even threatened. In engineering and science, it is thus increasingly important that managers monitor the methods their people use in their work. When professionals properly apply the proven techniques of their fields, they work more effectively and produce higher quality products.

EXAMPLES OF DISCIPLINED BEHAVIOR

Disciplined behavior is demonstrated in many fields. In medicine, for example, Dr. Mohs has developed a sophisticated surgical method for treating skin cancers. By the time physicians start their training in the Mohs method, they have already completed four years of medical school and a full internship. They then spend three years in training as dermatologists and another full year training for the Mohs specialty. Mohs surgeons must be both skilled surgeons and qualified pathologists. Besides studying surgical methods and soft tissue anatomy, they learn and practice the methods and techniques of pathology. The benefits of this discipline are extraordinary, for Mohs-trained surgeons have a cure rate of 98% as opposed to 85% for doctors with less rigorous backgrounds. When considered in terms of failure rate, this improvement reduces the failure rate from 15% to 2%, a 7.5 times reduction.

In music, discipline is also important. Before they are accepted as students at respected conservatories, aspiring musicians must be competent performers. Their rigorous conservatory training hones their skills until a flawless performance is routine. Only then can they develop the techniques of professional musicians. At this point, when they no longer worry about playing the proper notes, their concerns are with style and interpretation. When people attend professional concerts, they don't hear mistakes. Perfection is normal and expected, and a single wrong note would be cause for critical comment. Often, in fact, discipline enables creativity. Consider, for example, professional jazz musicians. They have, through rigorous practice, mastered their instruments and musical techniques to the point where they can improvise on a theme as they perform.

In many branches of engineering, science, sports, and the arts, aspiring professionals must learn and perfect the disciplines and techniques of their fields before they can be qualified to practice. Where health and public safety are concerned, qualifying boards administer rigorous examinations and only those who can demonstrate competence receive a license to practice. Disciplined behavior builds the skills and practices that are the ticket for admission.

INTELLECTUAL DISCIPLINES

With the steady advance of technology, purely intellectual disciplines have become increasingly important. In semiconductor chip design, for example, flawless initial designs are essential. Once a chip is designed, it often takes months to complete the masks and fabrication steps to produce the first chip. If that chip has even a single defect, months of preparation must be repeated.

Another example of discipline is the certification of physicists by the American Board of Radiology. To be qualified to handle radiation equipment and facilities, physicists must be certified by the Physics Credentials Committee. They first must achieve a Ph.D. degree in physics and then pass both oral and written examinations. They must demonstrate their ability to calibrate x-ray apparatus, know how to survey x-ray installations, and be qualified to conduct safety surveys of radioisotope laboratories. They must also have "at least two years of specialized training in radiologic physics including the study and measurement of ionizing radiation."[2]

In aircraft design, defect-free performance is even more crucial. The engineers consider all possible stress conditions to ensure that no resonance or flutter could cause metal fatigue and failure. In the Boeing 777, for example, the design engineers conducted rigorous pre-fabrication simulations and analyses. Even when aircraft development was far advanced, the Boeing engineers redesigned the tail assembly to ensure there would be no flutter problem.[3] Less disciplined engineers might not have anticipated the problem. Or they might not have had the courage to delay this multibillion dollar development program. Less disciplined groups would be tempted to overlook such "theoretical problems," until they became "real." In the case of Boeing, however, the engineers knew that theoretical problems can often turn into real, life-threatening problems. In spite of deadline pressure, these engineers were supported by their management in maintaining high standards.

Visibility

One of the most difficult problems with disciplined intellectual work is that it is invisible. Only the professionals know what they thought and how they reached their conclusions. Unless they keep comprehensive working notes or thoroughly measure their performance, they have no way to demonstrate that they have truly followed the appropriate methods. Doing disciplined work is hard enough, but when it is invisible, consistently superior performance is nearly impossible. That is why it is important that managers ask their professional employees about their work. What methods have they used and how can they demonstrate the effectiveness of their practices? Managers should look for outstanding work and then commend it when they find it. This will help make disciplined behavior both visible and rewarding.

THE IMPORTANCE OF DISCIPLINE

The disciplines professionals use in their work largely determine the quality of the products they produce. Professional disciplines capture the lessons that generations of prior professionals have learned. By learning and applying these disciplines, professionals avoid making common mistakes and reinventing solutions to previously solved problems. They thus start their practice where their elders left off. This saves them a great deal of time and it gives them a powerful advantage over their untrained and less accomplished peers. To quote Isaac Newton again, "If I have seen further, it is by standing on the shoulders of giants."[4]

Professional disciplines take a great deal of time and dedication to develop, as a comment by virtuoso Isaac Stern notes. A woman told him she would give her life to play the violin the way he did. Stern replied: "Madam, I did."

Some professionals argue that their work is creative and that disciplined methods would be a constraint. That is a serious misunderstanding. Even for relatively new fields like software engineering or biochemistry, much has been learned and many difficult problems have been solved. Often, in fact, lessons from other branches of engineering and science can point to effective practices in brand-new technologies. When professionals do not build on the available history, they must re-solve many of these old problems all over again. This wastes time they could otherwise spend being truly creative.

What sets technical professionals apart from craftsmen is the scientific foundation for their work. Extensive bodies of research define the most effective methods, training programs are approved, and there are standardized qualifying examinations. While craftsmen are often highly skilled, they generally learn through lengthy apprenticeships. Crafts also often have splinter groups that each practice private techniques. The methods craftsmen used were thus largely determined by where they were apprenticed. In fact, many ancient crafts were so adept at protecting their trade secrets that their methods have been lost in antiquity.

Software Engineering Discipline

Software engineering provides a marvelous example of the benefits of disciplined practices. While software engineering is a relatively new field, much has been learned about developing quality software. Unfortunately, there are few generally accepted software engineering practices. University computer science programs traditionally focus on products with little emphasis on skills and practices. Although they generally discuss various design practices and verification methods, they make no attempt to inculcate the skills and practices required to develop industrial-grade software.

When they graduate, most software engineers neither appreciate the importance of software quality nor understand quality principles. Few have been taught effective programming practices, and fewer still know how to plan or track their work. They rarely document their designs before they build them, and they rely on compilers and debugging aids to fix the defects they inject while designing and implementing their products.

Such practices produce poor quality products. The time and money spent finding and fixing product defects is generally more than it would cost to build the product properly in the first place. The American automobile industry learned to its sorrow that it could not be competitive building products of poor quality and fixing them in test. Emphasizing quality throughout the process yields higher quality products and reduces total costs.

THE PERSONAL SOFTWARE PROCESS

I have long believed that traditional software quality practices were inefficient and ineffective. When I retired from IBM, I joined the Software Engineering Institute (SEI), where I had the opportunity to develop what I called the Personal Software Process (PSP).[5] The PSP applies to software development the quality methods that have been proven in many other fields.

PSP-trained engineers know how to estimate and plan their work. Before they start every job, they make a plan and they gather data on the steps of their work. These data help them to meet their planned costs and schedules and to see how to make better plans in the future. Continuous learning is possible because these engineers learn to use their personal data to analyze their performance and to improve the methods they use.

With the PSP, engineers also practice effective personal quality methods. The PSP objective is to produce the highest quality software products at the earliest possible point in the development cycle. Their personal data show the engineers that they can produce higher quality products and improve their productivity when they seek and remove defects before they first compile or test their programs. Without the large and variable defect repair time, PSP-trained engineers also work faster and their performance is more predictable.[6] This makes their process more stable and helps them to make more accurate plans.

Some PSP Results

Even though the PSP is new, a growing volume of data demonstrates its effectiveness. Typical of the results are data from one of my PSP classes at Carnegie Mellon University. Figure 8.1, for example, shows the defects that 14 engineers found in compiling their programs. The engineers started the PSP course using their traditional software methods with program 1 at the left. Here, on average, they found a total of 88 defects per thousand lines of code (KLOC). Note that the engineer with the highest defect levels in compile found nearly 200 defects per KLOC while the minimum was 25. By program 10, at the right, the engineers were applying all the PSP methods in their work, and they had reduced the number of defects found in compile by 6.8 times to about 13 defects per KLOC. This is an 85% improvement. Note also that at the end of the course all 14 engineers had fewer defects than the best engineer had with program 1. In Figure 8.2, the same engineers reduced the numbers of defects they found in test from around 36 defects per KLOC to 4, a nearly 10 times improvement. These results are typical of those obtained by hundreds of engineers during PSP training.[7]

With current methods, large software systems are produced as assemblies of many small programs. Thus, the quality of large programs is almost

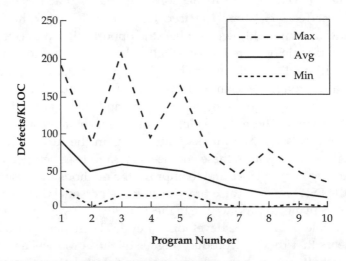

Figure 8.1   Defects Found in Compile Range

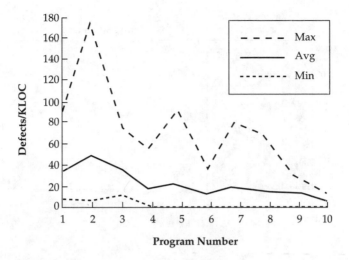

Figure 8.2   Defects Found in Test Range

entirely determined by the quality of the small program modules of which they are composed. During the final testing phases, project members today typically spend 40% to 50% or more of their time finding and fixing the defects in the program modules.[8] Because PSP training substantially reduces the numbers of defects engineers leave in their programs, the PSP methods can save substantial compiling, testing, and repair time.

The PSP also focuses on estimating and planning. One company, Advanced Information Services (AIS), has trained its engineers in the PSP. Figure 8.3 shows the estimated and actual times AIS engineers took to de-

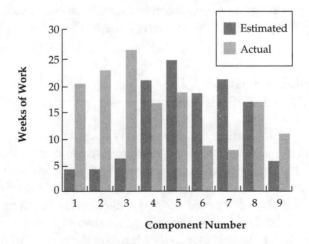

Figure 8.3   Estimated and Actual Weeks of Work

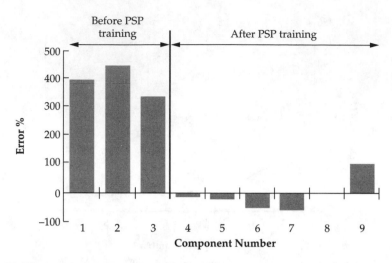

Figure 8.4   Error in Estimated Weeks of Work

velop nine components of a moderate-sized product. Figure 8.4 shows the estimating error for each of these components. Each component had about 1000 lines of code, and the engineers produced components 1, 2, and 3 before they were trained in the PSP. Their average estimating error for these first three components was 394%. The development time for component 3, for example, was estimated to be 6 weeks but ended up being 26. After PSP training, the average estimating error was −10.4%. That is, on average, the engineers completed their work about 10% ahead of their planned dates. Note that component 8 took 16 weeks, exactly as planned. Note also that estimating errors are normal. When engineers estimate their work in detail, and when their estimating errors are reasonably balanced around zero, they will generally complete the total job pretty close to when it was planned.

THE MANAGER'S ROLE IN PROFESSIONAL DISCIPLINE

Managers can profoundly affect the way their professionals behave. One would hope that trained and skilled professionals would act professionally at all times, but this is not the case. Some professionals have highly developed personal standards and will act professionally in spite of external pressures. Most professionals, however, need support and encouragement to consistently perform at their best. This is why even championship athletes have coaches.

Professionals generally prefer to do high-quality work. Their most common complaint is that the pressures of their jobs do not permit them to produce work of the quality they feel is needed. Their managers constantly press them for early deliveries and appear uninterested in product quality. Most professionals know that shipping poor quality work will cost more in the long run than doing the job properly in the first place. When managers only ask about schedules, they imply that the schedule is all that matters.

Quality and productivity are intimately related. Managers must recognize that if products didn't have to work, their people could develop them very quickly. When managers ask only about schedules, they foster sloppy work. While the products may get into test quickly, it will take longer to fix the product in test than it would have taken to do the job right the first time. A good rule of thumb is that it takes longer to fix a defective product than it would have taken to build it right in the first place. And when the engineers fix it, the best they can get is a patched up defective product.

When managers insist that their professional employees rigorously apply the recognized disciplines of their fields, they will do better work. And when they do better work, they will more consistently produce quality results. An early attention to quality saves the time that would have been spent debugging and fixing the product in test. Competent professionals soon learn that disciplined work is more satisfying and that it produces better products faster and cheaper than any other way.

MORE GUIDELINES FOR MANAGERS

If you are a manager, you can easily check to see if you are guilty of fostering undisciplined behavior. Do you ask only about schedules or do you demonstrate an equal interest in the quality of your professional employees' work? If you do not regularly consider the methods your employees use or the quality of the products they produce, consider the following guidelines:

1. When recruiting, focus on the disciplines the professionals have learned. Do they know how to produce quality products? What quality methods have they learned and what experience have they had in applying these methods? Do they know how to measure the quality of their work and do they have data to demonstrate their performance? Few schools train their graduates to answer such questions. If the schools where you recruit do not provide such training, ask them why not. Until industry demands suitably trained professionals, it will not get them.

2. If you cannot hire suitably trained professionals, you will have to train them. This requires finding or developing appropriate courses and arranging to have them taught. While there are not a great many such courses, there are a few good ones. Engineers and scientists who know how to write small programs, for example, could take an available course in the PSP.[9]

While this course uses software examples, the planning methods and quality principles apply to any engineering or scientific field.

3. While the professionals are being trained, treat training as part of their jobs. Track their performance and, if they fall behind, ask what help they need to get back on schedule. Recognize that professional training is hard work and celebrate their achievements when they finish.

4. Once the professionals have been trained, review their performance, daily if possible, but at least once a week. Do they plan their work and do they use historical data to make these plans? Do they use established disciplines to do the job and are they improving their personal performance? Have they defined measures for the quality of their work and do they record, analyze, and track these measures? Respect their personal data but monitor their use of quality practices. If the work is sloppy or defective, insist that the engineers correct it promptly. Never accept the excuse that there is no time to use proper methods. When there is no time to do the job right, correcting it later will always take more time.

5. When professionals finish each project, conduct a postmortem to see what worked and where problems arose. The professionals should suggest process improvements and these improvements should be incorporated in the process for the next project. Once the products are through development, require that every customer-reported defect be tracked. Also require professionals to measure defect repair costs, and participate in periodic defect reviews. The professionals should identify where each defect was injected and why it was not caught during development. Ask how these defects could better be found and prevented in the future.

Disciplined behavior is hard, but it is essential. If professionals do not know and practice the disciplines of their fields, their managers should get them trained. Once they are trained, the managers should insist that they rigorously apply the methods they have learned. The manager's job is to coach and support their professional employees in using effective disciplines and they must insist that they do. After all, if they don't nobody else will.

NOTES

1. These are the first three definitions for discipline, as listed in the *Random House Dictionary of the English Language*, 2nd ed. (New York: Random House, 1983).

2. Jack S. Krohmer, "Certification of physicists by the American Board of Radiology," published for the American Association of Physicists in Medicine by the American Institute of Physics, November 1995, pp. 1955–1960.

3. Karl Sabbagh, *Twenty-First Century Jet* (New York: Scribner, 1996), pp. 172, 204.

4. Stephen Jay Gould, *The Panda's Thumb* (New York: Norton, 1980), p. 47.

5. Watts S. Humphrey, *A Discipline for Software Engineering* (Reading, MA: Addison-Wesley, 1995).

6. Watts S. Humphrey, "The PSP and Personal Project Estimating," *American Programmer*, June 1996.

7. Watts S. Humphrey, "Using a Defined and Measured Personal Software Process," *IEEE Software*, May 1996.

8. In PSP training, even experienced engineers spend nearly 15% of their time compiling and 25% of their time unit testing their initial programs. Less experienced engineers often spend much more time.

9. My book, *A Discipline for Software Engineering,* is the text for a one-semester graduate course in disciplined process methods. Instructor's support materials are available from Addison-Wesley, and the Software Engineering Institute provides industrial support for introducing the PSP.

PART 3

The Identification
and Development
of Talented People

CHAPTER

9

Identifying
Talented
Professionals

A mong highly motivated people, the most talented generally do the best work. This assumes, of course, that their talents are directly suited to their work. Every field of specialty has a unique set of talents that provide the best chance of success. The talented have a special advantage; those lacking talent can also succeed, but it is much harder for them. As in the following example, most people would do well to find a calling that most closely matches their natural abilities.

On one of my early projects, Sam, a new engineer, had always wanted to be a circuit designer. He must have struggled valiantly in engineering school, for he had neither the mathematical talents of an engineer nor the instincts of a builder. After graduation Sam got a job with Sylvania Electric Products, where he was assigned to my project. I worked with Sam for several months, but he was unable to solve even the simplest design problems. After many discussions, I finally persuaded him to quit engineering and try his hand as a salesman. Some months later he proudly came back to thank me for urging him to change his career. He was selling paint and found he was a born salesman.

Gifted professionals can generally succeed as long as their talents are reasonably consistent with the needs of their work. As John Gardner has pointed out, however, finding such a fit is not as hard as it might seem, for "gifted individuals generally have many talents rather than a single talent. If the individual is promising in one line, the best guess is that he will be promising in a number of lines...."[1] The key is to identify the most talented people and put them in jobs that interest them. Their development is then best ensured by keeping their work continually challenging. The Peter principle says that employees tend to rise to their level of incompetence, but James Healey has proposed the far more important Paul principle: "For every employee who rises above his level of competence, there are several whose talents are not utilized."[2]

THE IMPORTANCE OF TALENT

Talented people are the organization's most important asset. They originate the creative ideas, solve the key problems, and produce the most successful products. The enormous difference between the truly talented and the average employee was demonstrated by a limited experiment with 12 programmers.[3] Each was given two identical specifications and told to produce a running program for each. Everyone was to use the same programming language and tools, and the results were carefully measured. Even though the programs were to perform identical calculations, the variation between the best and the worst was as much as 28 times. The data are shown in Table 9.1.

Table 9.1 Relative Test Results

	Algebra	Maze
Program size	6:1	5:1
Program run time	5:1	13:1
Programming hours	16:1	25:1
Debugging hours	28:1	26:1

In a course I have been teaching on the Personal Software Process (PSP), data on 104 engineers show quite similar results. Again, these engineers were all given the same specifications for 10 programs and they tracked their development time, program size, and defect levels for each program.[4] Table 9.2 shows the longest development time, the shortest development time, and the ratios of these times for the 10 PSP programs. While there is considerable variation in these ratios, the value is generally between 15 and 30 for all 10 programs. Note also that 11 different engineers accounted for these shortest and longest times. One of the 104 engineers had three repeats and another had five. It should be noted, however, that since short development time was not the principal objective of these exercises, these time differences are not entirely due to differences in native ability.

Table 9.2 PSP Development Times for 104 Engineers

| | Development Time (minutes) | | |
	Longest Times	*Shortest Times*	*Ratios*
Program 1	1355	50	27.1
Program 2	996	64	15.6
Program 3	1379	88	15.7
Program 4	1336	59	22.6
Program 5	1820	94	19.4
Program 6	1420	94	15.1
Program 7	1140	83	13.7
Program 8	1275	46	27.7
Program 9	2715	120	22.6
Program 10	1980	152	13.0

There is little question that such wide performance variations occur quite generally. Some professionals effortlessly accomplish exceptional work, while their less fortunate peers struggle to produce mediocre results. As Table 9.2 shows, we might be able to slightly reduce the differences between the high and low performers in a group, but we cannot eliminate them. On reflection, this is not surprising. Wide variations between the best and worst artists and athletes seem normal. Outstanding performance in circuit design, computer programming, or theoretical physics depends just as heavily on inherent talent.

THE AVAILABILITY OF TALENT

The ability to attract and develop talent is fundamental to organizational survival. Peter Drucker attributes the problems of the American railroads to their failings in this regard: "Before World War I able graduates of

American engineering schools looked for a railroad career. From the end of World War I on, for whatever reason, the railroads no longer appealed to young engineering graduates or to any educated young people."[5]

In every organization the limited supply of talent is clearly apparent to any manager who seeks candidates for an important assignment. An organization can address this problem only by attracting more and better engineers and scientists or by better utilizing those it already has. It is enormously difficult for an organization to make itself more attractive to the best people, however, because the most stimulating technical environments are most attractive; and this environment results from the caliber and reputation of the people who are already there. This means that the best groups attract the best people and thus become even more attractive. To become magnets for superior talent, technical organizations must both search for talent and make the best use of the talents they already have.

CHARACTERISTICS OF TECHNICALLY TALENTED PEOPLE

Of all technical talents, creativity is possibly the most important. Frank Barron has studied highly creative people, and in one test of 80 accomplished artists he found they were universally attracted by complexity.[6] They had a strong preference for asymmetrical drawings rather than simple figures, and they looked for "vital or dynamic" pictures that most other people thought chaotic. This same set of tests was then given to a group of doctor of science candidates at the University of California who had been ranked by the faculty on their originality. Barron was "somewhat surprised to discover that the more original scientists expressed preferences very similar to those of the artists." He concluded that "the creative response to disorder...is to find an elegant new order more satisfying than any that could be evoked by a simpler configuration."

Another of Barron's tests explored the relationship between originality and independence. He placed a test subject in a conference room with several people who were secretly part of the experiment. They were asked a series of simple questions, and the seating was arranged so that the subject was among the last to respond. Each was asked to look at a picture with several lines on it and to identify the line he or she believed was longest. Generally, the entire group gave the correct answer, but occasionally, at a secret signal, all the confederates gave the same incorrect response. Surprisingly, even though it was obvious which was the longest line, about 75% of the subjects contradicted the evidence of their own eyes and gave the same false response as the rest of the group.

At the completion of this test the subjects were separated into two groups according to their willingness to give the correct answer and again questioned to determine their tolerance for disorder. As shown by their responses to the following questions, the more independent-minded 25% showed a marked preference for complexity:

1. I like to fool around with new ideas even if they turn out later to be a total waste of time. (True)

2. The best theory is the one that has the best practical applications. (False)

3. Some of my friends think that my ideas are impractical, if not a bit wild. (True)

4. The unfinished and the imperfect often have greater appeal for me than the completed and the polished. (True)

5. I must admit that I would find it hard to have for a close friend a person whose manners or appearance made him somewhat repulsive, no matter how brilliant or kind he might be. (False)

6. A person should not probe too deeply into his own and other people's feelings but take things as they are. (False)

7. Young people sometimes get rebellious ideas, but as they grow up they ought to get over them and settle down. (False)

8. Perfect balance is the essence of a good composition. (False)

As a result of this work Barron has concluded that truly creative people must be sufficiently independent minded to suffer the personal discomfort and occasional ridicule that often accompany new ideas. It takes a high degree of self-confidence to challenge the existing order and even more strength of character to risk criticism. Those who are too timid rarely think up creative ideas, and when they do, they don't have the courage to support them. Barron found, however, that highly creative people were well aware of their own feelings and understood the risks they took to support them.

W.O. Baker, who was president and then chairman of Bell Laboratories before his retirement, adds an interesting dimension to Barron's findings:

> Not only must technical people possess the ego that gives them the self-confidence necessary for undertaking a very difficult mission, but they must also have some humility, because nature will have the last laugh. They must, in short, recognize the intrinsic difficulties of their task and be modest about the chance of success.[7]

Identifying Technically Talented People

Several years ago IBM established a special program to focus on the development of outstanding technical people. As a first step a survey was run of their leading technical professionals to learn how better to identify future technical leaders. A total of 25 senior professionals were questioned, including 18 IBM Fellows.[8] The responses to the various questions were scored by adding the positive reactions and subtracting the negative ones. For example, if two respondents felt that salary progression was a positive indicator and three felt it was negative, salary progression would be scored as –1. The maximum score would thus be +25, and the minimum –25. Using this system, the net scores for the most frequently mentioned leading indicators of superior technical performance are as shown in Table 9.3.

Table 9.3 Early Indications of Technical Leadership

Professional society activities

Publications	9
Awards	7
Presentations	6
Offices	–10

IBM technical committee activity

Presentations	3
Use on technical task forces	19
Special assignments	15
Technical memos	6

Academic history

Projects	4
Grade point average	3
Honors	0

IBM history

Awards	5
Performance rating	2
Salary progression	–1

These senior professionals clearly felt that highly talented technical professionals were best identified by the respect of their peers and managers. This respect was shown by the frequency of selection of the highly talented for task forces or special assignments. Publications, awards, and presentations were judged to be important, although opinions varied widely, with some strongly dissenting views. Involvement with professional societies was not felt to be a strong indicator, although this more likely reflects the limited technical society involvement of many industrial engineers and scientists than the value of such activities.

IDENTIFYING MANAGERIAL TALENT

Although the identification of technical talent is largely a matter of finding those creative people with motivation and self-confidence, the search for managerial talent is a different matter. Here, motivation and self-confidence are also needed, but other factors are equally essential. Edwin Gee, a senior vice president of DuPont, has listed the major reasons for the failure of research directors:[9]

1. Poor interpersonal relationships, difficulty in establishing rapport with subordinates, and pettiness. Where such problems exist, Gee feels they are inborn, ingrained, and irreversible.

2. Looking for intellectual solutions to managerial problems and not appreciating the subjective, human factors.

3. Overdedication to scientific discovery without the ability to use these discoveries to effectively support the organization's objectives.

4. The lack of financial, profit, or business orientation. Such managers devote the same effort to projects that have small potential dollar payoff as they do to ones with larger potential.

5. A lack of market orientation means such directors fail to get adequate marketplace feedback before dollar costs become excessive. As a result, a higher proportion of their projects become expensive marketplace failures because they were not previously stopped in the laboratory or plant.

6. Finally, many poorly performing research directors fail to establish goals, assessment programs, and a follow-up discipline.

Note that while I agree with Gee's other points, on point 1, he has over-generalized. In my experience, almost anyone can change, given the right motivation and support.

Gee also describes attributes of researchers which suggest that they will be good managers:

1. They are able to identify a problem, analyze it, and synthesize a solution.

2. They are willing to accept and even seek responsibility.

3. They view their current assignment as the most important single thing they have to do rather than as a step toward promotion.

4. They have good work habits, set personal goals, and plan ahead.

5. They are able to get results without upsetting people.

6. They have integrity.

7. In addition to technical talent, they have demonstrated at least some skill in such fields as marketing, finance, and employee relations.

8. Finally, the ability to make sound judgments is the key to both long-term potential and current readiness for promotion.

Harry Truman put it most succinctly when he said that a leader must act as if "the buck stops here."[10]

THE TAMED REBEL

Alon Gratch, while a doctoral candidate at Columbia University, made a psychological study of some 70 corporate leaders.[11] He ran a series of tests to identify their attitudes and to understand what he called their ego development. For this purpose, he divided them into Conformists and post-Conformists. The Conformist feels that rules are to be followed, but the post-Conformist sees them as guides that occasionally should be broken or changed. Gratch found that 95% of the successful executives in his study fell into the post-Conformist stage. This contrasts with the normal population, which is predominantly Conformist.

Gratch further divided the post-Conformist stage into the Conscientious and the Autonomous. He found that Conscientious managers are "interested in motives, consequences, long-term goals and ideals. They are self-critical but not self-rejecting." Most important, such managers are conscious of their own feelings and capable of managing issues objectively in spite of personal considerations. Such managers, he found

are ambitious and have a need for achievement

have the flexibility to see people and situations from several perspectives

act and feel like rebels but consciously hold themselves in check

The highest level of ego development is the Autonomous and Integrated stage where, according to Gratch, people "show a deep concern for the autonomy of others." None of Gratch's 70 successful executives fell into this Autonomous level. This is not surprising, because Autonomous individuals are more considerate of the concerns of others, more willing to accept problems as insoluble, and less inclined to strive valiantly for an unreachable goal. Great leaders are often great because they continue to struggle and often succeed even against apparently overwhelming odds.

RECOGNIZING TALENT

From all the studies on this subject a few criteria emerge as common identifiers of future leadership. It is clear that technically creative people must have the courage of their own convictions and be willing to face criticism. Similarly, future senior managers do not feel bound by the rules, and they have sufficient self-confidence to push for what they believe in. The personal courage to be different and the self-confidence to take the lone and often unpopular position are clearly basic characteristics of leaders in both management and technology.

This characteristic of talented people is the source of much of the difficulty with identification programs. All too often those who obey the rules and don't make waves are rewarded with steady advancement. The evidence suggests, however, that the most promising leaders are often the wild ducks, and that it might be wise to consciously look for talent among the ranks of the rebels.

This does not mean that every nonconformist will make a good leader. People choose to be different for many reasons, but some of them take this path because they see opportunities for improvement that the rest of us have missed. To avoid overlooking some of the organization's truly outstanding talent, the wild ducks should be reviewed to see what makes them wild.

Finally, an individual's dedication to work is vital. Based on a 20-year AT&T study, Ann Howard and Douglass Bray point out that the one characteristic that separated future top executives from their less successful peers was their continued willingness to work hard.[12] While no studies of the work attitudes of technical leaders have been made, there is no question that hard work is one of their common characteristics. Beyond these two simple measures of self-confidence and dedication, the only reliable guideline to future success is the opinion of the employee's peers and immediate managers.

The Identification Process

The first step in an identification process is to have the employees' direct managers evaluate their on-the-job performance and decide on their promotion potential. The managers than review these judgments with the next higher managers, who also talk with other managers to get as complete an opinion of the employees as possible. These individual judgments are made by the management team on all the people in the organization, and they are reviewed with the senior managers, who then select the most promising professionals for future development and promotion. The advantages of such an approach are as follows:

- It is simple, inexpensive, and timely.

- It accurately reflects current job performance and quickly eliminates those who obviously have low potential.

- It reflects the views of those managers who can most directly influence the employee's career.

- It is equally effective for both technical and managerial candidates.

- Finally, as Leavitt points out, the combined judgment and wisdom of many experienced managers is usually very sound.[13]

The typical problems with such direct managerial evaluations of employee potential are the following:

- One manager's views can seriously bias the evaluation. This risk is highest with the first-line manager, who is least experienced at making such judgments.

- Although junior managers can usually judge a professional's readiness for promotion, they rarely appreciate the needs of higher-level positions and are not reliable judges of long-term potential.

- Junior managers are often reluctant to identify their best people for promotion because they will likely lose them and have to find replacements.

- All managers are busy and rarely take the time to do these evaluations unless they are required to.

Even though doing so has serious drawbacks, there is no completely satisfactory substitute for using line management to do the basic identification work.

THE ASSESSMENT CENTER

The assessment center provides a practical and effective way to augment the immediate manager's judgment. It is typically used to evaluate a dozen or so high potential young managers by exposing them to several days of tests and exercises. Their performance is observed by an assessment staff of two or three trained professionals and four or more senior management observers. The program involves a number of individual exercises and presentations as well as unstructured team assignments. Each individual's performance is rated for each exercise, and at the end, the observers and the assessment staff combine their views on each individual's potential and career planning needs. These judgments are then discussed with the individual by the assessment staff. As is natural in such programs, the ratings tend to be relative, which necessitates that some people be ranked at the bottom. To protect them from potential career damage, only limited assessment results are shared with line management, and then only with the senior location executive for each attendee.

Badawy discusses such programs and gives an excellent summary of their strengths and weaknesses:[14]

1. Several assessors are likely to do a better job than a single supervisor.

2. The use of structured evaluation criteria helps to provide a more complete judgment.

3. Participation in such programs helps the senior management observers sharpen their assessment skills.

4. The candidates generally find that the exercises provide helpful perspective on themselves and their work.

5. Being chosen for an assessment exercise builds the candidates' morale and gives them an opportunity to show their abilities in fairly realistic situations.

Badawy, however, also points out some problems with assessment centers:

1. Assessment can be a self-fulfilling prophecy. Those who do best will get the greatest opportunities for promotion.

2. A candidate who does poorly can become discouraged and lose self-confidence, thus hurting an otherwise promising career.

3. Those who are not given the opportunity to attend such programs may object.

4. The stress of assessment can be serious, particularly for those who do not perform well in a competitive environment.

5. Assessment programs are generally expensive to operate.

Assessment Experience

During my years at IBM, the corporation ran an assessment program in engineering, programming, and product planning to identify and develop high-potential managers. In one survey of participants, 96% felt the assessment accurately measured the qualities crucial for management success, 92% were confident that observers' judgments were accurate, 96% rated the assessment effective in measuring their personal strengths and weaknesses, and 97% said it would help them in their own self-improvement efforts.

Regarding career progress, 51% of the participants felt assessment would help them, and 33% said it would neither help nor hurt. However, 16% felt their careers would be damaged by assessment. This probably explains why only 84% of the graduates would be willing to participate again.

At the time, approximately one-third of IBM's high-potential technical managers had been identified, in part, through this program, and even though the results were not made available to the immediate managers, subsequent promotional progress correlated well with the assessment ratings. Those rated very highly by the assessors were promoted an average of 2.1 levels in the six years following assessment, while those with lower ratings only moved 0.8 levels. The highly and moderately rated managers moved 1.7 and 1.2 levels, respectively.

Identification Programs

Immediate managers play an important role in assessment because they nominate the people to attend. They know their people best, are best qualified to judge their needs and talents, and will control their future development. The first-line manager's critical role, however, is also the greatest weakness of the identification process, because they are generally so busy with their daily priorities that they can rarely take the time to do this job adequately. That is why such programs are never effective unless higher-level management gets directly involved.

Direct involvement by senior managers is most effective when they take a strong personal interest in the program and are willing to spend their own time conducting periodic reviews with a top management team. For example, one division president would spend one full day a year with each location manager, reviewing the high-potential employee identification and development programs. When he found a program that was not up to par, he would explain to the manager that this was a basic requirement of the location manager's job and that he would be back for another review in a few months. The program was always in good shape for the second review.

NOTES

1. John W. Gardner, *Excellence* (New York: Harper & Row, 1961), p. 60.

2. M.K. Badawy, *Developing Managerial Skills in Engineers and Scientists: Succeeding as a Technical Manager* (New York: International Thompson Organization, Van Nostrand Reinhold, 1982), p. 274.

3. H. Sackman, W.J. Erikson, and E.E. Grant, "Exploratory Experimental Studies Comparing Online and Offline Programming Performance," *Communications of the ACM,* vol. 11, no. 1 (January 1968), pp. 3–11.

4. W.S. Humphrey, *A Discipline for Software Engineering* (Reading, MA: Addison-Wesley, 1995).

5. Peter F. Drucker, *Management, Tasks, Responsibilities, Practices* (New York: Harper & Row, 1974), p. 109.

6. Frank Barron, "The Psychology of Imagination," *Scientific American,* CXCIX (September 1958), pp. 151–166.

7. Michael F. Wolff, "Managing Large Egos," *Research Management,* July 1982, p. 7.

8. IBM Fellows are senior professionals who have demonstrated such outstanding technical ability that they are given the freedom to work on any project they choose. At any one time about 50 IBM professionals hold five-year renewable appointments to the rank of Fellow.

9. Edwin A. Gee and Chaplin Tyler, *Managing Innovation* (New York: Wiley, 1976), p. 172.

10. Merle Miller, *Plain Speaking: An Oral Biography of Harry S Truman* (New York: Putnam Publishing Group, Berkley Publishing Group, 1973).

11. Alon Gratch, "Tamed Rebels Make Good Managers," *New York Times,* February 10, 1985, sec. 3, p. 3.

12. Ann Howard and Douglass W. Bray, "A.T.&T.: The Hopes of Middle Managers," *New York Times*, March 21, 1982, sec. 3, p. 2.

13. Harold J. Leavitt, *Managerial Psychology*, 4th ed. (Chicago: University of Chicago Press, 1978), p. 100.

14. Badawy, *Developing Managerial Skills*, pp. 56–57.

CHAPTER

10

Developing
Technical
Talent

True excellence in any field requires a combination of talent, experience, and motivation. Even people with great natural talents must know how to use them to reach the first rank. It takes enormous effort to excel in any field, be it athletics, engineering, music, or science. Proper guidance can be very helpful in making these efforts most effective.

The late professor Herbert Simon, who won a Nobel Prize for his pioneering work in artificial intelligence, explained how expert knowledge is developed. Experts build a large store of remembered patterns; chess masters, for example, can remember as many as 50,000 or more combinations of chess pieces.[1] Simon called this their vocabulary, and he pointed out that average players can remember only several hundred such patterns. According to Simon, the human brain has separate short-term and long-term memories. The long-term memory holds a large volume of essentially permanent information, but it cannot save or retrieve it very quickly. Short-term memory is much faster but can only handle four to six "chunks" at a time.

Simon described a simple experiment that illustrates the expert's tremendous advantage over the novice. Several subjects are shown a chess board of a game in progress, which has 25 or so pieces upon it. They are told to look at this board for a few seconds and then to reproduce the positions of all the pieces from memory. Most novices can only place five or six of the pieces, but the experts can reproduce the entire board with about 90% accuracy. This works only with board positions from actual chess games, however, for if the pieces are placed at random, the expert does no better than the novice. The reason is that the novice needs to remember each piece individually, but the expert sees a chess game as logical groupings of pieces. Each such grouping is remembered as a single chunk of information, and since each chunk includes several pieces, only five or six chunks will often include the entire board. When the pieces are randomly placed, however, the expert now must also remember each piece individually; the experts can no longer draw on this store of 50,000 or so patterns. Experts thus do not necessarily have a better memory than novices, they just remember in more powerful chunks.

All experienced professionals have such expert "vocabularies" that provide them an analytic capability far greater than the average layman. The importance of powerful symbols can be easily visualized by trying to remember several eight-place binary numbers, such as 10010110, 11000101, and 10111010. Since most people are unfamiliar with this notation, they must memorize the positions of each individual bit. This means that each binary number must take eight chunks of short-term memory, thus making it impossible for many people to remember more than one such eight-place number. When the more powerful decimal notation is used, however, these same binary numbers become 150, 197, and 186, which most people can readily remember, at least for a few moments. The use of more powerful information chunks reduces the load on short-term memory, allows experts to deal with more information at one time, and thus permits them to think in far more complex and sophisticated terms.

As they accumulate large stores of knowledge in their respective special fields, experts are also increasing the power of the symbols they work and think with. All this takes a great deal of time and effort, as shown by the studies of the psychologist John R. Hayes of Carnegie Mellon University. He examined the careers of successful artists and found that none of them produced a world-class work until they had spent at least 10 years in their chosen medium.[2] Although artists are not scientists, their fields are similar in that they require special skills and a large store of relevant knowledge. With the increasing sophistication of science and engineering, it is progressively more difficult for anyone to become a first-class expert without taking the time to learn a large store of information about his or her chosen field. Although many people are able to do this on their own, a structured development program can help the promising professional spend this preparatory time to best advantage.

PROFESSIONAL DEVELOPMENT

No one questions the athlete's need for a trainer, but the corresponding needs of technical professionals are not as clearly recognized. Young engineers and scientists are eager to learn and willing to work hard, but they rarely have the perspective to direct their energies efficiently. A structured development program based on each individual's needs and career plans can help them select the assignments that will build their skills and give them the perspective to avoid dead-end jobs.

In addition to assisting the professionals, such programs also help make the organization more attractive to talented people. The best engineers and scientists are understandably concerned about career development and will be more interested in an organization that shows equal concern. Professional development programs also help to ensure an adequate supply of qualified candidates for key positions. Since there is always a shortage of skilled and capable people, this can be enormously valuable.

As part of its recruiting effort, DuPont had a corporate-wide professional development program that was administered by its Engineering Department. At the time I reviewed their program, 300 to 400 professionals were covered, with approximately 75 new college recruits enrolled in the program each year. In line with their interests, these young professionals were rotated through a series of two-year assignments across a range of technical activities. The full-time headquarters staff participated in performance reviews, ensured that the assignment continued to be appropriate for each individual, and arranged for new assignments. They reported no difficulty in finding these assignments and believed the program helped both to attract and retain good people. It also provided top-notch engineering talent to the company's operations. The professionals who had completed the program typically did well both in their initial assignments and in their future promotional progress.

CAREER MOVES

The typical technical professional has many latent talents, but only a few of them can be developed in any single assignment. While it would be impractical to attempt to capitalize on all the potential talents of any engineer or scientist, it is also clear that the most productive professionals have competence in several areas. This suggests that the most talented people should be given the opportunity to broaden their backgrounds, and this can best be done through multiple career moves.

Managers are always reluctant to let their best people go, but sometimes professionals are reluctant to move as well. When they get comfortable in one specialty, they often cling to its safety and resist management pressure to move. William Cohen describes such a case with Mickey, an aeronautical engineer who became a specialist in reciprocating aircraft engines during World War II.[3] Mickey stayed on with the same company after the war and over the next several years was given several opportunities to attend a six-month course on the new jet engine technology. He always claimed to be too busy, however, so he ended up staying with the old reciprocating engine technology and never did switch to jets. Despite his acknowledged talents, he ended up as the lone advisory staff consultant who handled the few remaining problems that came up with the old World War II vintage engines.

Professional development programs help to identify people like Mickey so that management can prod them into more promising career paths. Some people are reluctant to accept the challenge and stimulation of new technical assignments, but this is often exactly what is needed to maintain their professional development. Thomas J. Watson, Jr., once said, "Men who have accomplished great deeds in large organizations might have done less if they had been challenged with less."[4]

TECHNICAL DEVELOPMENT NEEDS

In one study, 25 senior engineers, scientists, and programmers were asked what experiences would have been most helpful to them in their careers.[5] As shown in Table 10.1, some experiences were supported by a clear majority, even though there was no general consensus. The wide divergence of opinion is shown by the fact that 11 were positive about research experience and only 2 negative; for assistantships, 10 were in favor, and 3 against. The strongest divergence of opinion concerned division and corporate staff positions with 9 in favor and 4 against. The one thing the responses of these 25 senior professionals all demonstrated was the wide range of potential career paths which can lead to success.

Table 10.1   Valuable Technical
             Development Experiences

Product development	14
Advanced technology	14
Management	13
An academic sabbatical	10
Manufacturing	9
Research	9
A technical assistantship	7
Corporate or division staff	5

The area of most general agreement concerned the value of identification and development programs in assisting the careers of promising technical professionals. Two respondents said they had succeeded on their own and felt everyone else should as well, but 23 of the 25 believed that early counseling and support would have helped them.

The most surprising finding of this study was the widely shared opinion that promising technical professionals should be given management experience. Sixteen of the 25 felt that management experience was important, while 3 felt it would have a negative effect on a promising professional's career, and 6 voiced no opinion. Even those technologists who had no continuing interest in a management career felt that early experience as a manager had better equipped them to deal with their superiors and had helped prepare them to lead their current small technical teams. With some exceptions, these technical leaders were currently managers of small advanced-technology groups, and they had found that people-management skills were important to them.

Technical Breadth

From his studies of technical people, Pelz concluded that the initial focus in developing scientists and engineers should be on building a deep understanding in one primary field of specialty. He says, "The younger Ph.D. should remain in one problem or research area, but learn as much as he can about many aspects of this area; he should not limit himself to a narrow facet."[6] Even with a high degree of concentration, it can take a lot of time for professionals to reach the limits of knowledge in their chosen topic, but until they do, they are rarely able to do leading-edge work.

Once they have established a career foundation, promising professionals should attempt to gain some breadth. How quickly they proceed must obviously depend on the individual, but broadening one's scope should not be delayed for long, for, to quote Pelz: "the key for mature scientists lies not in the dominance of breadth over depth, but rather in the presence of both breadth and depth."[7] The reason breadth is so important was best explained by the late Abraham Maslow when he said "To him that has only a hammer, the whole world looks like a nail."[8] Narrow technologists will spend too much of their time trying to fit the problems they face to their known but limited set of solutions.

Breadth also provides a rich foundation for intuitive judgment. In modern technology few issues are cleanly constrained to one special field, and the available data are rarely complete or even consistent. Under such conditions, good intuition is often the only reliable guide. Intuition, however, is best gained through hands-on experience in a variety of areas, and seasoned professionals can often sense the right answer while their less experienced colleagues are still struggling to define the problem.

Tracy Kidder described this phenomenon in his anecdote about the visit of Carl Carman, a Data General vice-president, to a computer test area. The engineers told him about a problem that had plagued them for weeks, and as Kidder says:

> The ALU was sitting outside Gallifrey's (the computer's) frame, on the extender. Gallifrey was running a low-level program. Carman said, "Hmmmmm." He walked over to the computer and, to the engineers' horror, he grasped the ALU board by its edges and shook it. At that instant, Gallifrey failed.[9]

The engineers suddenly realized that their problem was in the connectors that held the chips to the ALU, so they replaced them all, and the error that had plagued them for months was gone. In a few minutes Carman, with his broad experience, could "smell" the problem that these engineers had worked for weeks to find.

A similar problem came up in the early development of the SABRE airline reservation system. I had been asked to run an audit of the program to assess its status and identify potential problems. We assembled a team of experienced software and communications professionals. During the reviews, one of the communications experts asked about the system's maximum traffic capacity. The SABRE engineers explained that the maximum load was to be several transactions a second, which the system could easily handle. The communication expert then asked what would happen if the load was several times greater than expected. After objecting that such loads were not expected, the SABRE engineers did look at how their system would behave under a heavy overload. They found that the network protocol they had selected increased overhead sharply as the traffic approached maximum capacity. Under heavy overloads, the system would thus choke itself and cease handling any traffic at all. This expert review helped to identify a key problem in time to change the system design. This was fortunate since the SABRE system ultimately handled loads hundreds of times greater than originally planned.

Breadth permits engineers to apply knowledge from one area to problems in another. Technical intuition is often transferable between specialties, and the engineer or scientist with experience in several subjects invariably finds they have deep similarities. Much as an experienced linguist finds each new language easier to learn, broad-gauge professionals can grasp new issues and concepts far quicker than their less experienced associates. Patrick Winston, director of MIT's Artificial Intelligence Laboratory, suggests why this is true when he says, "You don't learn anything unless you almost know it anyway."[10]

An argument against broad exposure for engineers and scientists is that it reduces the time they can spend in their prime specialty. Pelz has shown, however, that professionals do better work when they are involved in several activities at the same time.[11] He found that only 6% of their time need be spent away from their prime project, but there was a decided peak in performance when they were involved in four to five activities. With 75 research Ph.D.'s, for example, those who spent one-half to three-quarters of their time on strictly research work were more scientifically productive than the ones who devoted full time. Even when the balance of this nonproject time was spent on nontechnical matters, the part-time researchers still did better work.[12] This characteristic of broad exposure and interests seems to apply quite generally. For example, my brother reports that when he was a museum director at the University of Kansas, his best staff members had the heaviest teaching loads, counseled many graduate students, maintained high publication rates, and managed major grant commitments.

CONTINUING MANAGEMENT CONTACT

Managers can also help to develop their outstanding people by managing them in a stimulating way. Exposing them to multiple challenges and providing them with a high degree of control over their own work enables them to grow most quickly. By showing continuing interest in their people's work, managers also reinforce its importance. This helps to maintain their enthusiasm during the long periods of drudgery between the occasional moments of excitement. Managers must be careful, however, to handle these contacts in the right way; for if they are excessively critical or highly directive, they can cause the professional to worry more about the manager's opinions than about the technical issues.

George Farris reports on a study of NASA scientists that compared the supervisory styles of high- and low-performing groups.[13] He found that the supervisors with the best groups had a great deal of interaction with the members of their groups and behaved more like collaborators than traditional managers. Because of this their employees were also more interactive with one another and maintained a more open and informal atmosphere. In the low-performing groups, conversely, the supervisors were seen as dominant figures unlikely to be influenced by their employees. Although these managers were often highly competent, their employees did not see them as helpful and thus looked outside the group for assistance. Managers are responsible for the working environment of the people they oversee, and the evidence is overwhelming that the best managers provide goals, stimulation, and guidance but let their people manage themselves.

CAREER COUNSELING

One of the technical manager's most important responsibilities is to help the personnel under his or her supervision formulate their career plans. Since few engineers or scientists have a very good idea what they want to do, the manager's first step should be to talk with them about their interests and aspirations. Many will probably feel that a move to management is necessary for their continued advancement, but they may be reluctant to take such a step. It takes a great deal of self-confidence to direct the work of someone else, and many professionals don't feel comfortable having that kind of personal power. On the other hand, some professionals have natural leadership ability, and a move into management in their first three to five years can accelerate their long-term development. Although these questions can only be settled by employees themselves, a frank discussion with the manager can suggest experiences that will help them crystallize their thinking on this question.

Badawy suggests five major topics employees should consider as they analyze their career options:[14]

1. The basic career choice between technical specialization and management

2. An understanding of the specific work people do in each job which seems interesting

3. The relationship of these working roles to the professional's personal goals and interests

4. Understanding why one role is more attractive than another and taking care not to move into management or any other job solely because someone has urged them to, because it pays more, or because it carries more prestige

5. The necessity for the employee to discuss career plans with his or her family so that they can jointly understand the sacrifices likely to be required and be better prepared to make them if and when they are asked

Each job choice will likely have a profound long-term effect on the professional's career, so it should be made with great care. For, as Badawy says, "You are what you do."[15]

STEPS IN TECHNICAL DEVELOPMENT

For professionals who decide on a technical career, the manager's next step is to work with them on a personal development plan. Although it is impractical to try to make such plans very far in advance, temporary staff positions or technical committee participation should be considered for every promising professional. Other than that, only a general direction should be established, with one or two short-term actions identified. Figure 10.1 shows the career path of a scientist who ultimately became an IBM Fellow. Since he had a Ph.D. before joining IBM, he moved quickly into a technical staff position. Thereafter, his assignments remained in his specialty, with some broadening staff moves and technical committee and university involvement. The design engineer's career, shown in Figure 10.2, started with several years in advanced technology before he took a leave of absence to get a Ph.D. Thereafter, he held a number of management and technical assignments before becoming an IBM Fellow.

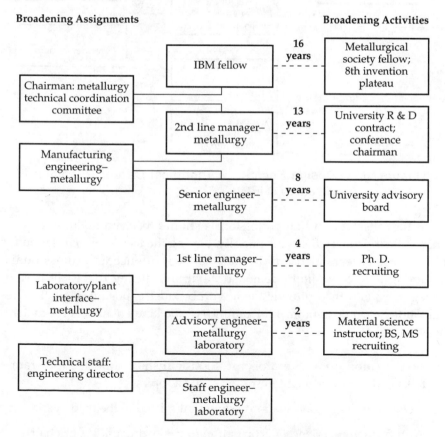

Broadening Assignments

Broadening Activities

	IBM fellow	**16 years** — Metallurgical society fellow; 8th invention plateau
Chairman: metallurgy technical coordination committee		
	2nd line manager–metallurgy	**13 years** — University R & D contract; conference chairman
Manufacturing engineering–metallurgy		
	Senior engineer–metallurgy	**8 years** — University advisory board
	1st line manager–metallurgy	**4 years** — Ph. D. recruiting
Laboratory/plant interface–metallurgy		
	Advisory engineer–metallurgy laboratory	**2 years** — Material science instructor; BS, MS recruiting
Technical staff: engineering director		
	Staff engineer–metallurgy laboratory	

Figure 10.1   Metallurgist's Technical Career Roadmap (Courtesy of IBM)

Broadening Assignments **Broadening Activities**

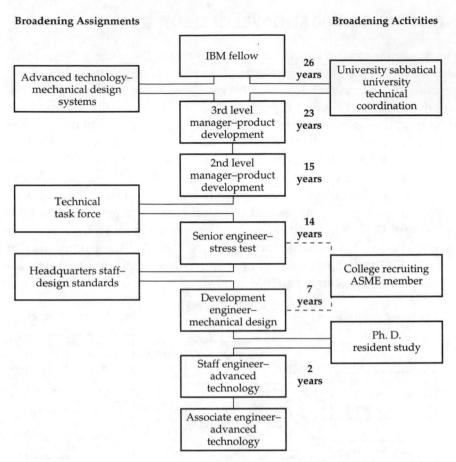

Figure 10.2   Design Engineer's Technical Career Roadmap
(Courtesy of IBM)

At the outset, promising professionals should focus on building competence in their primary fields of specialty. Laying the technical foundation for
their future careers also builds their self-confidence as professionals.
Assuming they continue to demonstrate ability during this early period,
managers should then provide them with broader exposure while they remain in the current assignment. Examples of the kinds of exposures that are
most helpful are

1. Participation on a laboratory professionalism committee to arrange
   talks and seminars on interesting technical topics

2. A company-wide coordination assignment related to the field of specialty

3. With further experience, participation in reviewing papers or chairing a
   session for a technical society conference

4. Work with a local university to arrange a joint technical program in an area of interest

5. Spending a month in a field sales office to learn about customer and marketing issues

6. Participation in a short "shadow" program with a technical or general business executive in order to gain appreciation of some of the key issues such executives face and better understand how a successful executive operates

7. Participation in occasional task forces both inside and outside the field of specialty

There is rarely time to arrange for more than a few of these broadening activities during a professional's first few working years, but almost any such exposure can be enormously helpful.

After this initial period, broadening assignments should continue, but there should also be a move to a job outside the immediate area of specialization. Although this move should generally be temporary, the intent is to provide broader perspective on both the company and its technology. There can, of course, be no firm guideline on when to make such a move, but it is often best to take this step within the first five to ten years. If it is delayed too long, the professional will be at too high a level to be easily spared, and there will be fewer appropriate temporary positions available. Examples of the kinds of assignments that can be most helpful are the following:

- A temporary assignment in research

- A teaching sabbatical at a college or university

- A technical staff assignment at corporate or division headquarters

- A one-year assignment as a technical or administrative assistant to a senior executive

- An educational fellowship to complete an advanced degree

Potentially useful broadening assignments are numerous. The key to maximizing benefit from them is to reach agreement with the professional on the areas he or she would like to explore and to establish an orderly plan to do so. The manager can both assist in implementing this plan and periodically review progress with the employee, but it must be the employee's plan.

The most important rule, however, is this: All broadening assignments must be temporary with a clearly defined line job at the end.

NOTES

1. Jill Larkin, John McDermott, Dorothea P. Simon, and Herbert A. Simon, "Expert and Novice Performance in Solving Physics Problems," *Science,* vol. 208 (June 20, 1980), p. 1336.

2. Howard Gardner, "Science Grapples with the Creative Puzzle," *New York Times,* May 13, 1984, sec. 2, p. 1.

3. William A. Cohen, *Principles of Technical Management* (New York: AMACOM, a division of American Management Associations, 1980), p. 11.

4. T.J. Watson, Jr., *A Business and Its Beliefs* (New York: McGraw-Hill, 1963), p. 27.

5. This survey and the grading system used are described in Chapter 9.

6. Donald C. Pelz and Frank M. Andrews, *Scientists in Organizations: Productive Climates for Research and Development* (New York: Wiley, 1966), p. 207.

7. Ibid.

8. Professor Joseph Weizenbaum of the MIT computer science department cited this Maslow quote in the April 4, 1982, *New York Times.*

9. Tracy Kidder, *The Soul of a New Machine* (Boston: Little, Brown, 1981), p. 265.

10. Tom Alexander, "Teaching Computers the Art of Reason," *Fortune,* May 17, 1982, p. 87.

11. Pelz and Andrews, *Scientists in Organizations,* p. 65.

12. Ibid. p. 56.

13. George Farris's article is included in Michael L. Tushman and William L. Moore's *Readings in the Management of Innovation* (Marshfield, MA: Pitman, 1982), p. 345.

14. M.K. Badawy, *Developing Managerial Skills in Engineers and Scientists: Succeeding as a Technical Manager* (New York: International Thompson Organization, Van Nostrand Reinhold, 1982), pp. 82–105.

15. Ibid., p. 87.

CHAPTER

11

Developing Managerial Talent

M anagement development programs give future leaders the broad business and technical intuition they will need to advance to the top of their organizations. Peter Drucker describes a Sears Roebuck experience that shows how important this can be.[1] Shortly after World War II, Sears divided one year's MBA hires into three groups and put one-third in large stores, one-third in small stores, and one-third in the headquarters mail-order department. Five years later they found that many of those who had started in the small stores were moving into store management positions, while those in the larger stores had not progressed as fast. In the mail-order department, however, the best of the trainees had left. Drucker concludes that the more complete business environment of the small stores allowed trainees to relate their work to understandable business issues and to gain an intellectual grasp of their jobs. They then began to think and act more like store managers. The trainees in the more isolated mail-order department, however, saw less, understood less, and grew more slowly. When faced with such constraints, the best soon became impatient and left for better opportunities elsewhere.

This is typical of large organizations where many jobs do not relate to such clearly necessary tasks as designing, manufacturing, servicing, or selling products. The larger the organization, the narrower the scope of each lower-level job and the harder it is for people to appreciate the value of their work. Although large companies can offer greater opportunities, the complexity of their operations often confuses and discourages the people. In smaller organizations the assignments are necessarily broader and easier

117

to grasp; therefore, the people can more readily appreciate how their work fits into the overall operation.

Management development programs are progressively more valuable in the larger environment because they help to counteract this organizational complexity by showing the professionals how their work relates to the broader needs of the business. Like technical development, it also makes the organization more attractive to ambitious people, reduces management hoarding of talent, more fully develops the most promising candidates, and helps to uncover high-potential people. Such programs also help to keep an organization alive and stimulated, for, in John Gardner's words, "Nothing is more vital to the renewal of an organization than the system by which able people are nurtured and moved into positions where they can make their contributions."[2]

MANAGEMENT DEVELOPMENT OBJECTIVES

When technical professionals become managers, they also join the management team. Changing roles from employee to employer requires a different viewpoint. This point was made very effectively by a senior executive's response to a management trainee who asked why "management" had made a particular decision. The trainee kept referring to management as "they" until the executive told the trainee that now that he was a manager, management was no longer "they" but "we."

It is hard for many new managers to learn that they are part of management. In large organizations it is tempting to believe that some omniscient authority can make all the decisions. As they gain experience, most professionals see many things that could be improved if only some senior manager would decide to improve them. Some see this as evidence of management's ineptness, and it never occurs to them that the problems that seem so important to them are not even visible at higher levels. No all-seeing manager can possibly solve all the problems, because in any large organization there are far too many issues for any one person to understand or resolve. The only practical solution is for the managers on the spot to take the responsibility for fixing their own problems. If they don't, nobody else generally can.

A good example of this is the way Neal Reizer launched a new project at the Software Engineering Institute (SEI) at Carnegie Mellon University. He had taken a course I was then teaching on the Personal Software Process and felt that SEI should build an industrial training program around this course.[3] Newly hired by the SEI, he came to me to talk about his ideas. I asked him why he didn't do it himself. He argued that he was a new employee, didn't know the SEI organization, did not have the authority, etc. I told him:

1. If he didn't do it, probably nobody else would.

2. He should start with a plan of action. If he wanted, I would be glad to help him put it together.

3. He should tell everybody what he planned to do, particularly his immediate manager.

4. He should then work aggressively to get the job done, asking for help from all the involved groups when he needed it.

5. If his concept and plan made sense, and if he kept his supervisors informed on his progress, nobody was likely to stop him.

Neal was excited by the challenge and decided to do it. He launched a successful SEI project and got some useful experience in the bargain.

The sense of ownership is an essential characteristic of future managers and executives. The management development process should couple this attitude with the hands-on experiences needed to build the managers' willingness to act independently. Valentine sums up such programs as a way to find out if "the manager is capable of using authority...to achieve improvements."[4]

STARTING THE DEVELOPMENT PROCESS

The first step in the management development process is to talk with employees about their goals and objectives. Have they thought through their careers, and do they understand the personal sacrifices they must make to reach an executive position? If they are not willing to work harder than everyone they know, they are not likely to progress very far, so there is little point in designing an aggressive development plan. If young managers are eager to learn, are doing something about their own development, and are willing to work hard, they are probably good candidates. If, however, they express interest in senior management but haven't done anything to improve themselves, their chances are much less. They may be excellent employees, but they will not likely make it to the top rank unless they use their own time for self-improvement and demonstrate unusual drive and initiative.

Motivation is easy to spot, and with a little encouragement the best candidates will stand out. Even highly motivated employees, however, may not be good management material. McClelland and Burnham have conducted management workshops with over 500 managers from 25 different U.S. corporations to see what traits accompany high management effectiveness.[5] They found that the better managers had a stronger need for power than for being liked. Candidates who feel uncomfortable about taking unpopular actions are probably not emotionally equipped for senior management. Note, however, that power can be a positive force for accomplishing results but a negative force when the objective is personal control.

THE EXECUTIVE PERSONALITY

Assuming the employee is highly motivated and willing to step out of the crowd, Lee Iacocca identifies "two really important things about a candidate that you just can't learn from one short job interview. The first is whether he's lazy, and the second is whether he's got any horse sense."[6] The ability to make sensible decisions is often a question of maturity, and McClelland and Burnham found that the better managers were more mature and less egotistical. They could deal impersonally with issues and keep their own problems in the background. They were less defensive, more willing to consult experts, and more inclined to help others. This suggests that the most promising candidates should get largely positive responses to the following questions:

1. Do they take charge and act like leaders, do people listen to their views, and are they followed?

2. Do they tactfully use their authority instead of bulling ahead regardless of suggestions and problems?

3. Are they capable of trusting personal relationships with their co-workers, and are they willing and interested in helping others?

4. Can they handle setbacks, heavy pressure, and criticism without getting defensive or discouraged?

5. Can they take management direction in an open and interactive way rather than either blindly accepting or resenting authority?

Professionals who do well with these questions are probably excellent management material. The key, however, is not so much management's opinions of employees as the employees' understanding of themselves. If employees have important shortcomings but recognize them and are willing to work on improvement, they deserve management support.

Quite apart from their personality traits, promising candidates should also meet certain basic criteria before they are ready for accelerated promotion:

1. Have they demonstrated sound technical judgment, with a record of project success?

Project failures are not always the professional's fault, but the best people are usually found on the most successful projects. If they don't have a winner under their belt, it is best to wait a little longer to see what they can do.

2. Do they plan their work, manage their time, set targets, and drive to meet them?

3. Do they drive beyond the confines of their jobs, show initiative, and treat rules as guidelines that can be changed?

4. Can they communicate?

5. Do they know when to seek help and how to do it?

6. Do they have the integrity and negotiating skill to work effectively as part of a team?

7. Are they pragmatists? Can they face the facts and sort out the operative from the theoretical issues?

Although weaknesses can be addressed through experience and counseling, professionals should understand their problems and be willing to work on them. Such discussions are hard work, but managers who are willing to make this effort can be an enormous help to their high-potential candidates.

ALTERNATING ASSIGNMENTS

The development of promising managers is best accomplished through a carefully planned sequence of line and staff assignments. The line positions build confidence and add deeper understanding, and the staff assignments provide perspective and broadened awareness. Harold Leavitt points out that management development should be "an interactive, back-and-forth process between outside educational programs and inside active experience."[7] As with technologists, however, technical managers should start with a solid grounding in their respective technical fields. Only after they have demonstrated competence and some initial success should they be considered for broadening. Even then, most of their learning should come from within their specialty, with only brief development assignments in other areas. At least for the first 10 or so years these broadening assignments should be followed immediately by a longer assignment back at home base.

It is almost always a mistake to give a young manager two broadening assignments in a row. A young engineering manager had worked on the corporate headquarters planning staff for two years, and it was time for him to return to his home laboratory. This assignment had been stimulating, however, and he now felt that an international assignment would give him valuable added exposure. When asked about his personal goals, however, he saw his future in technical management but felt that a two-year assignment in Europe would help him understand the corporate international business. He had thought about this for some time and had even lined up a potential assignment in Paris. His manager felt that he was wrong, however, and enlisted the help of his prior manager in the home laboratory. After much discussion, they finally convinced him that in two more years he would be out of touch with his technical specialty and would be an unknown to the senior managers in the laboratory. He reluctantly decided to return. Within a few months he was put in charge of the New Product Introduction Department in the manufacturing organization. His corporate planning experience was all the exposure he needed for this important promotion.

There are so many functions in any large business that an entire career could be spent in broadening assignments. The result would be an accumulation of analytical knowledge, but senior managers need an action orientation that can only come from line experience. As Lee Iacocca says, managers must "know how to look for the pressure points and how to set priorities. They're the kind of guys who can say: 'Forget that, it'll take ten years. Here's what we gotta do now.'"[8]

With the rapid pace of modern technology, people who stay in staff assignments for more than a couple of years are soon out of date and hard to place in line positions. One example was a promising young systems engineer who took an assistant's job for a division executive. He did well, and in the next two years he caught the eye of the division president and moved to a job in his office. Again, he performed with skill, and in only two years was made administrative assistant to the company president. He held this job for three years before being moved to a corporate staff position. During this time his salary and job level had progressively advanced until he was making more money than most laboratory directors. He had been out of technical work for so long, however, that he no longer had the knowledge to compete with technical managers at this level. His line experience was too limited to fit him for an executive role, and he could no longer take any job that would give him the experience needed for further advancement. In spite of his enormous potential, he spent the rest of his career in various middle-level headquarters staff assignments.

THE PRODUCT DEVELOPMENT EXECUTIVE

Once it seems likely that employees have executive potential, it is necessary to decide on the kind of broadening assignments that would most help them. In one study, approximately 90 technical vice presidents, laboratory directors, and product managers were asked to identify the experiences they felt would have best prepared them for their present positions.[9] The results show general agreement on the need for product management and product development experiences, as shown in Tables 11.1 and 11.2. There were some wide divergences, however, for fewer executives saw such areas as testing, component development, product engineering, and laboratory support as important. When these executives were asked about the relative value of areas where they had not worked, those without business planning experience uniformly judged it to be important, with software development a close second. Another set of questions explored the value of exposure to different parts of the organization, with 85% rating an assignment in more than one division as valuable, 83% stating that work in more than one location was important, and 60% judging an assignment on corporate or group staff as worthwhile.

Table 11.1 Valuable Technical Management Experiences

Technical Area	Percent
Product or system management	92
Business planning and management	91
Hardware development	85
Hardware design and architecture	84
Software design and architecture	79
Software development	70
Hardware product planning	65
Advanced technology	59
Software product planning	52

Table 11.2   Ranking of Technical Work Experiences

Technical Area	Relative Rank	
	Areas Worked In	Areas Not Worked In
Product or system management	1	4
Hardware development	2	6
Business planning and management	3	1
Advanced technology	4	5
Component development	5	11
Hardware design and architecture	6	9
Software development	7	2
Software design and architecture	8	3

As shown in Table 11.3, this survey also explored the value of nondevelopment experiences. Here, marketing was generally viewed as important, while those who had worked in manufacturing ranked *it* as even more important. Those who had not worked in business planning, however, uniformly ranked it most valuable. Even though manufacturing, marketing, and business planning were judged to be the most important areas for outside experience, only 19%, 17%, and 15% of the executives, respectively, had such backgrounds. There was, however, general agreement on the value of broad career exposure as preparation for a technical executive position, as shown in the idealized career path for a laboratory director in Figure 11.1.

Table 11.3   Ranking of Nondevelopment Experiences

Function	Relative Rank	
	Areas Worked In	Areas Not Worked In
Business planning	3	1
Marketing	2	2
Manufacturing	1	3
Finance	5	4
Field service	4	5

Broadening Assignments   **Broadening Activities**

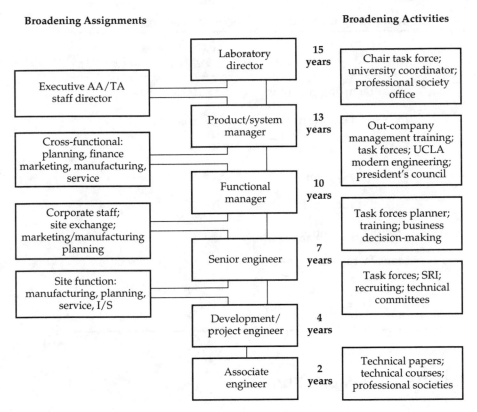

Figure 11.1   Laboratory Director's Career Roadmap (Courtesy of IBM)

THE MANUFACTURING EXECUTIVE

A similar study, made of 36 manufacturing executives, is shown in Table 11.4.[10] Although this group gave somewhat different priorities, they also agreed on the importance of breadth. Unlike the development executives, however, they did not view marketing as particularly valuable, although they viewed development experience as important. Business and financial backgrounds continued to get high ranking, though few actually had such exposure.

Table 11.4   Manufacturing Experience Ratings

Area	Extremely Valuable	Actual Experience
Manufacturing planning	100%	50%
Industrial engineering	91	45
Finance	91	4
Business planning	91	19
New products (mfg.)	78	14
Production control	74	22
Manufacturing engineering	67	4
Direct manufacturing	58	50
Information systems	56	9

THE DEVELOPMENT PLAN

After defining the professionals' high-priority development needs, the next step is to formulate a development plan. This should be done quite early, because high-potential future executives need exposure to so many areas that time is the primary development constraint. Although no particular format is important, the plan should be documented and should clearly spell out who will be responsible for each step. The first development question to resolve is the timing of the professionals' moves to next assignments. Although every case must be considered separately, some of the key considerations apply to all:

1. They should not move until they have established a firm grounding in the basic disciplines of their technical fields.

2. If they do not have a successful project under their belts, they should stay in the laboratory until they have gained the reputation and self-confidence from at least one success.

3. Nonmanagement professionals who have three or more years' experience and a good record of success should be given their first management assignment in the laboratory.

4. After they have demonstrated their ability to manage people, temporary broadening moves to headquarters or other laboratory and manufacturing functions should be considered.

Since engineers' first years set the critical foundation for their entire careers, they should not be moved until they have demonstrated their competence as first-line managers. Once they have this foundation, however, they should be moved quickly. There is not a great deal of time, since the most successful senior managers generally reach their first executive positions before the age of 40. Wherever possible, high-potential technical managers should thus make their first broadening moves within 5 to 10 years of starting work and there should be a continued emphasis on broadening developmental experiences for the next several years.

TEMPORARY ASSIGNMENTS

While future executives are in their early, foundation-building phase in the laboratory, they should be given many of the same exposures as technical professionals. After they move into management, however, their broadening exposures should be focused more directly on management topics. Some examples of valuable short experiences are the following:

- Short management education courses can provide useful perspectives as well as exposure to people with a wide variety of backgrounds.

- Executive "shadow" programs give a brief snapshot of a technical executive's work and also help to provide the promising young manager with added visibility.

- Technical task force assignments are particularly valuable developmental experiences, so they should be staffed with high-potential people whenever possible.

- Most technical organizations have a variety of committees and coordination groups for such topics as process improvement, strategic planning, education, and awards. Rotating these assignments among the promising future executives will give them better appreciation of a broad range of laboratory activities.

After the career foundation is laid, the high-potential manager should be moved to a new assignment at least every two or three years. As illustrated by the case of one programming manager, this can involve quite a lot of effort on the part of several executives. This manager had worked in the laboratory for 10 years, and he was increasingly concerned about his chances of reaching a senior management position. He had taken some evening courses for his MBA and felt that he was ready for a temporary assignment on the corporate financial staff. He discussed this with his immediate manager, but nothing seemed to happen; so he raised the point with me when I was an executive observer at a management assessment program he attended. I called the manager's laboratory director, and we agreed to arrange such a move. I contacted several headquarters associates and finally found an appropriate job. The laboratory director made the final arrangements, and the programming manager had his temporary assignment with the corporate finance and planning staff.

Although this assignment was arranged fairly easily, it took several months and dozens of phone calls to find the right assignment and make the final arrangements for this temporary move. Since a manager can expect to spend a couple of hours a week over a period of several months arranging for one such assignment, few managers can afford to make such an effort for more than two or three promising candidates each year. In this case the results were well worth the effort. After his broadening staff position, this manager was rapidly moved to a technical executive position.

MANAGEMENT DEVELOPMENT REVIEWS

Since most working-level managers have to defer almost every activity that has not reached crisis proportions, personnel-development programs must be made sufficiently important to get their attention. This can only be done if a senior executive is interested enough in the subject to get personally involved. Without such high-level commitment, no bureaucratic process can possibly make the lower-level managers take this subject seriously. Thus, the most effective way to make such programs work is for senior executives to hold periodic one-on-one reviews with each of their most senior department heads. These sessions should focus exclusively on personnel development, with a specific discussion of each manager and key professional. The agenda should include the following items.

1. Identify candidates for early promotion with their likely next positions.

2. Identify potential replacements for the senior department heads themselves, assessing their readiness for the job.

3. Name candidates for temporary assignments and suggest areas and dates of availability.

4. Track the movement of people between functions as well as within the same organization, for the departmental promotion summary.

5. Review the goals for interfunctional movement, and compare actual performance with prior goals.

6. Identify key management positions and give reasons for any that are not occupied by high-potential managers. (A key management position is one that provides important background for future executives, significant exposure to senior management, or essential preparation for an immediate executive promotion.)

7. Review the promotion table for each key position, with particular focus on the candidates' readiness and the number of people on the list from other locations and divisions.

8. Separately review the performance of high-potential managers, summarize their development plans, and list their promotion table entries. At least some of these potential positions should be in other line organizations.

The key to this entire process, however, is the senior executive's personal involvement. Many managers mistakenly think that management development can be handled by the personnel department, but as Peter Drucker says, "To depend on the personnel department to do management development is basically a misunderstanding. A marriage counselor can help with a marriage, but it's your job."[11]

SUPPORTING MANAGEMENT DEVELOPMENT

Since management development takes a great deal of time, some support is required both to ensure that it is handled properly and to take care of follow-up tracking. Typical support duties are to

• Schedule and attend the executive reviews.

• Ensure that the key positions are identified and replacement tables prepared.

• Retain the master file of development plans and replacement tables.

- Ensure that a reasonable number of high-potential management candidates are identified in each department and that each has a development plan.

- Track implementation of the development plans and provide assistance where needed.

- Keep track of replacement activity and record how often the replacement tables are used.

- Suggest candidates for promotion when requested.

- Periodically report on the management development performance of each department and suggest areas where added management attention is required.

In organizations of several hundred to a thousand people, one personnel specialist should be able to handle these functions as part of his or her job. In larger organizations, however, one full-time support specialist or more will often be needed. Regardless of the size of the staff, the principal task is to ensure that promotion reviews are periodically conducted and that no high-potential candidates are overlooked or forgotten.

If these mechanics are not properly handled, management development will be a hit-or-miss affair. The problems this can cause are illustrated by the case of a young engineer who worked for a large oil company. When he was recruited, he was told about the management development program that prepared promising engineers for senior management positions. Each candidate's career was to be personally planned and reviewed, starting with a six-month assignment in headquarters. He or she would then move to an overseas location for two years' experience before reassignment to another domestic staff. This orderly job progression was to be carefully tailored to the trainee's personal interests and experiences.

One day a trainee who had been posted to the Middle East unexpectedly arrived at the home office. His initial two-year field assignment was over, and since no one in headquarters had communicated with him about his next move, he came back to see what was wrong. For several confusing days his file could not be found, and all the trainees soon realized that the story of a carefully orchestrated training program was pure fiction. As one remarked, "It was obvious we were so much meat."

Minor goof-ups are understandable in parts lists, production schedules, or even financial statements, but when it comes to people, a higher standard is needed. All people are special, at least in their own eyes, and they will never excuse a management that overlooks or forgets them. This is why development programs must be managed with the greatest of care and staffed with experienced senior professionals.

DEVELOPMENT CONSIDERATIONS

One problem with programs to develop high-potential managers is that they tend to separate people into classes. Since this is clearly undesirable, an attempt is generally made to keep such programs confidential. Unfortunately, the number of people who must be involved renders this largely impractical. The other option, open disclosure, has a number of attractive advantages: The program will become public knowledge anyway, so open disclosure ensures that it is properly explained. The program can help with recruiting, but only if it is public knowledge. It is hard to discuss development plans with people who don't know why they are needed.

The disadvantages of publicizing such programs, however, are equally compelling: The employees will quickly learn who is "in" and who is "out," thus creating a potential elite. The professionals who have been dropped from the program will find out and be unhappy. Since only a few people can be helped by such programs, public knowledge will negatively affect many more people than will be helped.

John Gardner describes this last problem with the example of a military commander who had an extremely effective way of recommending noncoms for officer candidates school. This, however, turned out to have a devastating effect on those who were not selected. As long as they could say he was unjust, they were relatively happy, but "the commanding officer's scrupulous search for talent had deprived them of those comfortable defenses. They had no place to hide. It was now clear to all concerned that they were enlisted soldiers because that was where they belonged."[12]

No simple answer meets all objections. Probably the best compromise is to keep the existence of a formal program confidential while publicly requiring managers to have development plans for all their people. This permits open discussion of development plans, but it also means the managers will have much more work to do. If they try, on the one hand, to work out comprehensive plans with each of their employees, they will be swamped in so much paperwork that none of the plans will be adequate. On the other hand, someone who was thought to have little potential occasionally turns out to be a star when given the chance. Thus, managers should spend at least some time on the development of every one of their employees.

When everyone has a development plan, there is no question of an "in" and an "out" group. Although the management review process will naturally focus on the small number with highest potential, no one will be ignored. If employees complain about an inadequate development plan, managers can tell them that development is largely *their* responsibility; and although management will gladly help, the work is largely up to *them*. If employees take this challenge seriously, managers should assist them, for motivation is the key ingredient of self-development; and all employees who are willing to work at improving themselves should get their management's help.

THE PROFESSIONAL DEVELOPMENT BUREAUCRACY

Since development programs necessarily involve many procedures, checkpoints, reviews, and forms, they can easily become bureaucratic. There are some steps that can help to minimize this tendency:

1. Restrict the number of different development programs. Separate programs for young executives, females, minorities, new managers, and the various technical specialties will each have their own forms, procedures, and reviews; and this proliferation will both confuse and overburden line management.

2. Since many of the same managers are involved in each review, one staff person should handle all resource programs and make sure that they are reviewed simultaneously.

3. The professional development support job should be rotated every two to three years so the incumbents don't develop a bureaucratic mentality.

Finally, senior executives should identify the key jobs that cannot be filled without their approval and require that the proposed promotion be reviewed by the management development support person before they will agree. If this is not done, the management development support personnel cannot be effective.

NOTES

1. Peter F. Drucker, *The Practice of Management* (New York: Harper & Row, 1954).
2. John W. Gardner, *Excellence* (New York: Harper & Row, 1961).
3. W.S. Humphrey, *A Discipline for Software Engineering* (Reading, MA: Addison-Wesley, 1995).

4. Raymond F. Valentine, *Initiative and Managerial Power* (New York: AMACOM, a division of American Management Associations, 1973), p. 94.

5. David C. McClelland and David Burnham, "Power Is the Great Motivator," *Harvard Business Review*, vol. 54, no. 2 (March-April 1976), p. 101.

6. Lee Iacocca and William Novak, *Iacocca: An Autobiography* (New York: Bantam Books, 1984), p. 23.

7. Harold J. Leavitt, *Managerial Psychology*, 4th ed. (Chicago: University of Chicago Press, 1978), p. 249.

8. Iacocca and Novak, *Iacocca*, p. 60.

9. This study was conducted in 1980 by the IBM Corporate Engineering, Programming, and Technology Staff.

10. This study was conducted in 1977 by J.H. Motes and A.D. Wolfson of the IBM Corporate Manufacturing Staff.

11. John J. Tarrant, *Drucker: The Man Who Invented the Corporate Society* (New York: Warner Publishing, Warner Books, 1976). This quote from Peter Drucker appears on p. 316.

12. Gardner, *Excellence*, p. 72.

PART

4

Innovation

CHAPTER

12

The
Importance of
Innovation

anagement guru Theodore Levitt once said:

> Creativity is thinking up new things. Innovation is doing new things. A powerful idea can kick around unused in a company for years, not because its merits are not recognized, but because nobody has assumed the responsibility for converting it from words into action. Ideas are useless unless used. The proof of their value is only in their implementation. Until then, they are in limbo.[1]

While innovation requires creativity, it also involves a great deal of hard work. The lonely inventors with bright ideas take the essential first steps, but their efforts will be totally wasted if someone with the necessary drive and energy doesn't pick up each idea and turn it into a business success. Innovation is the process of turning ideas into manufacturable and marketable form. In Peter Drucker's words, "Business has only two basic functions: marketing and innovation. Marketing and innovation produce results. All the rest are costs."[2]

Although we all know about such great laboratory advances as the transistor and the laser, few realize that it was manufacturing innovations that produced the major economic changes of the modern industrial age. It was a manufacturing innovation that reduced the cost of electric light bulbs by 80% and made electric lighting commercially viable. It was also Henry

Ford's use of high-volume manufacturing methods for the Model T Ford that cut automobile prices by a factor of three and changed the face of modern industry.[3] Innovation spans every phase of technology from research through development, manufacturing, and marketing, and its prime role is to economically couple creative technology to the needs of the marketplace.

INDUSTRIAL INNOVATION

Today, more than ever before, a strong market position must be based on an organization's technical competence. Brian Smith has examined what the loss of this competitive race has meant to much of industry in Great Britain.[4] He found, for example, that the British textile industry led the industrial revolution before World War II but then started looking to foreign suppliers for textile machinery. This was not because the foreign machines were cheaper or had better service, but because they were more reliable, more productive, and more efficient than the British units. Smith concludes that in textiles, as in shipbuilding and motorcycles, the foreign manufacturers were simply better at designing innovative products and that this is what caused British industry to lose its leadership position.

Such dramatic changes have also happened in the United States, as demonstrated by the development of the portable transistor radio.[5] In 1956 the U.S. portable radio market was dominated by domestically manufactured 20-ounce units that cost $57 each. This was a big improvement over the earlier 6-pound units, but the Japanese quickly introduced smaller capacitors, miniature loudspeakers, and lightweight power supplies, which resulted in compact 10-ounce portable sets. In the next three years the Japanese captured 68% of the U.S. portable transistor radio market.

Behind these major innovations were invariably a few key technical decisions that made the crucial difference. In the case of the Lockheed Electra, a fleet of 72 aircraft were in service in 1961; only seven years later the Lockheed fleet had dwindled to 28, while the newer Boeing 727s numbered over 400.

The dramatic reversal in Lockheed's fortunes was the result of a series of decisions made in the design of the Electra and the 727. Since the Lockheed engineers aimed for an aircraft to operate out of small local airports, they picked propellers that provided more thrust than traditional jet engines, even though this limited maximum aircraft speed. The Boeing engineers, instead, conceived of the fan-jet engine that would accelerate a cylinder of cold air around a hot central jet and produce far higher takeoff thrust than had previously been possible. They also introduced wing flaps and slats for high-lift takeoff and landing and high-speed cruising. The result was an aircraft that could operate out of smaller airfields, with the speed and comfort of a jet. Even though Boeing was a late starter, its innovative 727 rapidly beat the Electra in the marketplace. By the time the last 727 was rolled out in 1984, Boeing had produced 1832 aircraft in 24 years, and the 727 accounted for 37% of total Boeing jet aircraft production. In the 24 years, these planes flew a total of 21.4 billion miles, or the equivalent of "115 round trips to the sun."[6] Although the Boeing 727 was a remarkable marketing success, its battle with the Electra was won in Boeing's laboratories and plants.

THE RISK OF FAILURE

Since a true innovative success must be both economical to manufacture and responsive to customer needs, it must necessarily combine the high risks of technology with the uncertainties of the competitive marketplace. A 1968 Booz, Allen, and Hamilton study found that two-thirds of all new product development funds were spent on failures and that only about 2% of new product ideas made it through development to become successful in the marketplace.[7] Bronislaw Verhage et al. reported that 40% to 80% of all new product developments were commercial failures.[8]

Introducing a new product is like riding a surfboard: You need to catch the crest of the wave. The case of IBM's OS/2 is a good example of this problem. When this system was first introduced, it was too big and slow to work with most available personal computers and it was not compatible with existing DOS programs. By the time the IBM engineers had fixed these problems, Microsoft's Windows had taken the market and IBM's arguably superior product was never able to catch up.

Among the many reasons for research and development failure, one problem shows up with the most regularity. It is the persistent tendency of technical people to confine themselves to the laboratory and not to seek a detailed understanding of the user's needs. High technology is always risky, but the technical solution in search of a problem faces the highest risks of all. From a study of 23 organizations Knut Holt found that every single company had product failures and that they were all caused either by the failure to study the user's needs or by the misuse of such studies. He said:

> Four of the firms had made no inquiries to potential users, six had made too few inquiries, two ignored the results, two had misinterpreted the answers, six were committed to preconceived designs and three failed to understand the environment to which their products would be subjected.[9]

Edwin Mansfield, a University of Pennsylvania economist, has studied the reasons behind project failures and has similarly concluded that successful product development depends more on market astuteness than on technical competence. He estimates that only from 12% to 20% of all R&D projects produce a marketing success, even though their technical objectives are generally met.[10] He found that when the development and marketing functions were closely coupled, product innovation was generally successful.

Eric A. von Hippel has examined the sources of innovative ideas in several industries and found that when the users were technically competent, they originated the bulk of the innovations.[11] As shown in Table 12.1, for example, the users in instrumentation and process equipment had their own technical experts and were responsible for every single new advance during the entire period of the study. Even after these new innovations were introduced, the users continued to originate most of the new ideas, while the manufacturers made only incremental improvements. By contrast, in polymers and chemical additives, the users did not have the technical staff or facilities to do innovative work, and consequently the important advances were all made by the manufacturers.

Table 12.1 Originators of Innovation

Field of Innovation	User	Manufacturer
Instrumentation		
First of a type	100%	0%
Major improvements	82	18
Minor improvements	70	30
Process Equipment		
First of a type	100	0
Major improvements	63	21
Minor improvements	20	29
Polymers		
All major since 1955	0	100
Additives		
All since 1945	0	100

Abernathy and Utterback referenced eight studies that all reached a similar conclusion.[12] On average, 75% of all the innovations reviewed by these studies came from market sources, but the highest percentage of technically driven innovations given by any single study was only 34%. In one study of the sources of 567 innovations, 75% came from a recognized need, but only 21% originated from a new technical opportunity.[13] The breakdown of these figures is shown in Table 12.2.

Table 12.2 Sources of Innovation

Innovation Source	Percent
Technical feasibility	21
Market demand	45
Production need	30
Administrative change	4

While no similar study has been made of software innovations, my observations are as follows.

The development and enhancement of operating systems is done almost exclusively by software firms or the hardware manufacturers. With the single exception of UNIX and the Bell Telephone Laboratories, computing system users do not have the skills or resources to develop such systems.

New system applications are originated by a research or user-associated group. This was true of IBM's IMS and CICS programs, which were later brought into the development laboratories. The same is true of network management protocols, spreadsheets, and original application programs.

Departures like electronic mail, Lotus Notes, groupware, and the World Wide Web can originate almost anywhere, but they are invariably driven by someone who understands the users' environment and has a vision for how the system should work in operation.

The key to recognizing successful innovations is that they invariably start with a small system that is designed around an integrating concept. Users are then attracted by this concept and find it easy and convenient to use. As system use explodes, the initial developers learn from this early experience and provide enhancements that further accelerate acceptance. This happened with the initial MIT time-sharing system in the early 1960s and it happened with Microsoft Windows 30 years later. It is also happening with electronic mail and the World Wide Web.

REVERSE ENGINEERING

The risky nature of technical innovation has led to something called reverse engineering. This practice occurs when an organization waits for somebody else to do the expensive pioneering and then attempts to improve on or extend their work. Westinghouse is reported to have followed this path with gas turbine technology. They felt that ceramic turbine blades could be superior because they could operate at higher temperatures and efficiencies than metal blades. The research costs, however, were estimated to exceed $80 million for the seven-year program to solve the brittleness problem. They thus decided to wait to see what GE would do. *Fortune* quotes George Mechlin, Westinghouse's vice president for R&D, as saying,

> There are really two risks in research and development....One is whether the technology will succeed. The other is whether it will satisfy some market requirements. If you hang back and wait, you can be in a position where you can know the answer to both questions, and catching up can take a lot less time than the original effort.[14]

Although the Westinghouse decision looks good in hindsight and certainly made good business sense, planning to copy someone else's innovations is far from risk free. The fast pace of today's technologies doesn't allow much time for catching up. Once an important advance is "in the air," many organizations will be working on it. One will necessarily be first in bringing it to the market, but others will be close behind with the necessary technical competence. Any organization that waits for others to do the pioneering will often not have the knowledge or talent to catch up. Further, if they haven't been active in the field, they will not likely have an adequate patent portfolio and someone else will own the key technology trade secrets. It is not as important to be first to announce a new advance as it is to have the technical capacity to capitalize on new ideas when their time has come.

It is interesting to note that in those technologies that directly affect users, it can be important to be first. With computer operating systems, network protocols, and data base systems, for example, the users' operations are closely tied to product features. Thus, the first supplier builds a loyal band of users who demand a compatible growth path before they will move to a competitor.

In technology, as everywhere else, there is no free lunch. The leaders take the greatest risks and stand to reap the greatest rewards, while the followers couple lower short-term risks with loss of technological control. To keep control of its own destiny, the technical organization must maintain a skilled team of innovators in close touch with its marketplace. An organization that is not in control of its key technologies cannot be master of its own destiny.

NOTES

1. Thomas J. Peters and Robert H. Waterman, Jr., *In Search of Excellence: Lessons from America's Best-Run Companies* (New York: Harper & Row, 1982), p. 206.

2. Peter Drucker, *Management, Tasks, Responsibilities, Practices* (New York: Harper & Row, 1974), p. 61.

3. W.J. Abernathy and J.M. Utterback, "Patterns of Industrial Innovation," in Tushman and Moore, *Readings in the Management of Innovation* (Marshfield, MA: Pitman, 1982), p. 97.

4. Brian Smith, "Design Management and New Product Development," *European Journal of Marketing (UK)*, vol. 15, no. 5 (1981), p. 52.

5. George R. White includes this description of the introduction of Japanese portable transistor radios and the following Lockheed Electra example in his article "Management Criteria for Effective Innovation," *IEEE Transactions on Professional Communication*, vol. PC-22, no. 2 (June 1979), p. 79.

6. *Wall Street Journal*, August 15, 1984, p. 25.

7. D.A. Guidici, "Evaluation—How Can It Aid Innovation?" *ISA Transactions*, vol. 19, no. 4 (1980), p. 33.

8. Bronislaw Verhage, Ph. Waalewijn, and A.J. vanWeele, "New Product Development in Dutch Companies: The Idea Generation Stage," *European Journal of Marketing (UK)*, vol. 15, no. 5 (1981), p. 73.

9. Knut Holt, "Idea Generation—Key to Successful Management of Change," International Conference of Product Research, Amsterdam, August 1979.

10. Tom Alexander, "The Right Remedy for R & D Lag," *Fortune*, January 25, 1982, p. 67.

11. Eric A. von Hippel, "Users as Innovators," *Technology Review*, MIT, January 1978.

12. Abernathy and Utterback, "Patterns," p. 97.

13. Ibid.

14. Alexander, "The Right Remedy," p. 62.

13

The Innovators

I saac Auerbach, who once taught a course in entrepreneurship at the University of Pennsylvania, observes that "a Class A person with a Class B idea has a better chance for success than a Class B person with a Class A idea."[1] The people involved in innovation and the roles they play are beautifully illustrated by Elting E. Morison's story of the introduction of continuous-aim firing in the United States Navy.[2] Until the end of the nineteenth century, naval gunners had to adjust their aim for the ship's roll, and if their timing was poor or the fuses burned unevenly, their shots would miss.

In 1898 British Admiral Sir Percy Scott, commander of *H.M.S. Scylla*, was watching gunnery practice and thinking about the problem of accuracy when he noticed one pointer trying to adjust his gun's elevating gear in time with the ship's roll. He suddenly realized that this could be the answer and he had the elevating gear on all his ship's guns changed so that the guns could be more easily raised and depressed. His men then started making fleet gunnery records. Shortly afterward, Scott was sent to the British China station, where he met Lieutenant William S. Sims of the U.S. fleet. When Sims heard about the technique of continuous-aim firing, he changed the guns on the *U.S.S. Kentucky*, and soon his gunners were making fleet records as well.

Sims quite logically felt that the entire U.S. Navy should adopt this method; therefore, he prepared and sent 13 detailed reports to the Navy Department in Washington. At first, his suggestions were ignored, but when he didn't give up, Washington argued that the U.S. equipment was as good as that of the British and that the problem must therefore be with the officers. When Sims persisted, however, they claimed that his proposal was impossible. Shore tests had shown that gunners could not crank the guns fast enough to compensate for the roll of ocean waves. The testers failed to realize, however, that at sea little power was required to adjust the guns so that they could stay stationary while the ship rolled beneath them. When none of the arguments silenced him, the Navy finally claimed that Sims had falsified the evidence. This so infuriated him that he took the extraordinary step of writing to the president of the United States. Theodore Roosevelt was so intrigued that he brought Sims to Washington and ultimately made him inspector of naval target practice. Morison explains the impact of this change:

> In 1899 five ships of the North Atlantic Squadron fired five minutes each at a lighthouse hulk at the conventional range of 1600 yards. After twenty-five minutes of banging away two hits had been made on the sails of the elderly vessel. Six years later one naval gunner made fifteen hits in one minute at a target 75 by 25 feet at the same range; half of them hit in the bull's-eye 50 inches square.

The key roles in this story were played by Scott, Sims, and Roosevelt. Scott was the inventor who saw the importance of adjusting the gun's elevation to compensate for the ship's roll. His creative imagination was essential, but it wasn't enough for the U.S. Navy. Sims, although not the inventor of continuous-aim firing, saw its potential and decided to champion its cause in the U.S. fleet. His dedication and obstinacy finally took him to the president of the United States, where he found a sponsor to overcome bureaucratic resistance. These roles—the inventor, the champion, and the sponsor—are critical to the success of just about every significant innovation.

NEW IDEAS

Patrick Haggerty best defined the innovative role of creative people when he said that "organizations neither possess imagination nor generate ideas."[3] Organizations are, however, communities of people. We can therefore refer to an organization as innovative if its management effectively motivates and supports its innovative people.

The idea that starts the innovation process often appears in a sudden flash of insight. Nineteenth-century German chemist August von Stradonitz Kekule had such a vision when he solved the problem of the molecular structure of organic chemicals. The arrangement of the oxygen, carbon, and hydrogen atoms in organic compounds was one of the great chemical mysteries, and Kekule had worked on it for many months without success. One evening he fell asleep before the fire and dreamed of atoms dancing like snakes, and then "he saw one snake forming a loop and eating its own tail. Kekule awoke with a start. In that instant, his imagination conjured up a hexagonal ring, each corner taken up by a carbon atom—six atoms in all.[4] Kekule had literally dreamed up the benzene ring, the basic building block of organic chemistry.

After he had worked for many years in a vain attempt to perfect the sewing machine, a similar incident happened to Elias Howe. He fell asleep one day and dreamed he was the prisoner of a medieval tyrant.

> One morning, he was led out for execution: drums beating, the king on a dais, a huge crowd waiting by the block. As he stood there trembling, Howe looked round at his guards, each of them toted a long spear; the broad, leaf blade of every spear punctured by a hole—the hole in the sewing needle should be at the tip, not in the middle.[5]

The Inventor

Although these flashes of creative genius may seem mere accidents, studies have shown that creativity is a logical and structured process.[6,7] Insight, the first step, is where the germ of the problem originates. This intuitive process rarely includes any hint of the solution, and it may actually come years before the final answer. Next, the preparation, or manipulation, stage is a logical period of problem definition and analysis that generally involves exhaustive studies or experiments. In modern science and engineering, inspiration is often found by digging out prior work on a subject. This both helps to prevent repeating earlier mistakes and occasionally actually produces an answer to the problem. More often, however, such structured efforts are fruitless, and the problem is temporarily relegated to incubation, a stage in which it continues to receive subconscious attention. When something next happens to trigger the inventor's imagination, however, the manipulation phase is reentered to test it out. If the trial doesn't work, incubation is resumed. This alternating cycle may continue many times as a host of ideas are tried and discarded. Each cycle, however, gradually increases understanding until some idea suddenly crystallizes with a seeming flash of insight.

Alexander Graham Bell's invention of the telephone is a well-known example of this incubation process.[8] Bell developed the theory for electrically reproducing speech while vacationing with his parents, but he could not figure out how to make an electric current change in proportion to the sound of a voice. As he told his father at the time, if he could solve this one problem, he would be able to transmit speech telegraphically.

Bell did not forget the problem, but he put it aside for about a year while he worked on the development of a harmonic telegraph. On June 2, 1875, while attempting to transmit fixed-frequency telegraph signals with magnetized steel reeds, Watson, Bell's assistant, accidentally clamped one reed to the magnet so tightly that it would not vibrate. He plucked at it and it came loose with a "twang." Bell, at the other end of the telegraph line, saw *his* reed vibrate while he also heard a faint twang. He shouted excitedly: "What did you do then? Don't change anything. Let me see." The vibrations from Watson's plucked reed had caused an electrical current in the electromagnet to be transmitted through the wire and make Bell's reed vibrate in exactly the same way. These vibrations then reproduced the "twang" that Bell heard.

Working at Creativity

Illumination, the fourth creative stage, follows insight, preparation, and incubation. At this stage the inventor suddenly puts the pieces together into the full-blown solution. As in Bell's case, lucky accidents often provide the trigger, but while luck is involved, it is not blind luck. Because Bell had been incubating the problem of electrically reproducing sound, he was prepared and waiting for just such an event to suggest the final solution.

This was the case in the early days of General Motors when Charles Kettering headed G.M.'s research. He was working on the problem of engine knock and had his engineer put a window in a gasoline engine cylinder so they could see the flame and possibly better understand what was going on. They found, however, that the gasoline flame was invisible, so Kettering looked around for something they could use to give it color. He found a bottle of iodine in the first-aid cabinet, and when the iodine was put in the gasoline, the engine knock disappeared. This stroke of luck led to the completely new industry of gasoline additives.[9]

Another such lucky accident happened when Dr. Alexander Fleming was examining a culture plate that had been contaminated with mold. As he looked at the culture under the microscope, he saw colonies of bacteria, looking like islands surrounded by clear spaces. Fleming reasoned that the mold might be preventing the spread of bacteria, and this observation led to the discovery of penicillin. A lucky discovery? Perhaps, but how many other biologists given the same culture would have dismissed the observation as irrelevant?[10]

Chance plays an important part in the creative process, but it is not just blind luck. If these accidents had happened to someone else, their significance likely would have been missed. The inventor, however, had a prepared mind with all the ingredients of the solution just waiting for some trigger to suggest the proper arrangement. If these particular accidents had not happened, the discoveries were so nearly ripe that something else surely would have triggered them just the same.

Verification

Verification is the final, and often most tedious, part of the creative process. In this stage the wild and impractical ideas are culled out by extensive testing and analysis. Although an occasional intuitive insight will point directly to the full-blown solution, most often it provides only a teasing suggestion of what might work. The idea must then be developed, refined, and molded before it has practical value. Thomas Edison is reported to have unsuccessfully tried over a hundred ways to perfect one of his ideas: "When asked if he was discouraged, Edison scoffed at the idea, pointing out that he was making progress. He now knew one hundred things that didn't work."[11]

There is a fine line between invention and development. At one extreme, invention is pure illumination, and development may seem to be all verification. Although true inventions are usually characterized by some single identifiable concept, most of them must undergo extensive development before they can be economically produced and marketed. Product development work, on the other hand, often starts with a well-known concept and refines and improves upon it. During this process, however, many new ideas and novel approaches must be introduced before a significantly improved final product will result. No single concept stands out as the most crucial idea, but many smaller creative cycles have been combined to produce a superior total result.

THE NATURE OF CREATIVITY

The first step in the innovative process is thus a creative one. Creativity, however, has not been well understood. In fact, it was once viewed as a magical power arising from divine inspiration. This view is now largely obsolete, due in part to the work of Harvard philosopher Nelson Goodman on Project Zero. In 1967, when Goodman was asked to study the creative process in the arts, he quipped, "There's nothing known about that," so he called it Project Zero.[12] This turned into a 17-year effort to examine the skills of artists, the way they worked, and what had most deeply influenced their careers. The conclusion was that creativity is merely a way of thinking and that the seeming sudden insights were not sudden at all but were preceded by early premonitions and hints, which were then developed through an orderly and logical process.

Goodman also found that many of the artists he studied were strongly influenced by what he called an early crystallizing experience, such as when Yehudi Menuhin attended a concert at age three and then asked for a violin for his fourth birthday. This gift was the start of a lifetime of dedication by this man who became the greatest violinist of his time. Such crystallizing experiences focus geniuses on their chosen careers and help to build the motivation needed to devote their lives to this one subject.

Stimulating Ideas

Project Hindsight looked further into the creative process to see how important prior work can be in stimulating creative ideas.[13] The investigators found that each of the eight military projects they studied depended on several prior innovations which, though separately quite modest, together reinforced one another to produce a significant total project effort. Since most of the prior innovations were made long before these projects started, the team's awareness of this prior work turned out to be critically important to their creative success.

Another way to stimulate ideas is to have a group with a common problem get together and discuss it. This is the principle of the quality circle, where a team of workers discusses common problems and suggests solutions. The enormous power of this approach was shown by Toyota's experience, when in 1980 each production worker averaged 17.8 suggestions, of which 90% were accepted. General Motors was slower to adopt this approach: In the same year less than one suggestion was submitted per worker, and only 31% of them were adopted.[14] The number of adopted suggestions per 1000 workers in General Motors was thus about 300 per year, while Toyota had over 16,000. This 50-to-1 advantage in useful per-capita worker suggestions must have increased innovation in Toyota's factories and importantly influenced their performance in the U.S. automobile market.

IMAGINATION AND NERVE

Arthur C. Clarke, who is best known for his *2001: A Space Odyssey*, points out that otherwise competent professionals often make serious blunders when they project the future.[15] In one case an 1878 British parliamentary committee declared that electric lighting was "unworthy of the attention of practical or scientific men." Lord Rutherford, who won the Nobel Prize in 1908 for his "Theory of Atomic Transmutation," similarly argued that nuclear reactions could not release more energy than they consumed. He died just five years before Enrico Fermi demonstrated the first self-sustaining nuclear chain reaction at the University of Chicago.

Clarke argues that these miscalculations are due to either a failure of imagination or a failure of nerve. Failure of imagination is most likely when all the available facts point in one direction but some limitation blocks the way. Even trained observers are often unable to imagine that a single break-through can clear up all remaining obstacles.

One example of this occurred in the early days of computers when machine designers failed to visualize the need for vastly larger memories. When IBM designed the 360 system in the early 1960s, the maximum addressing capacity was set at 16 million bytes of memory. This seemed so enormous at the time that one technical committee could not visualize this ever being a limitation. Memory demands have consistently exceeded available capacity, however, and the enormous advances in semiconductor technology have made vastly larger memories practical. Today, addressing capacities of billions of bytes are essential even for small desk top computers.

Failure of nerve occurs when all the facts are available but the observer is somehow unable to accept their inevitable conclusion. This reaction is a surprising and very common fact of technical life, and it is often the prime reason for so much resistance to change. This is what led Edward R. Murrow to remark: "The obscure we see eventually. The completely obvious, it seems, takes longer."[16]

THE CHAMPION

Modesto Maidique has concluded that new ideas either find a *champion* or they die.[17] Conard Fernilius and W.H. Waldo, in a study for the National Science Foundation, also found that the successful projects invariably had champions.[18] Texas Instruments studied 50 of their completed projects and found that none of the failures had a voluntary champion. As a result, they now require every new project to be run by someone who has, in effect, volunteered for the job.[19]

Thomas Edison's enormous inventive genius often overshadows his impressive performance as a champion, but he was every bit as effective in this sphere as well. In the summer of 1878 he publicly declared that he would invent the electric light bulb, and he lined up the needed initial capital and started to work. In December he told his backers that he had "just about got it." A couple of months went by and nothing happened until, in February, he invited his backers out to see a demonstration. They came and saw all the bulbs blow out in less than 10 minutes. This happened several times during the next 18 months, and every time the backers would say, "That's Edison; we know he can do it." And, of course, he did.[20]

Champions maintain a focused drive to overcome every obstacle, and their unshakable confidence both inspires their team and maintains their momentum. Often, the champion's singleminded refusal to give up is what keeps the project moving in spite of all the doubters. Although champions don't always win, winners, it seems, always have champions.

THE SPONSOR

After the inventor and the champion, the third key person in the innovation process is the sponsor. The sponsor may not share the knowledge, skill, or conviction of either the champion or the inventor, but he or she does have imagination and nerve. At the outset, most technology projects look very promising; but when, as often happens, they run into trouble, dedicated sponsors can be invaluable. Any backer can handle the good news, but it takes courageous sponsors to stick with their original convictions when the schedules are slipping, project members are discouraged, and the budget is nearly exhausted.

RCA's David Sarnoff demonstrated his remarkable capacity as a leader and a sponsor both with color television and again at the forty-fifth anniversary celebration of his radio career in 1951. In his speech to RCA's technical elite, he challenged them to produce a magnetic tape recorder for both black-and-white and color television. This was one of the leading technical problems of the day, and few people were confident that it could be solved, at least not very quickly. Sarnoff, however, had the confidence to ask for a demonstration on his fiftieth anniversary five years later. The scientists were staggered, and many wondered if he knew what he was saying. The project, however, instantly became a top RCA priority, and all worries about failure were submerged in the drive to meet this aggressive target. Five years later when they gave Sarnoff his demonstration, he said, "I had no doubts that they could solve these problems....I have often had more faith in these men than they have had in themselves."[21]

NOTES

1. Nancy Stern, "From Eniac to Univac," *IEEE Spectrum*, vol. 18, no. 12 (December 1981), p. 61.

2. Elting E. Morison, "A Case Study of Innovation," *Engineering and Science Monthly*, California Institute of Technology, April 1950.

3. Patrick E. Haggerty, "The Corporation and Innovation," *Strategic Management Journal*, vol. 2 (1981), pp. 97–118.

4. Lee Edson, "Intuition," *Across the Board*, June 1982. p. 7.

5. Graeme Fife, letter to the editor of the *New York Times*, November 21, 1984.

6. W.J. Abernathy and J.M. Utterback, "Patterns of Industrial Innovation," in Tushman and Moore, *Readings in the Management of Innovation* (Marshfield, MA: Pitman, 1982), p. 97.

7. Michael LeBoeuf, *Imagineering: How to Profit from Your Creative Powers* (New York: McGraw-Hill, 1980), p. 56.

8. American Telephone and Telegraph Co., "The Mad Idea," in *Communicating and the Telephone*, July 1979.

9. Alfred P. Sloan, Jr., *Adventures of a White Collar Man* (Garden City, NY: Doubleday, 1941).

10. LeBoeuf, *Imagineering*, p. 189.

11. Ibid., p. 26.

12. Howard Gardner, "Science Grapples with the Creative Puzzle," *New York Times*, May 13, 1984, sec. H, p. 1.

13. C.W. Sherwin and others, *First Interim Report on Project Hindsight*, U.S. Department of Defense (Washington, DC, June 30, 1966). Reference in A.J.A. Sparnus's "Uncertainty Reducing Techniques in Technological Innovation," *IEEE Engineering Management Review*, vol. 9, no. 4 (December 1981).

14. "Putting Workers into Workmanship," *Business Week*, February 23, 1981, p. 132D.

15. Arthur C. Clarke, *Profiles of the Future* (New York: Holt, Rinehart and Winston, 1984), pp. 16, 29.

16. LeBoeuf, *Imagineering*, p. 19.

17. Modesto A. Maidique, "Entrepreneurs, Champions, and Technological Innovation," *Sloan Management Review*, Harvard University, Winter 1980, p. 59.

18. W. Conard Fernilius and W.H. Waldo, "Contribution of Basic Research to Recent Successful Industrial Innovations," Industrial Research Institute Research Corporation, St. Louis, MO. Prepared for the Division of Policy Research and Analysis, National Science Foundation (Washington, DC: September 1979).

19. Thomas J. Peters and Robert H. Waterman, Jr., *In Search of Excellence: Lessons from America's Best-Run Companies* (New York: Harper & Row, 1982), p. 203.

20. Nancy Stern, in "Eniac to Univac," quotes from an interview she held with Robert Friedel, the director of the IEEE Center for the History of Electrical Engineering.

21. *RCA Executive Biography: David Sarnoff* (New York: RCA Corporation, 1970).

PART
5

Innovative Teams

CHAPTER

14

Team Structure

A team is a group of people who are working together toward a common end. The internal structure of a team largely governs the relationships among its members and often determines their behavior. When its internal structure is effective, the team will concentrate on its official objectives, but when the structure is ineffective, performance generally suffers. Even though each individual member has a unique role, the overall character of a cohesive team is much like a collective personality.

Teams develop codes of conduct that influence their behavior. Fred Brooks referred to this when he said that the members of a great team run a little faster and try a bit harder. Team spirit "provides the cushion, the reserve capacity, that enables a team to cope with routine mishaps."[1]

CONCEPTS OF TEAM STRUCTURE

Early efficiency expert Fredrick Winslow Taylor proposed that work be divided into precisely specified tasks, each task examined in detail, and the best working methods defined for each. A worker is then told both what to do and precisely how to do it.[2] In early factories this may have been essential, but Mayo found at Hawthorne that even routine jobs can be improved if the workers are treated with respect.[3] Peter Drucker has best explained the reason why Taylor's methods are not effective: "Machines work best if they do only one task...[but] for any one task and any one operation, the human being is ill suited."[4] People are adaptable and intelligent, and if their work doesn't use both these traits, they quickly find it dull and uninteresting. As Drucker adds, "What is good industrial engineering for work is exceedingly poor human engineering for workers."

It is desirable to make work interesting for the people, but this is hard to do with large groups. The job must then be subdivided, each piece handled separately, and the results somehow coordinated. Some managers attempt to follow Taylor's philosophy of rigidly defining these tasks, but this is rarely practical. In addition to demotivating the people, technology is too unpredictable. Something new invariably causes the plans to change. A rigid management style both wastes the skills and talents of the workers and consumes managers' time. If managers persist in this style, they will generally be too busy to handle all the necessary details and will thus become the limit on their organization's performance.

With experience, managers learn to involve their professionals in dividing up team assignments into individual tasks. This allows the engineers and scientists to adjust their daily work according to the progress of their co-workers, and thus to maximize their total performance. Superior technical teams maintain a high level of internal communications, provide one another with informal support, and readily adjust their own assignments, all with little or no management involvement.

TEAMWORK

One of the finest examples of teamwork I know of was displayed on my very first development project. The contract was for a large digital communications system that was planned for U.S. Army field use by the Signal Corps. The eight engineers on the team were mostly raw recruits, but the two technicians were old hands. Once, when we burned out the last precision resistor, they saved the day. The Signal Corps was coming for a review in one week, and the early demonstration model wouldn't work without these parts. When Purchasing said they couldn't get new resistors in time, the technicians found some in only half an hour. We never asked where they came from, but we learned to trust their "midnight requisition" system.

This team did whatever was needed without question or direction. Just after we finished the first system and put it under test in the basement laboratory, a hurricane struck, and floods were predicted for the weekend. Even though no one was called, everyone showed up on Saturday morning. By late afternoon, water was actually squirting up through cracks in the cement floor, and all power had to be shut off. Everyone splashed around in that cold, dark basement, moving heavy equipment onto improvised stands; but none of it was damaged.

At the end of the project, volunteers were needed to help with the environmental tests. The equipment had to operate from minus 10°F to plus 132°F while the humidity was maintained at a constant 90%. This wasn't too bad during the heat-up cycle, but on the way down, it actually snowed in the chamber! Since someone had to be in there with the equipment all the time, this promised to be a tough assignment. Everyone wanted to go, however, but the medical department allowed only four of the team into the chamber. The equipment came through the tests with flying colors and so did the people.

TEAM CREATIVITY

In an effective team, the combined intellects of the members make more total knowledge available. When all the professionals fully participate, the team performs better than the individuals could do alone.[5] Two engineering groups from different laboratories exemplified this principle when they cooperated in building a computer system for retail stores. The group from the printer organization was to build a small print unit for the receipts and transaction listings, and the communications department was responsible for the rest of the check-out terminal. These separate teams were soon in violent disagreement. The printer people found that no existing mechanism would fit in the required space, meet the cost targets, or provide adequate print quality. There wasn't enough time to design a completely new unit, so they began to argue about the specifications. Engineers designing the terminal, meanwhile, were convinced that their needs could be met because they had seen competitive terminals that had the kind of functions they wanted.

The debates grew increasingly acrimonious until finally the two groups went to their respective laboratory managers for help. The two executives got together and agreed that the best chance to solve the problem would be to form one team with the best engineers from the two groups. This new team was then told to focus on the technical and cost issues but to leave the organizational and funding questions for the laboratory managers to resolve. The engineers started out arguing about the requirements, but they soon realized that the targets were proper and started to work cooperatively on solving the problem. They next reassessed the technical assumptions of each of the groups and found that, contrary to their prior experience, the printing no longer had to be done on flat sheets of paper. Although it had always been done this way, this was not necessary for the narrow strips to be used in this terminal. Instead of the bulky mechanism to move the print head, they could now mount an existing print element on a simple swivel to print against a curved platen. This new design was not only within the cost targets but also could be quickly made from available parts.

All the knowledge required to solve this problem had already existed in these two separate groups, but as long as they were defending their preconceived positions, they were unable to think objectively about the problem. Once they were merged into a common effort, their multidiscipline skills quickly produced a creative result. The laboratory managers knew that a single group with a crisply defined technical goal was far more likely to produce an innovative solution. Once the technical issues were resolved, the organizational and funding questions were quickly cleared up as well.

TEAM SUPPORT

From his studies of technical teams, Eugene Raudsepp concluded that the effective team honors the individualism of its members, but acts as a unit. All the members are encouraged to contribute their knowledge to the overall effort. This communication of experiences and trading of ideas enables members to learn more, consider a greater number of variables, and improve their skills. An effective and challenged team also brings out the members' latent abilities and provides an atmosphere for continuing growth and development.[6]

Team membership satisfies the members' need for affiliation and provides them a safe haven for developing their ideas. The lone worker needs incredible stamina and self-confidence to single-handedly struggle with difficult technical problems while simultaneously facing personal insecurity. In high technology the projects are generally controversial, and the advocate of change is often subjected to personal attack. The social support of a team can thus provide professionals with reassuring security while they continue their crusades.

BASIC TEAM STRUCTURES

According to Eric Berne, groups typically have three organizational structures: the official, the individual, and the private.[7] The official structure describes how things are supposed to work according to the organizational charts and the procedure manuals. Problems change so rapidly, however, that reorganizations can rarely keep pace, and most technical work is far too complex to describe in reasonably sized manuals. As a result, the official structure is always out of date and far too simplistic to be useful. The only people who really know what is going on are the professionals and their immediate managers. They have learned to largely ignore the official structure and to operate through the host of private understandings and agreements that make up the individual structure.

Even with the rapid pace of modern technical change, the difference between the individual and the official structures rarely causes any trouble. In electronics, for example, engineers traditionally designed machines with circuits and wires, and programming was typically considered a support function. With the introduction of integrated circuit technology, however, sophisticated microprocessors cost less than wired logic, and the engineers found they could save time and money by making their logic from processor chips and microprograms. In the space of a few years, most engineers' jobs changed from designing and testing circuits to writing and testing microprograms. This called for new skills, new support systems, different release and change procedures, new service concepts, and a host of advanced tools and methods. The professionals themselves had little trouble with this change, even though the official organization and procedures manuals continued for several years to treat engineering as an exclusively hardware discipline.

In contrast to the work focus of the official and individual structures, the private structure concerns the social relationships among the team members. Each group generally has some informal spokesperson who speaks up when secretarial service is inadequate, purchasing is late, or supplies are exhausted. There is also a wise counselor who provides advice on personal or business problems and a social secretary who arranges for group activities. These roles are never officially stated, but they are well known just the same. This private structure makes up the members' personal support framework, and it is what makes the group cohesive and interdependent. Each member must support and contribute to the team's private structure to earn the full benefits of membership.

STRUCTURAL CONFLICTS

The interaction between the official, the individual, and the private organizations rarely causes much trouble because most professionals are more concerned with doing their jobs than with following procedures. Occasionally, however, an officious manager may try to work "by the book" and disrupt an otherwise smooth operation. Charlie had managed a large technical support department before his promotion to head of the headquarters engineering standards staff of half a dozen senior professionals. According to the book, every standards change was to be issued in preliminary form, reviewed by all affected parties, approved by every level of division management, and finally signed off by the staff head. These professionals knew, however, that most of these issues were far too minor to warrant all this formality, so they had long since developed the practice of reaching informal telephone agreements with their divisional associates and then issuing informal "clarifications."

Charlie, however, was accustomed to running a larger organization, and he felt most comfortable with a daily stack of mail and a full schedule of appointments. The first thing he did on assuming his new job was to read all the organization and procedure manuals and require his staff members each to review their project plans with him. He was horrified to discover that none of the recent changes had any of the required documentation required to support them. He immediately instituted periodic status reviews and a rigorous follow-up system. In no time his calendar was filled with meetings, and he was happily presiding over endless reviews of every detail of his people's work. The book was now being followed precisely, but little real work was actually being done. After a few months he was quietly reassigned to a less sensitive position.

GROUP ETHICS

The behavior of team members is influenced by their positions in the team's private structure, and each of them has a vested interest in preserving this role. When any member's position is threatened, there is an unwritten team ethic that all the members will rally round in support and so preserve the team as a social entity. Another tacit understanding requires the members to settle their own disputes without appealing for outside help. When one engineer, for example, has a dispute with a co-worker, they should settle the issue themselves or with the help of another team member. An appeal to the team's manager or an outsider is often seen as breaking this rule and can thus be counterproductive.

Although he had never really thought about these matters, one older engineer unconsciously followed this ethic when a new member took over his accustomed role of chairing the annual technical conference. He had enjoyed being the unofficial professional coordinator, and he had already started planning the next conference. When a new member joined the group, however, he inserted himself in this planning process. The old hand complained loudly to all the other team members, but never went to the department manager for help. The newcomer was energetic and ambitious, and he did a good job of the initial conference planning. He had, however, expected some kind of recognition for his efforts. When he found that the other team members were not the least bit impressed, he concluded that the work was not worth the effort and quietly let his older associate resume his traditional role.

GROUP BEHAVIOR

Three basic kinds of groups have been called the work group, the process group, and the combat group.[8]

The Work Group   The *work group* has no major internal conflicts, good communication between members, and a positive and friendly atmosphere. Its energies are directed toward the job, and the members subordinate their personal interests to the group's objectives. From the manager's point of view, this is ideal group behavior, and interestingly enough, it is also the ideal for the group.

The Process Group   Groups with internal conflicts are called *process groups*. A member may be disruptive, there may be a leadership challenge, or someone may violate the group's ethics. In any of these cases, the group must devote at least some of its energies to resolving the problem. This is often a completely informal process and is generally handled without resorting to outside help. Since this kind of group action is rarely possible without consensus, such process problem solving can immobilize a group for long periods.

An example of process problem solving is the case of 10 managers who were attending a two-week seminar on business management. Although none had previously worked together, they were now to listen to a series of lectures and work out a number of case studies. At the opening session one student, Bob, was the first to raise a question. His rambling comments soon showed that he was more interested in talking than in getting an answer, but the discussion leader politely handled the interruption and proceeded. Bob interrupted repeatedly, however, and by the end of the day he had done almost as much talking as the instructor. The other members were thoroughly disgusted with this performance, and their annoyance increased when the same behavior continued on the second day. On the third day, without any prior agreement, the members developed an effective way to handle the problem. Whenever Bob raised a question, one of them would interrupt for clarification, and then the others would join in. As soon as Bob was silenced, a member would ask the instructor to continue. Initially, Bob tried to talk over this competition, but he was completely ignored. His questions soon ceased and the group returned to normal.

Most groups sense their internal dynamics and intuitively know how to coordinate their actions to solve process problems. When operating in the process mode, task forces, discussion groups, classes, and juries quickly learn to speak with one voice against the lone miscreant. Such group pressures can be enormous, and few members can withstand them unaided for very long.

The Combat Group   The last team classification is the *combat group*. Regardless of its internal problems, this group loyally closes ranks and directs all its energies to defending itself from an external attack.

An example of this involved a technical staff that was to be split between two divisions. The staff manager had opposed the split from the beginning and argued that he should keep the entire function in one division and provide service to the other. Division management, however, rejected this approach and asked an organizational consultant to recommend how the split should be made. The staff manager brought his entire management team to an all-day meeting with the consultant, but none of them said a word. The consultant was frustrated by his inability to learn anyone's views but the staff manager's. He next met individually with some of the department's managers. Everyone, however, merely repeated what the staff manager had already said. While the consultant was sure that some of them agreed with the change, not one of them would say anything that even implied acceptance of a split. Finally, after many meetings, the consultant had learned enough about the department's operations to make his own recommendations, but nobody on the team had said anything that was counter to the staff manager's initially stated position.

This is classic combat behavior. Even though the group had previously faced serious internal conflicts, all process issues were submerged in the face of this external threat. Everyone closed ranks behind the staff manager. Leaders of strife-torn groups often find this combat behavior helpful in suppressing internal friction, and some even create external threats just to consolidate their positions.

NOTES

1. F.P. Brooks, *The Mythical Man-Month* (Reading, MA: Addison-Wesley, 1995), p. 155.

2. Fredrick W. Taylor, *The Principles of Scientific Management* (New York: Harper & Row, 1911).

3. The Hawthorne studies were discussed in Chapter 7.

4. Peter F. Drucker, *Management, Tasks, Responsibilities, Practices* (New York: Harper & Row, 1974), p. 183.

5. A number of studies have shown that close and sustained technical interaction between professionals stimulates their innovative performance: Frank Barton, "The Psychology of Imagination," *Scientific American*, CXCIX (September 1958), pp. 151–166; Patrick H. Irwin and Frank W. Langham, Jr., "The Change Seekers," *Harvard Business Review*, January/February 1966; Rensis Likert, *New Patterns of Management* (New York: McGraw-Hill, 1961); Eugene Raudsepp, "Teamwork: Silent Partner in the Design Group," *IEEE Engineering Management Review*, vol. 9, no 4 (December 1981).

6. Raudsepp, "Teamwork," p. 94.

7. Eric Berne, *The Structure and Dynamics of Organizations and Groups* (New York: Grove Press, 1966), p. 64.

8. Ibid., p. 73.

CHAPTER

15

Managing
Innovative
Teams

Many of the techniques for managing creative people carry over to managing teams. Managers, for example, play the key role in determining their team's attitudes. The way managers assign the work, evaluate performance, and set the pace heavily influences the feelings of the members of their departments or groups. When managers ensure that each person feels personally valued, the team is most likely to coalesce into an effective working entity. If not, the group will likely split into factions with each competing for the boss's favor.

A strong and cohesive spirit greatly improves team performance. This cannot be achieved, however, unless the members feel loyal to the group and comfortable with their roles within it. Loyalty builds personal responsibility for team performance. If the members feel comfortable with their team roles, they will more likely voice their views and contribute their ideas. The team members then do what is needed without worrying about job responsibilities or whether everyone is doing their part.

THE NEEDS OF CREATIVE TEAMS

A study reported by Donald Pelz and Frank Andrews found that employees whose managers tightly control the work are generally less creative than employees whose managers have a looser and more informal style. The major differences in performance occurred because "some scientists were in situations where their creative ability 'paid off' for them, but others were in situations where creative ability seemed to hurt their performance."[1] The major factors that caused this result were managers' willingness to give their people adequate control over their own work, the people's ability to influence the managers' decisions, and their ability to communicate new ideas both within the group and with other groups. Pelz and Andrews concluded that "creative ability was less likely to pay off, and may even hurt a man's performance if he was in a restrictive situation."[2]

An example of how the manager's behavior influences team performance occurred when Barbara joined a research project at a leading university. This group was starting an industrial training program and Charlie, the project director, asked Barbara to help with class registration. When he described how to handle the registration process, Barbara saw some problems. When she voiced her concerns, however, Charlie was visibly annoyed. Barbara saw that he was not interested in her views so she quickly shut up and did the job as Charlie directed. As she had expected, the registration process was inefficient and took much longer than planned.

SIGNING UP

The way team members are recruited is also important. If they voluntarily choose the job, they will more likely maintain their energy and enthusiasm through the many routine phases of the project. Tracy Kidder describes the way Tom West handled recruiting for the Eagle computer.[3] Tom was looking for candidates who would perform well under the pressure of his crash program, and he wanted people who were excited by the challenge of designing and building an advanced computer. Any engineer who signed declared, in effect: "I want to do this job, and I'll give it my heart and soul." Although signing up was not a formal process, when old hands said, "Yeah, I'll do that," they had signed up. West carefully picked the best and the most motivated of the engineers, and although the pressure was intense, they worked incredibly long hours and produced a very successful machine.

THE TEAM LEADER'S STYLE

George Farris and Frank Andrews have found that the way managers deal with their employees makes an enormous difference in the quality of their work.[4] The groups they studied were separated into the most and the least innovative. In the most innovative, the managers personally involved themselves in the work and maintained close technical contact with their people. For the least innovative, the managers were less active and more remote. Although they occasionally provided ideas and information, they were not deeply involved and had little close interaction with their groups.

Farris and Andrews then looked more deeply to see what kind of close involvement was most effective. They found that if the manager had only limited ability, innovation was highest when the group was given the greatest freedom. If the manager was highly skilled in administration, personnel management, and technology, however, the results were mixed; sometimes freedom helped, but sometimes it did not. As they said: "If you don't know what you're doing, then stay out of the way!"[5]

This is the age-old conflict between top-down direction and bottom-up participation. For managers who are more competent and their people less so, top-down direction is most important. In the extreme, the employees merely carry out their manager's detailed instructions. At the other extreme, where the managers' technical talents are more limited and their employees are highly capable, managers should focus on goals and objectives and leave the technical details to their employee.

TEAM DYNAMICS

As shown in Figure 15.1, Larry Constantine has identified four team styles, as follows:[6]

1. The *closed* group is managed from the top down. The manager gives direction and the troops perform. This group is highly effective in well-

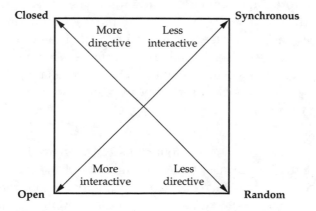

Figure 15.1   Team Styles

defined situations. Examples are military combat or a football scrimmage. When the objective is to make a touchdown or to neutralize an enemy machine gun nest, there is no time for debate. The leader had better know what to do and everyone else had better do their jobs without question or hesitation.

2. The *random* group is at the opposite extreme. The key is independent thinking and creativity. The objective is to produce an innovative result. This is best done by ensuring that all the members' ideas are considered. Brainstorming is a formal way to encourage such behavior and it is generally most effective when facilitated by someone who knows how to get all the team members to contribute their ideas and to stay open minded. The random style is often most effective when identifying and resolving requirements uncertainties or finding a solution to a difficult problem—like a mountaineering group deciding on the best route to the top. They thoughtfully share the knowledge and wisdom of all the members before they make a decision.

3. The *synchronous* group consists of people who can work effectively by themselves. They have well-defined interfaces but no need to interact dynamically. An example would be an electrical engineer, a power systems designer, and a packaging designer who cooperate on designing a product. Although they must communicate their results, and these results must interrelate, they need not discuss the details of their work. As in a wrestling or track team, while team spirit provides support and motivation, there is no need for dynamic interaction.

4. In the *open* group, each member does a job the others are capable of performing. They can switch positions, support each other, or review each other's work. This is often the situation in a software project where several engineers develop the modular parts of a common system. Although they each separately design and code their modules, they must work together to establish the module interfaces. They also must integrate their pieces into a coherent whole. The sports analogy is the tennis team, where the players back each other up and may even switch positions during the play.

As shown in Figure 15.1, these four styles can be viewed as the four corners of a square. The corners are the extremes and the areas within the square are combination behaviors. Constantine points out that these extremes are appropriate under different conditions. Managers should thus use whichever style is most appropriate to the situation at hand, recognizing that many style gradations are possible.

A SOFTWARE DEVELOPMENT EXAMPLE

In software development, for example, each of these style extremes might be appropriate under the following conditions:

1. The closed style could make most sense during the last minute crunch to get a product through system test and delivered. There is no time for extended debates or to review alternatives. The manager/leader must know what to do and ensure that each team member has a clearly assigned role, defined tasks, and specific objectives.

2. The random style could be appropriate during the requirements phase or while searching for the best product design strategy. Here, the engineers might hold extended design sessions where they trade ideas and explore alternatives. These are often free-form discussions that jump from high-level conceptual design to great detail, depending on the topic at hand.[7]

3. The synchronous style can be effective at many times in a software project. During the planning phase, for example, the members' roles are established before each produces a personal plan to do the work. While these plans must be consistent with each other, they should each be based on the member's personal data and development strategy.

4. The open style is also effective during many phases of a software project. When engineers have problems or need support, they call on their peers for assistance. They may review each other's designs, help with environment problems, or assist with a difficult test defect. When engineers find their jobs are bigger than planned, open groups are more likely to adjust their work to compensate and thus to improve overall team performance.

One style does not fit all. Managers who use any one single style for all situations will not effectively use their teams. Capable managers know when to make difficult decisions and when to call for debate. They know how to utilize their employees' knowledge and they are directive when quick and decisive action is needed. As managers learn to mix their operating styles effectively, the people they lead will be happier, more productive, and will produce better results. This combination should be the manager's ultimate objective.

THE MANAGER'S RESPONSIBILITY

Managers must strive to get the job done, and when their groups do not perform, they must step in and straighten things out. Unfortunately, even with capable workers, many pressures drive managers toward autocratic or closed behavior. At the start of a project, the managers know what is needed, and they must inform the project members. Often, the managers are both more experienced and better informed, so when the work load is heavy and the budget tight, they may lose patience and tell their people *exactly* what to do. Doing so may quickly resolve the current problem, but it demonstrates the manager's superiority, reduces the engineers' self-confidence, and limits their initiative. This tends to further reduce team performance and causes the manager to become more authoritarian.

The best guideline is for managers to recognize that different styles are appropriate under different conditions. When invention is required, for example, the manager should consider Constantine's random style. During a final delivery crunch, however, a closed style would likely be more effective. Most of the time, however, some combination of synchronous and open styles is probably more appropriate.

THE TEAM'S PERSONAL NEEDS

In addition to the nature of the work, it is important to consider the personal needs of the team members. The principles of situational leadership discussed in Chapter 7 suggest that managers consistently strive to build the team members' task and relationship maturity. Although managers may need to be directive at the outset, they should gradually provide more latitude. The objective is to stay closely involved and to show continuing interest in the engineers' work.

Keep pushing the engineers to do the work by themselves and encourage them to take the initiative. While they should know how and when to interact with their peers and managers, it is important that the engineers learn how and when to take action by themselves. Technically competent managers should make suggestions when they feel inclined, but they should emphasize that these are only suggestions. They should ask probing questions but gradually reduce their level of explicit direction. When managers urge their group's members to make their own decisions and then ask them for the data to support their conclusions, the members will learn to think for themselves. This will help them to do better work while it builds their task and relationship maturity.

The team leader should also set goals, review performance, and instill a sense of urgency. Few people can perform at peak capacity unless they feel their work is needed. As Farris and Andrews found: "Performance is lowest when there is little time pressure."[8] By pushing for aggressive schedules, managers not only maintain their group's energy; they demonstrate the importance of the work.

One example of the way management pressure stimulates team performance was a programming interface standard. The three groups involved had been unable to reach agreement on their own. When the laboratory manager learned of the disagreement, he decided to exert pressure. He gave the three department heads three weeks to solve the problem. They chartered a technical group with a senior staff professional as the chairman. The six experts were drawn from the involved departments, and they devoted full time to the problem. By six o'clock on the night before the deadline, they had settled all but one of the points. The chairman had checked, and the manager insisted that the review meeting be held the next morning. The chairman therefore told them they would have to work all night, if necessary, to finish. It was almost midnight before they reached agreement. Even though they each had given some ground, they all agreed that the final solution was a good one. The work had been intense, and the entire team was exhausted. The laboratory manager's deadline had been met with a good technical result.

POLITICAL VERSUS TECHNICAL SOLUTIONS

In their drive to get consensus agreement, managers must recognize the difference between political and technical problems. With political problems, such as allocating job assignments, agreeing on project schedules, setting prices, or achieving agreement on administrative procedures, it is important that all key parties be represented. The team should then be managed with a random style to ensure that everyone's views are considered. While resolutions reached this way invariably involve compromises, the agreement of all the members is generally sufficient to sell the solution to the rest of the organization. It is then most likely to work in practice.

For technical questions, however, it is important to avoid political solutions. The need here is to use the skills and abilities of the team members to identify the criteria for a superior solution. The team should then brainstorm possible approaches and examine them to see which best meet the criteria. Superior technical solutions often have a coherent simplicity that can be destroyed by compromise. While proposed solutions are often modified during team debates, new and better ideas often result. It is important to distinguish between improved solutions to the stated problem and compromises to reach team agreement. Again, a random style will likely be most effective, but the key is to consistently focus on reaching a superior solution.

TEAM SYNERGISM

Educational exercises called survival games are often used to demonstrate the principles of team performance.[9] In one example in the late 1960s a group of 20 managers was asked to pretend they were on the first Apollo moon landing mission two years hence. They were given a list of 40 items—such as a life raft, an oxygen bottle, and canned food—and asked to decide, in priority order, which they should take in case they were marooned. This same test had been given to the NASA astronauts in Houston, and their combined answer was to be used as the grading standard.

First, the class members took the test individually and turned in their answers. The group was then arbitrarily divided into two 10-person teams, and each went to a separate meeting room for an hour to produce a team answer. In one case, a team member quickly took charge and guided the group through an orderly process of establishing criteria, evaluating the items, and assigning priorities to each. By coincidence this team included all the engineers and scientists from the class. One of them had even worked on the space program. This total process was orderly and efficient, each point was discussed and unanimously settled, and the group was finished in only 45 minutes.

The second team had no technically trained members, and none of them knew anything about the space program. Several viewed this class as a way to demonstrate their leadership skills, so they each tried to take charge. As a result, the meeting quickly degenerated into a series of arguments with no discernible order or plan. When the hour was up, they were still arguing over the final items and had to be called back into the meeting room.

When the results were compared, the technical team members had individually done quite well, but their overall team result was little better than the average of their individual scores. On the disorderly team, none of the individual scores had been very good, but the team result was better than their best individual score. What is more, it was even better than the score of the technical team, even though their individual members had not done nearly as well.

Team exercises generally produce similar results. When strong leaders take charge, their views tend to dominate the process. While they may request everyone's opinions, their views set the agenda and largely control the final result. A managed agenda and a firm chairman can be very effective in gathering facts, but they seriously inhibit the generation of new ideas and the open communication needed to reach complete agreement. With an established agenda, members are often reluctant to disrupt the proceedings. Even when they have very good ideas, they will hold back out of shyness or deference to the leader. With no strong leader, open communication is fostered by the resulting equality.

This is a good example of the way Larry Constantine's random team behaves. A disorderly environment is a great equalizer, and although total chaos is rarely desirable, the resulting high level of communication certainly is. When the team members feel strongly enough about the subject to participate, less structure and more interaction is more likely to produce agreement on an innovative result. If the members don't feel strongly enough about the subject to participate, it is the wrong team.

CRYSTALLIZING THE TEAM

When a team is initially formed, it is a loosely coupled collection of individuals. As the following example shows, there are various techniques for building such groups into cohesive units. A corporate task force was charged with recommending how to make a number of the company's communications products more compatible. These machines each used different message formats and processing rules, and although they had all used the same line signaling and addressing schemes, the content and structure of the messages was uncontrolled. As a result, each product's analysis and processing equipment had to be specially designed, and the customers had limited options on how to interconnect them. While everyone knew that this situation was undesirable, prior agreement had been impossible because some units were intended for low-cost applications, while others were for sophisticated high-performance systems.

The leading communications technologists from each product area were assigned to this task force, as were several staff experts. Because of the number of organizations involved, this produced a 16-member group that was near the limit of manageability. It was essential, however, to include knowledgeable representatives from each involved area. The task force leader was an experienced engineer from the corporate staff who had not been previously involved in this issue, so he was viewed by all the members as a neutral party.

At the opening session, Ray, the chairman, suggested that the work be divided into three phases. The first phase would be devoted to fact finding, and he would arrange for any presentations the members wanted and would schedule discussions with any requested technical or business experts. The second phase was to be a free-form period with no agenda and no chairperson. Ray would act like any other task force member except that he would arrange for the meeting facilities and refreshments, keep the discussions from getting too disorderly, and ensure that every member had an equal chance to speak. When someone tried unsuccessfully to break into the conversation, for example, he would make a note and later ask for that person's comments. The third phase was to start only after all the members had agreed on the conclusions and were satisfied on all important points. Ray would then assume the more traditional leader's role for the production of the final presentation and written report. After some discussion all task force members agreed with this approach.

The task force met for four consecutive days every few weeks and held about 30 days of meetings over the next several months. The data-gathering and free-form discussion phases were interspersed for much of this time, and only two heated arguments required Ray's intervention. Many of the members had strong and conflicting views, so the discussions were lively, and Ray often had to call on members who had been unable to make themselves heard. This management style crystallized the group into a coherent team within the first few days. They quickly developed several "in" jokes and a shorthand mode of communication. Often, for example, a single word or phrase would get quick agreement or cause a general laugh.

At the outset Ray had scheduled the final report presentation to the corporate technical director. As this date neared, the task force members became increasingly concerned. After all the presentations and outside discussions had been completed, only two weeks remained, and the group was far from agreement. Although they urged Ray to delay the final report, he felt the time pressure would be helpful, so he refused. Under this severe constraint, the group worked late many evenings and soon settled all the smaller issues. The one remaining question was how to achieve compatibility between the smallest and the largest machines. The small-product advocates argued that compatibility was undesirable because it would require them to add more costly features. This position was unacceptable to the high-performance representatives, however, because their machines would either be functionally constrained or be limited to communicating with only a few other machine types. They finally agreed to set up a subcommittee to see if an acceptable approach could be found to balance these conflicting needs.

A four-man subgroup was put to work on this one issue while everyone else started on the final report. The subcommittee was surprised to find that a standard compatibility format for all devices was possible with only modest cost impact for the smaller machines. The larger machines could then incorporate optional additional functions, but all units would be able to communicate at least at a basic level. The entire task force accepted this conclusion, and the report was completed on time and accepted by all the product groups. Even though many of the task force members had initially held opposing views, they finished in unanimous agreement. Because of the unstructured meetings, everyone had a chance to speak and the high level of communication fostered both creativity and understanding.

COMMUNICATION

Since communication between team members is so important, it is not surprising that communication with the manager is, if anything, more important. Eugene Raudsepp, however, found that "lack of communication is one of the most frequently cited complaints against managers."[10] It is through communication with their leader that the team members learn their goals, the tasks they are to perform, and what their manager thinks of their performance. If this communication link is inadequate, the team will be in the dark, they will not think objectively, and their work will not seem rewarding. Regardless of their task maturity, poor management communication invariably damages the team's relationship maturity.[11]

The essence of good communications is two-way interaction. If managers merely share information with their people, they are just talking, and there is no guarantee that they are understood. True understanding is rarely possible without some level of interaction. Leavitt's analogy to artillery spotting explains why this is so important:

> If an artilleryman had to fire over a hill at an invisible target, he would have to fire blind and hope that by luck one of his shells would land on the target. He would spray the area with shells and go away, never being certain whether he had or had not destroyed his objective. But by the simple addition of a spotter standing on the hilltop, the likelihood of accurate shooting can be greatly increased. The spotter can feed back to the gunner information about the effects of the gunner's own shots. "Your last shot was a hundred yards short. The second was fifty yards over." And so on. The advantage is obvious and it is precisely the advantage of two-way over one-way communication—the communicator can learn the effects of his attempts to communicate and can adjust his behavior accordingly.[12]

There is, however, one big difference between communication and artillery. When a gun misses in wartime, there is generally little lost except for some wasted ammunition and possible damage to the militarily unimportant countryside. Misses in communication, however, can both confuse and mislead. Once a manager miscommunicates, the resulting confusion is often hard to correct. When the manager then provides accurate information, the recipient may be confused and not know what to believe. When this confusion is coupled with normal conversational imprecision and the human predilection to interpret what we hear in terms of our own needs, miscommunication is more the rule than the exception.

Open Communication

James Brian Quinn has said that "high morale occurs when team members intensely share a common goal."[13] This requires that managers not only inform their people but also share with them their goals and plans. When managers have worked out an explicit set of goals and shared them with their people, their people can translate these objectives into their own personal actions. Thoroughly informed professionals invariably have many ideas on what to do and how to do it. Leaders who respect their views will be rewarded with loyal, cohesive, and productive teams.

Open communication, however, does not mean that managers should share everything with their people. The professionals are busy and have limited need for, or interest in, many of the topics that concern managers. Eugene Raudsepp states the following four ground rules for honest and open communication with team members:[14]

1. Is the issue important enough to require group discussion? It is much more efficient to communicate minor issues with brief notes or memos and then invite comments and questions.

2. If the problem only concerns management, it will be of little interest to the team in general.

3. If the members are unable to contribute to the issue because they don't have the necessary knowledge or skill, involving them will only embarrass them.

4. If the decision has already been made, it must be honestly presented that way. If not, group agreement will be a sham, and group disagreement will be a problem.

Open communication between managers and their teams also helps to improve the communication links between the members themselves. Poor management communication, on the other hand, adds to worries and causes minor issues to be blown out of proportion. As Theodore H. White has observed: "Rumors will grow in any large organization without open communication."[15]

A TECHNICAL PROPOSAL TEAM

An IBM proposal team for the FAA Enroute Air Traffic Control System in late 1963 shows how effective open communication can be. This group had grown quickly to approximately 50 engineering, marketing, and financial people, and space had become a serious problem. The local IBM laboratory was overcrowded, so a dance hall was rented from the nearby volunteer fire department. Since there were no offices and everyone had to work in one large room, the facilities would normally have been considered inadequate for professionals. It was the only space available, however, so everybody moved in for the final 60 days before the proposal due date.

In spite of the noise and lack of privacy, this turned out to be a remarkably efficient arrangement. A large blackboard on a stand was put in the middle of the room. Everyone worked at tables set around the walls. When any issue needed discussion, it was announced to all hands, and everyone involved would congregate around the blackboard. Most people came to the opening of every meeting, but those not involved quickly returned to their work. If people were needed, however, they could readily be called over and the point quickly resolved.

This free and open communication came about largely by accident, but it produced a remarkably cohesive team. Everybody knew what was going on and where they fit in. The excitement and enthusiasm grew as the deadline neared, and at the last minute there were many volunteers for the final review. This was surprising because, as a result of the tight deadline, it had to be held at the printer's in New York City on Christmas Eve. Because of this team's effectiveness the proposal was judged so superior that IBM won the competition for the 9020 system, which was to control U.S. air traffic for the next 30 years.

MANAGING TEAM CONFLICT

Nothing can destroy the effectiveness of a team more quickly or more completely than unresolved conflicts between the members. Inevitable differences and disagreements will crop up in any fast-paced organization, but the members themselves can generally work them out. Occasionally, however, the problems are too complex or pervasive, and a highly destructive process ensues. Rather than face continuing unpleasantness, the disagreeing parties start to avoid each other. The reduced contact that results causes a total break in communication. This temporarily reduces the unpleasantness, but it also makes it almost impossible for the parties themselves to resolve the problem.

Under these circumstances outside intervention is generally required. Here, Roger Fisher's basic principles for third-party conflict resolution can be helpful.[16] First, avoid early polarization. The resolution of most nontechnical problems calls for compromise on both sides, and early fixed positions make the later accommodation more difficult. Win/lose situations are the hardest to resolve, so they should be tempered by showing both parties how little they have to lose and what they can both gain from reaching agreement. Wherever possible, the stakes should be reduced so that neither party feels pressed to give up too much.

Attention should also be focused on the issues rather than on personalities, motives, or blame. Information should be obtained from several sources, and all parties made aware of all the pertinent facts. The disagreements should be focused on verifying the data and identifying additional information to clarify the remaining points in contention. When people get angry or defensive, it often means that there are hidden issues that cannot be easily resolved. Thomas Harris's wonderful book *I'm OK—You're OK* provides practical guidance in handling such situations.[17]

Finally, no conflict between team members can be resolved by dealing with either of them separately. They must both be equally involved and must both openly accept the conclusions. Since silence is not a reliable indicator of consent, both parties should air their opinions and restate the final agreement. Often, when the entire issue cannot be resolved in a single step, some points should be deferred for later consideration. It is important, however, to end each meeting with some agreement, even if it is only on the time and agenda for the next meeting.

Some conflicts cannot be resolved to everyone's satisfaction, of course. This is normal in any fast-paced organization. Different people have different priorities, and each job has its own unique objectives. Generally, however, both sides will accept a decision that goes against them if they can see how the greater good is served. This is true only if their views have been heard, and if they were told precisely why the decision was made.

In one example, the lack of skilled resources forced IBM to move the data management functions for the OS/360 programming system from Poughkeepsie, New York, to the IBM laboratory in San Jose, California. While everyone agreed with the move, they could not agree on the specific interface between the two functions. After several technical studies, there was still no agreement and the issue was brought to me. Though I was probably the least qualified person in the room, I had to make the decision. After listening to the arguments and asking questions of both sides, I settled the issue. Since everyone's position had been heard, this decision was accepted by everyone. To this day, I do not know if this was the right decision or not. The engineers, however, made it work.

No group of active and intelligent professionals can function for very long without generating friction of some kind. Disagreement is natural, and Pelz and Andrews, in a study of 83 technical groups, found it often stimulated performance.[18] When a group of professionals are personally compatible but intellectually competitive, friendly rivalry generates the highest overall group performance. When the disputes become personal, however, performance invariably suffers.

INTERGROUP CONFLICTS

The process of resolving conflicts among groups follows essentially the same rules as for conflicts among individuals. There are, however, a few additional considerations. Some general guidelines for intergroup conflict resolution are as follows:

1. The managers of the conflicting groups should first attempt to resolve the issues themselves.

2. If the managers reach an impasse, the issues should be informally explored with each manager separately, and then the parties brought together. This meeting is not to settle the issue but to agree on a way to settle it.

3. If the managers are well informed and deeply committed to their own positions, it is often helpful to form an expert subcommittee with members taken from each department. The chairperson, however, should be neutral; otherwise this group will become polarized at the outset and will likely make little progress.

4. To reduce the stakes, this subcommittee should address a portion of the issue. An example would be to focus on technical questions and ignore organizational or staffing concerns.

5. In most cases, once there is an agreed technical solution, the managers can quickly resolve the remaining questions themselves.

An example of this was the selection of a disk storage system for a new low-cost computer. The storage group had a new disk file in development, and they wanted it used both to increase its market and because they didn't have the resources for a new disk file project. The computer group, however, was convinced that this existing unit would be too expensive. The disagreement continued for some time with no resolution. Finally the two managers formed a joint subcommittee and put a respected planner in charge. He was told to focus the group on finding a technically superior solution and not to dismiss the group until they found it. After a couple of days of rehashing all the prior arguments, they each understood everyone's point of view. By that time they realized that neither of the prior proposals would do the job, so they looked for a different answer. They soon found they could modify an older existing machine to meet the performance targets. The costs would be reduced because the machine was already in production, and the tools and most of the parts were already available. An aggressive schedule was needed to meet the announcement date, and some added development resources would be needed; but everyone agreed this was the right answer. With this agreement, the managers were soon able to get the needed staffing, and the product was completed and announced on time.

NOTES

1. Donald C. Pelz and Frank M. Andrews, *Scientists in Organizations: Productive Climates for Research and Development* (New York: Wiley, 1966), p. 171.

2. Ibid., p. 172.

3. Tracy Kidder, *The Soul of a New Machine* (Boston: Little, Brown, 1981), p. 63.

4. Michael L. Tushman and William L. Moore, *Readings in the Management of Innovation* (Marshfield, MA: Pitman, 1982), p. 344.

5. Ibid., p. 347.

6. Larry L. Constantine, "Work Organization: Paradigms for Project Management and Organization," *Communications of the ACM*, vol. 36, no. 10 (October 1993), pp. 35–43.

7. Bill Curtis, Herb Krasner, and Neil Iscoe, "A Field Study of the Software Design Process for Large Systems," *Communications of the ACM*, vol. 31, no. 11 (November 1988).

8. Tushman and Moore, *Management of Innovation*, p. 346.

9. The game described here was conducted by Dale Zand, of New York University, at the IBM Sands Point Executive School in 1968.

10. Eugene Raudsepp, "Teamwork: Silent Partner in the Design *Group*," *IEEE Engineering Management Review*, vol. 9, no. 4 (December 1981), p. 94.

11. Task and relationship maturity are elements of situational leadership, which is discussed in Chapter 7.

12. Harold J. Leavitt, *Managerial Psychology*, 4th ed. (Chicago: University of Chicago Press, 1978), p. 122.

13. Tushman and Moore, *Management of Innovation*, p. 556.

14. Raudsepp, "Teamwork."

15. Theodore H. White, *In Search of History* (New York: Harper & Row, 1978).

16. Roger Fisher and William Ury, *Getting to Yes* (Boston: Houghton Mifflin, 1981).

17. Thomas A. Harris, *I'm OK—You're OK, A Practical Guide to Transactional Analysis* (New York: Harper & Row, 1969).

18. Pelz, *Scientists in Organizations*, p. 152.

16

The Innovative
Team
Environment

T he nature of the work environment can make a big difference in workers' creativity. When he compared the most and the least successful departments in several mining companies, Tom Peters found that the most innovative looked like "nothing so much as structured chaos. Buzzing, blooming environments."[1] Controlled chaos can stimulate interaction among team members, free them from mental constraints, and enhance their creativity.

One reason that seemingly free-form environments are so creative is that random behavior stimulates discovery. Karl E. Weick describes an experiment with flies and bees that demonstrates how this works.[2] Half a dozen bees and an equal number of flies are put in a bottle placed on its side with the base against a window. The bees will try to get through the base of the bottle to the light beyond, continuing this struggle until they die of exhaustion or hunger. The flies, instead, randomly buzz around, and in a few minutes they have all found the opening in the neck of the bottle and escaped.

New solutions frequently involve seemingly irrational ideas. If the search is confined to the known dimensions of the problem, no one will notice the open end of the bottle, and they will continue, like the bees, in their fruitless direct attack. While the organization is engrossed in this valiant assault, it is rarely able to hear the lone voice suggesting an unconventional new and creative solution. But what an organization needs in order to be truly innovative is the tolerance to support unconventional voices and the wisdom to listen to them.

THE SKUNK WORKS

To explore the relationship between laboratory size and innovative performance, Veronica Stolte-Heiskenen did a study of 50 research laboratories.[3] The slight correlation she found was negative. That is, smaller organizations often produced more innovative work per capita, and some even had a greater total output than their larger counterparts. This is why many companies establish special organizations, or "skunk works," to house their most creative people. These are small, informal teams given considerable freedom from the constraints normal to the rest of the organization. Lockheed, for example, had a six-engineer group in a dingy building seven miles from corporate headquarters, which, over a period of many years, was responsible for three of the corporation's five major products. Ms. Stolte-Heiskenen also found that an eight-person Spanish subsidiary of another company produced as many new products as the 400-person central product development organization.

Some years ago Thomas J. Watson, Jr., emphasized IBM's need to encourage and support its "wild ducks." As a result the company set up its special IBM Fellow program to allow engineers and scientists with proven ability to pursue their own creative ideas. When I retired from IBM, between 50 and 60 Fellows were working under five-year renewable appointments in the various company laboratories. Each had a budget, laboratory facilities, and a small technical staff to assist in the work.

Regardless of management's best efforts, however, the wild ducks in any organization generally have a hard time. Established manufacturing and development groups do not readily accept outside ideas. Committed to meeting an established plan, they view new ideas as diversions and often brush them off without an objective review. If management does not support innovators, the main-line organization will invariably reject them, and their valuable efforts and potential will be wasted. Nelson Goodman's Project Zero described in Chapter 13 found that "creative activity is only possible if one lives in a society where it is tolerated, if not encouraged."[4]

FINANCIAL JUSTIFICATION

The problems of management style and communication were discussed in Chapter 7, but another important constraint is the rigidity of tightly controlled organizations. When there is a strict focus on main-line projects, seemingly sound financial measures can cause serious problems. Hard-headed business managers generally demand financial justification for each new project. Since new ideas can rarely be financially justified at the outset, they are often killed before they can prove their worth.

Larry, a software manager, was trying to introduce a process improvement program in his organization. In a presentation on the importance of software process improvement, his senior manager asked what the return on investment of this work would be. Although Larry did not have a dollars-and-cents answer, he knew that the executive had worked as a hardware engineer. So Larry explained that even though the proposed software process methods were new, they were much like the standard hardware methods of releasing products for manufacturing. The needed software procedures, for example, were the equivalents of producing a hardware release schedule, generating a parts list, establishing a change control system, producing assembly drawings, and specifying the test procedures. It would be pointless and probably impossible to calculate the return on investment of such work. Once the executive understood that the proposed methods were merely sound technical management, he dropped his demand for cost justification and agreed to the proposed work.

Cost justification is appropriate for capital investments, but it should never be applied to new or advanced technical methods. The key is to do the job using sound and effective technical methods. If properly introduced and managed, such work will generally pay off, but there is no way to justify it at the outset. When executives are convinced that the work is needed and that it makes technical sense, they rarely ask for a cost justification. Such questions should thus be treated as symptoms of deeper problems rather than as the need for a financial analysis. It is important to know what the work will cost and to have a clear understanding of the potential benefits, but the key is to first convince management that what you propose is technically sound.

REMOVING INHIBITORS TO INNOVATION

One way managers can improve their organizations' performance is to look for and remove the inhibitors to innovation. Physical facilities, while not of paramount importance, can be a problem. When professionals have inadequate or inconvenient working conditions, they can easily be distracted by annoying details. The lack of a contiguous work space limits interteam communications and reduces team effectiveness. Poor technical support can waste a lot of the professionals' time. It is hard to focus on tough technical problems when instruments are out of calibration, computer systems are inconvenient, or purchasing is unresponsive. When a dedicated team spends hours on a job that should take a few minutes, their performance is bound to suffer.

Finally, as Pelz and Andrews have pointed out, total dedication to one job will reduce the professional's performance.[5] The best professionals have cosmopolitan leanings.[6] They want to know what is happening in both their organizations and their technical fields, and they need the stimulation of broad technical exposure. When management insists that its technical professionals work exclusively on their immediate assignments, the professionals will feel trapped and their performance will suffer.

NOT INVENTED HERE

The "Not Invented Here" syndrome can be a serious problem, particularly in large organizations. When I first joined IBM, I was both surprised and amazed by the tremendous breadth and depth of the company. If you had a problem and were willing to make a modest effort, you could find someone in this worldwide organization who was a leading expert on that specific subject. While this breadth was often very helpful, it also had a serious downside. Few IBM people were involved in or even aware of work outside the company. As long as IBM was well ahead of its competitors in all important technologies, the problem was not significant. As various technologies became generally available, however, technically competent competitors sprang up in most areas of the company's business. The lack of external awareness then meant that IBM was frequently surprised in the marketplace.

The Not Invented Here syndrome is a threat to any organization, particularly one that is successful. The larger and more successful the firm, the more its members' feelings of superiority are reinforced. Most successful organizations, however, are successful because they had the good luck to be in the right place at the right time. As long as one or two key managers used good judgment and properly made a few critical decisions, their success was almost assured. Most organizations, however, have good people and none have a monopoly on the technology. If organizations don't stay in touch with their customers, aware of their competitors, and current with their key technologies, they will sooner or later face unpleasant surprises. A few years ago, IBM seemed invincible, but they weren't. And neither is anyone else.

MAINTAINING AN INNOVATIVE ENVIRONMENT

Managers can take many steps to establish and maintain an innovative environment. For example:

1. Establish a technical resources program and take special pains to identify and help develop the most promising people.

2. Support a few of the best innovators by providing them with both the time and resources to pursue their own interests.

3. Recognize the need for sponsors and seek out and support promising inventors and champions.

4. Maintain a reasonable level of ferment and change in the organization so groups do not become stagnant and resistant to new ideas.

5. Keep a sharp eye on outside technical and market developments.

6. Set up a communication program to ensure that managers interact with their people.

7. Provide adequate facilities and support so the professionals can work in contiguous space and have modern tools and support.

8. Establish a formal program to recognize and reward outstanding work.

NOTES

1. Thomas J. Peters and Robert H. Waterman, Jr., *In Search of Excellence: Lessons from Best-Run Companies* (New York: Harper & Row, 1982).

2. Ibid., p. 108.

3. Thomas J. Peters, "The Rational Model Has Led Us Astray," *Planning Review*, March 1982. This paper cites the study by Veronica Stolte-Heiskenen of 50 public and private-sector research laboratories, p. 16.

4. Howard Gardner, "Science Grapples with the Creative Puzzle," *New York Times*, May 13, 1984, sec. 2, p. 1.

5. Donald C. Pelz and Frank M. Andrews, *Scientists in Organizations: Productive Climates for Research and Development* (New York: Wiley, 1966), pp. 56, 65.

6. The local and cosmopolitan behavior of engineers and scientists is discussed in Chapter 5.

17

Rewards and Recognition

Although the fertile imaginations of creative people are enormously valuable, their imaginations can lead them to anticipate difficulties where none really exist. When people aren't adequately recognized, for example, they may suspect something is wrong and get upset. Pelz and Andrews's study of the people who had left a major government laboratory found this to be the case.[1] They compared the people who had resigned with those who stayed. A series of interviews with previous peers revealed general agreement that those who left had been fully as productive, but their talents had not been as well appreciated by their management.

Consider the example of a very creative engineer who resigned in spite of his good record and his management's high opinion. They had readily agreed to his taking a one-year leave at a university to do research and teaching and quite naturally assumed he would need little supervision. The engineer, however, became increasingly concerned as his year drew to a close. Since no one had seemed very interested in his future, he finally decided to take a job with another company. It took a great deal of management effort to get him to change his mind.

AWARD PROGRAMS

On any project, a very few people generally make the difference between success and failure. Someone has the initial idea, another champions the program to management, and one or two key people spearhead the design and implementation. Although managers invariably know who these people are, they rarely tell them how much they appreciate their work. Some of them will be sufficiently self-confident not to worry, but most professionals need more direct evidence of their managers' approval. These engineers and scientists are the lifeblood of the organization, and it is important to reassure them frequently that their managers recognize their unique value.

The basic idea behind recognition programs is to reward significant achievements as promptly as possible. The famous Foxboro Award was conceived late one evening when one of the Foxboro Corporation's scientists solved a crucial technical problem. He excitedly raced to the president's office to show what he had done, and the delighted president looked through his desk to find something he could give in recognition. As Peters says, he "found something, leaned over the desk to the scientist and said, 'Here.' In his hand was a banana."[2] This was all he could find, but it turned out to be enough. From then on, the "golden banana" pin was awarded by Foxboro to those company engineers and scientists who were responsible for the highest technical achievements.

RECOGNITION PROGRAMS

Although recognition of the top people is essential, the professionals routinely make hundreds or even thousands of smaller contributions every day. In aggregate these little changes can have an enormous impact. Since none of them stand out, however, they rarely get special attention. Even minor advances should be encouraged in some way, if only by a letter from the boss or a pat on the back.

Rene McPherson, who headed the Dana Corporation before he became dean of the Stanford University Business School, has observed: "The real key to success is helping the middle 60 percent a few steps up the ladder."[3] When a reasonably large portion of the population know their efforts are recognized, they will continue their creative work, and the organization will continue to improve.

AN EXAMPLE AWARD PLAN

During my years with IBM, the corporation's award plan combined both "informal" and "formal" awards to recognize a wide spectrum of achievements. The "informal" awards ranged from $50 to $1500 and could be given at the manager's discretion. Once the manager got the approval of his or her immediate manager, the award could be given, even on the same day.

The larger awards were more formal. Divisional management could grant sums of up to $25,000 for important achievements and corporate awards ranged up to $100,000 or more. These large awards were reserved for unique accomplishments and were presented at an annual gala recognition dinner. The award recipients and their spouses were joined by senior IBM executives at a three-day affair equivalent to that given the most productive salesmen.

The amount of these awards may seem excessive, but the achievements they celebrate are equally significant. When someone comes up with an idea that is worth literally millions of dollars, an award of $100,000 is not out of line. One of the largest awards IBM has ever given is the $225,000 presented to an IBM Fellow and eight of his prior associates for conceiving and implementing FORTRAN, the first widely used programming language. In the five years before I retired, over $4 million in corporate awards was presented to approximately 150 employees. Twelve of these awards were for $100,000 or more.

INDUSTRY AWARD PLANS

Many companies have similar plans. For example, Edwin Gee and Chaplin Tyler describe the awards a chemical company gave to the team that created a new fertilizer product. The team's idea for a novel urea nitrate compound turned out to be a significant advance over the standard nitrate of soda or sulfate of ammonia formulations then used for commercial fertilizers. An immediate success, the urea product netted a $300,000 profit in the first 12 months of commercial operation. Management decided that 4% of this amount should be divided among the 5 key contributors on the 20-person team:

- Dr. A, agronomist, conceived and defined the product characteristics and marketing strategy, leading to an important advance in the fertilizer mixing art, thereby laying the groundwork for the company's successful entry into a new and opportune sales field. Allocation of 30% of the award was recommended.

- Mr. B, A's supervisor, proposed a modification of A's initial product concept, thereby significantly reducing costs of manufacture and distribution and strengthening the claims of the patent subsequently issued to B and A. Allocation of 10% of the award was recommended.

- Dr. C, research chemist, established the principles of the product synthesis, which theretofore had not been exploited commercially in the United States. Allocation of 20% of the award was recommended.

- Mr. D, chemical engineer, scaled up C's synthesis to the pilot stage and established design criteria for a full-scale commercial plant. This design embodied novel features resulting in substantial reduction in cost and in significant quality improvement. Allocation of 30% of the award was recommended.

- Mr. E, sales technologist, devised a facsimile mixing unit whereby the novel applications technology was demonstrated successfully to prospective customers. Allocation of 10% of the award was recommended.[4]

Following the success of the product in its first year, a total of five annual awards were planned which were expected to total $80,000 to $100,000.

Many other companies have similar award plans, and it is not unusual for them to set the award amounts in much the same way, as shown in Table 17.1.[5]

Table 17.1   Six Corporate Compensation Awards

Company	Award Amount	Annual Savings	Award (%)
United Technologies	$2,900	$19,791	14.6
United Technologies	2,500	40,000	6.3
Western Electric	3,910	26,000	15.0
Schering Corp.	1,125	5,000	22.5
Johnson & Johnson	6,978	46,500	15.0
GAF Corporation	3,580	29,000	12.3
Total	$20,993	$166,291	12.6

AWARD GUIDELINES

To qualify for an award, the achievement should be clear, significant, worthy of special recognition, and reasonably consistent with other awards for similar achievements. Take care when recognizing managers not to imply that the engineers and designers do the work and the managers get the rewards. Give the awards in public with plenty of publicity. This follows a maxim of Charlie Beacham, Lee Iacocca's mentor at Ford: "If you want to give a man credit, put it in writing. If you want to give him hell, do it on the phone."[6]

Large teams' achievements require special care; and when an entire project deserves recognition, it is best done with a special event, such as a dinner or an outing. Depending on the achievement, everyone can be given a special memento, such as a wall plaque, an engraved paperweight, or a specially designed tee shirt. Avoid giving cash to large groups.

When a large team's success also includes several important individual contributions, it is essential to provide both types of recognition. The entire team deserves the dinner and memento, but the unique achievements should receive significant dollar awards. The two events need not be held at the same time, but they should not be too widely separated. Presentation of the cash awards should be made at a meeting of the entire group, and the specific achievements should be described in enough detail to make their unique nature completely clear.

Finally, never give awards before the achievement has actually been completed. All too often, the manager will eagerly propose an award for something that is "as good as done," only to have an unforeseen snag nullify or delay the success. It is wise to wait until the achievement has been clearly demonstrated but then to be prompt and generous with the reward.

INCENTIVE PLANS

Award plans seek to meet the employees' need for recognition and thus facilitate self-actualizing performance. Incentive programs, on the other hand, are aimed at the more fundamental demands for sustenance and comfort. Even though these basic needs fall much lower in Maslow's hierarchy, all incentive systems include some element of recognition. This is because they are invariably based, at least in part, on the management's appraisal of the employee's performance. Since this is generally well known, an incentive payment thus is tangible evidence of the professional's worth to the organization.

Various types of incentive pay systems are commonly used by high-technology firms, particularly those newer organizations that need to attract and retain technical talent. In one survey of 105 firms in the Boston area, over 80% of those in high technology had bonus pay plans as opposed to only 33% of the rest.[7] Typically the plans granted cash bonuses to all technical professionals based on such nonfinancial criteria as project completion. This approach was particularly prevalent in start-up firms that were not yet sufficiently profitable to use profit sharing.

Such plans appear to be both widespread and relatively popular with employees, but there is only limited evidence to support their economic value to the organization.[8] In the case of Analog Devices, for example, a two-dimensional management incentive plan was well received by the workers, although there were a few complaints. No clear cause-and-effect relationship could be demonstrated, but sales did increase by 40%, and return on assets grew from 16% to 21% during the first four years of the plan.[9]

An interesting sidelight of incentive plans is that they can be used to stimulate peripheral behavior. At Raytheon, for example, a plan was introduced to motivate engineers to write technical papers and give talks at technical conferences.[10] An award of $250 plus $100 per page was given to every engineer who published a paper. The award was limited to a maximum of $750. Although no papers had been published in the 12 months immediately preceding the program, five papers were published and three more were started in the next three months.

Depending on the needs of the organization, both award and incentive programs can be highly effective.

A CAUTION ON RECOGNITION PROGRAMS

As W. Edwards Deming emphasized in his famous 14 points for effective quality management, various recognition and reward systems can be counterproductive.

> Remove barriers that rate people in management and in engineering of their right to pride of workmanship. This means, inter alia, abolishment of the annual merit rating and of management by objectives.[11]

While recognition is important, it is essential to keep the focus on the work. As soon as the reward becomes the objective, some employees will stop striving to do a better job and will start viewing the reward as the goal. Reward systems can be seen as an attempt to manipulate the employees, saying in effect: You do this and I will give you that. Even worse, unless you keep giving the rewards, they can become a disincentive. This is best illustrated by an apocryphal story from the *Kansas City Star*:

> An elderly man, harassed for weeks by the taunts of neighborhood children, devises a scheme. He offers to pay the children a dollar each if they'll return the next day and yell their insults again. They do so eagerly and he pays them as promised. "If you come back tomorrow I'll give you 25 cents," he tells them. They do and collect their quarters. "From now on I'll pay you a penny," the old man announces. The children are contemptuous. "A penny? Forget it!" they reply, and they never return.[12]

By all means, use rewards and recognition, but make sure they do not become disincentives.

NOTES

1. Donald C. Pelz and Frank M. Andrews, *Scientists in Organizations: Productive Climates for Research and Development* (New York: Wiley, 1966), p. 110.

2. Thomas J. Peters and Robert H. Waterman, Jr., *In Search of Excellence, Lessons from America's Best-Run Companies* (New York: Harper & Row, 1982), p. 70.

3. Ibid., p. 269.

4. Edwin A. Gee and Chaplin Tyler, *Managing Innovation* (New York: Wiley, 1976), p. 204.

5. *New York Times*, March 24, 1974.

6. Lee Iacocca and William Novak, *Iacocca: An Autobiography* (New York: Bantam Books, 1984), p. 56.

7. David B. Balkin and Louis R. Gomez-Mejia, "Compensation Practices in High Technology Industries," *Personnel Administrator*, June 1985, p. 111.

8. Reuven Shapira and Shlomo Globerson, "An Incentive Plan for R&D Workers," *Research Management*, September-October 1983, p. 17.

9. Ray Stata and Modesto A. Maidique, "Bonus System for Balanced Strategy," *Harvard Business Review*, November-December 1980, p. 156.

10. Dan Anderson, "Getting Engineers to Write," *IEEE Transactions on Professional Communication*, vol. PC-26, no. 4 (December 1983), p. 170.

11. W. Edwards Deming, *Out of the Crisis* (Cambridge, MA: MIT Center for Advanced Engineering Study, 1982), ch. 2.

12. Alfie Kohn, "Rewarding Kids May Be a Mistake," *Kansas City Star*, September 5, 1990.

18

The Management Team

The top manager and immediate subordinate managers make up the management team—the most important single group in the entire organization. They make the key operating decisions, set priorities, and determine the quality of the working environment. Unless they can work closely together, the organization will be a loosely coupled, and often contentious, group of largely independent departments.

CONTENTION MANAGEMENT

The operation of any organization of even moderate size necessarily involves a great many conflicts. Resources are never adequate, and schedules are always tight. Some central group is thus needed to resolve issues and set priorities. Senior managers are naturally responsible for everything in their organizations, but they should involve their management team in most of the issues. If they do this effectively, they can strengthen this team; but if not, the group will fragment, and the organization's energy will be dissipated in internal friction.

Paul Lawrence and Jay Lorsch have found that a contention management style leads to the most effective group performance. Of the organizations they studied, those with the highest performance used contention extensively, the medium performing groups used it to a moderate degree, and the lowest performers the least.[1] The basic ground rules for contention management are as follows:

1. Top managers make sure their management team is aware of all important decisions before they are made and invite comments and reactions in advance.

2. The team member who advocates the proposal is held responsible for informing the other members in advance.

3. Those in disagreement are responsible for resolving or escalating their issues.

4. All concerned parties are present when decisions are made, and they all have an opportunity to state their views.

5. When no opposition is voiced, the top manager makes sure the issue has been thoroughly explored and is well understood by everyone involved. If not, the decision is deferred until there is a healthy level of contention.

The reason contention is so effective is that it both exposes the organization's latent conflicts and helps to keep the discussions on a rational plane. When decisions are made in secret, the debates become political, and a feeling of distrust invariably develops among the top managers. Distrust not only damages management's effectiveness, but it also damages the professionals' working environment. Since the professional workers are entirely dependent on their manager's ability to resolve interdepartmental issues, their lack of trust in management makes resolving issues very difficult.

A further advantage of contention is the motivation it provides to find all the facts and to understand their implications. When there is a disagreement, each party works hard to find anything that will support his or her point of view. This is why Alfred P. Sloan, founder of General Motors, used to say that no important decision should be made unless there is some contention.[2]

THE IBM PERSONAL COMPUTER

In the late 1970s, IBM was clearly behind in the newly emerging personal computer business. Despite several attempts to produce a competitive system, nothing had resulted. In each case the designs were too conservative, the technology not sufficiently advanced, or the functions pedestrian. Frank Cary, the IBM CEO at the time, decided to address this problem in a radical way. He personally chartered a group in one of the product divisions to produce a personal computer at flank speed. This group was to break any IBM rules standing in the way and to bypass all the checks and balances of the corporate contention system.

Don Estridge was given this assignment, and he did a remarkable job. His first step was to move the entire development group to a dedicated location where they could work as a closely integrated team. He then involved them in project planning and had all the professionals use personal computers in their work. These were not IBM machines but tangible daily reminders of the competition. This small, hard-driving team made many innovations and broke many previously sacred IBM traditions to bring out a new machine in only one year. In just three years, they took IBM from ground zero to the undisputed leadership of the industry.

While this dramatic action on CEO Cary's part had a remarkable and very positive impact on IBM's business, it was a long-term disaster. There were many concerns about the PC strategy but no forum in which to voice them. The DOS program used to provide PC programming support, for example, was obtained from a small start-up company called Microsoft. No provisions were made to ensure that IBM retained a controlling role in the future development and marketing of DOS. This would have been entirely possible, it turns out, since Bill Gates at Microsoft did not even own the DOS program. He went out and bought full ownership from the original developers. IBM could have done the same thing.

Many of IBM's staff experts anticipated from the very start of the PC program that its software would likely become the most critical and profitable part of the entire system. While the machines ultimately became low-margin commodities, the software grew into an enormously profitable industry. Within 12 years, the great and seemingly invulnerable IBM was losing money, while Microsoft had become a multibillion dollar software giant.

A second disastrous consequence of the PC program concerned the hardware itself. At the time of the PC's development, the dominant microprocessor was the 6800 from Motorola. After much discussion, Don Estridge and his team decided to use a new Intel Chip for the PC. Again, however, because there was no in-depth review of this decision, no provision was made to ensure IBM a strong continuing position in the chip technology. Subsequently, Intel produced a growing family of increasingly powerful PC microprocessor chips that they marketed to all comers. IBM's role as a PC supplier was soon reduced to assembling commercially available parts and marketing the assembled machines through distributors. Offering no unique components or functions, IBM soon dropped to a relatively modest position in a market largely controlled by Microsoft and Intel.

THE PC JUNIOR

Contention in system development can be a mixed blessing, however. Within two years of announcing its product, the IBM PC development group lost its special privileges and was subjected to the rigors of the corporate contention system. Now, however, the problem was to meet the growing demand for a lower priced PC. To get approval for the new machine, the development group had to show the various staffs that the new PC Jr. would not seriously detract from the original PC, which was still selling very well. The staffs were concerned that informed customers could buy the cheaper PC Jr. and add a few parts to get equivalent PC performance at lower cost. If this were possible, the argument went, the price difference between the PC and the PC Jr. would be limited to the cost of the incremental parts. If the price difference between the PC and the PC Jr. were too large, people would buy the PC Jr. and upgrade. Conversely, if the price difference were restricted to the cost of the upgrade parts, either the PC price would have to be cut or the PC Jr. price would not be low enough to satisfy the market need for an entry-level machine.

To settle this debate, the development team designed the PC Jr. so it could not be upgraded beyond its initial limited capability. When this crippled machine was introduced, purchasers soon found that its limitations made it totally inadequate for the increasingly sophisticated applications becoming available. The PC Jr. was the first of several largely uncompetitive IBM personal computers. While it would be an overstatement to blame all these problems on the contention system, that system certainly contributed.

BUSINESS PRINCIPLES AND STRATEGIES

Each organization must develop its own principles and strategies. In doing this, technological firms should consider the following guidelines:

1. Assume that technology will continue to improve at least as fast and probably faster than in the past. This would have helped IBM recognize that the initial PC was near the end of its life at the time of PC Jr.'s announcement. If the PC Jr. had been a "barn burner" instead of a cripple, the face of the PC industry would likely have been quite different.

2. Always try to do what is best for the customers. The PC Jr. customers were consciously sold an inferior product. Hurting these customers ultimately hurt IBM.

3. Watch for fundamental changes in technology. Rapid technical advances inevitably cause unexpected changes in the way products are built, distributed, or used. Organizations that do not look for and anticipate these trends will be surprised by changes and ill-prepared to respond to them.

For the 10 years before the IBM PC was introduced, a growing number of IBM experts had warned of the fundamental changes to be expected both from integrated circuit technology and from software. In the early 1970s it was clear that the hardware portion of customer budgets was being supplanted by software and service. While these trends were well known, IBM's strategies continued to assume steady growth in the hardware business. With expected 10 to 15% annual growth rates, the company continued investing in hardware manufacturing plants. Within five years, they were closing plants and laying off thousands of employees.

An important management lesson is the need to encourage the technical experts, wild ducks, and dissidents to speak up. The contention system, if properly managed, provides an appropriate forum. It is also essential to think about what the wild ducks say. Fundamental changes often seem unthinkable right up until they happen. Then they are so obvious everyone wonders how they were missed.

MANAGING THE CONTENTION SYSTEM

Although no simple solution can solve all problems, the contention system can be helpful if it is managed properly. Some guidelines are the following:

1. Put product managers in charge of the product programs and ensure they have the clearly defined responsibility to make critical product decisions. Make sure they use the advice and council of all the appropriate staffs.

2. When any staff feels strongly that a decision is wrong, that staff can take their disagreement with the product manager to higher management.

3. While senior management should be reluctant to overrule the product managers, they must protect the organization's long-term principles and strategies.

The last guideline, of course, assumes that the business has clearly enunciated principles and strategies.

The example of Janet, the development manager for a compiler program, shows how effective these guidelines can be. In carrying her product through a review for announcement, a marketing staff threatened to disagree with announcement if she didn't add several new features to the compiler. Janet's group was aware of marketing's desires but had studied the issue and concluded that the cost and time required to add these features would not make business sense. Janet told the marketing people that she did not agree with the features and would proceed without their concurrence. If they wanted to stop her, they would have to escalate the issue to higher management. The staff was surprised by this strong stand and decided not to escalate. The product turned out to be a success without the features the marketing department desired.

MANAGEMENT ROLES

Since technical teams generally make better decisions than the members do separately, it would seem logical that management teams should do the same. This, however, is not always the case. The reason is that the members of technical groups represent themselves; but managers must consider their departmental constituencies. While technical teams may be limited by their managers on administrative or resource questions, their technical views are rarely constrained. This is why, when purely professional groups have the time to thoroughly explore a technical issue, they rarely have trouble reaching agreement.

On a management team, however, the members are each representatives. Their people depend on them for support, and the managers know that their people will be concerned if they do not vigorously defend their interests. Managers, therefore, must insist that their departments get fair treatment in all organizational trade-offs. Every department needs space, people, computer support, services, and many of the other resources that are often in short supply. Since these zero-sum trade-offs always have winners and losers, they can rarely be settled by consensus.

A simple experiment in group dynamics demonstrates the constraints of having a constituency. A group of 16 people is first divided into four 4-person teams. Each team is asked to make some simple decision like selecting the name for a new product. To give the experiment some realism, a meaningful prize is offered to the team whose selection is unanimously accepted by the entire group. It doesn't make much difference what this prize is, however, since experience shows that no one can win it. Once each team has made its separate choice, one member is selected from each group to sit on a new 4-person team that will select the winner from these four initial candidates. This final team now holds its discussions in view of the entire group. Invariably, not one of the members of this new team will agree that any solution is superior to the name selected by his or her initial group. Since they each feel constrained to support their constituencies, their loyalty to their constituents destroys their ability to make an objective selection.

TEAM COOPERATION

Managers face a complex array of pressures that they must resolve. On occasion, managers must compromise their department's interests to meet the broader goals of their organizations. This, however, puts them in a difficult position. If they compromise too easily, their employees will sense a lack of support; but if they do not work cooperatively with the other managers, their management peers and superiors will see them as parochial.

Managers sometimes feel they must choose between these extremes. Those who choose loyalty to their employees lose influence in the management team. On the other hand, when managers honestly try to cooperate with their peers, they can have the reverse problem. The other managers will see them as cooperative, but their own employees will suspect they are currying favor with the boss at their expense.

Departments need the help and support of effective managers, and when they are too anxious to please the boss or don't have the guts to fight for the department's interests, their jobs become more difficult. At the extreme, such managers are even reluctant to talk openly with their employees because they can't explain what they have done in terms that are acceptable to them. As a result, managers who do not fight aggressively for their groups often become distant, uncommunicative, and, eventually, totally ineffective.

Obviously, some middle ground is desirable. Managers each represent knowledgeable groups, and they should vigorously defend their group's interests in their dealings with the management team. If the manager doesn't speak up, decisions that involve the group will not be as informed, and overall organization performance will suffer. On the other hand, the managers' parochial focus on the needs of their people must be tempered by broader considerations. When a decision must run counter to their department's interests, managers' views should be respectfully heard and considered. If the decision still goes against them, the logic behind the final conclusion should be clearly explained so they in turn can explain it to their people. The people will then see that their interests have been considered and more likely accept and support the final decision.

A DECISION A MINUTE

One laboratory director was technically competent but had no prior experience running a large organization. He was used to dealing with every issue as it came up and he continued to work this way in running the new larger group. When an issue arose in his staff meetings, he would energetically dig in to understand the pros and cons and then make a decision. He was thus personally involved in both global issues like the five-year plan and detailed decisions like where the copy machines should be installed.

The director's behavior had several unfortunate consequences. It disenfranchised the management team: Everyone knew that if they could get an issue raised with the director, he would settle it, regardless of prior decisions by the management team. It clogged the management team's agenda with trivial issues: In any organization, there are so many minor issues that, if the management team deals with them all, there will be no time for important topics. Practically nothing got done: Because every issue was settled by the director, nobody else had clear responsibility for doing anything. Since the director was too busy to follow up on these details and since no one else felt responsible, no one followed up to ensure the decisions were implemented. As a consequence, even though the director appeared personally decisive, his organization actually accomplished very little.

The director had not learned to delegate authority. He should have defined his subordinate managers' responsibilities and held them accountable for doing their jobs. He would then have had to scrupulously avoid making decisions he had delegated to subordinates. The best rule for senior managers is to delegate every possible operating decision. Then, deal only with setting and tracking goals, resolving contentions between subordinates, and with planning for the long range. While executives must occasionally dig into operational issues, delegating authority properly will always make clear which subordinate is responsible for each issue and who is accountable for its implementation.

MANAGEMENT SCOPE

Job descriptions and tables of organization typically define the scope and responsibilities of jobs. This formal structure helps the managers understand their relationships with each other and it defines the actions they can take on their own. The way job scopes are defined, however, can make an enormous difference. Too rigid a structure provides little management flexibility, while loose definitions can be confusing. The managers will be unsure of their roles and less willing to act on their own initiative. The key is for managers to recognize that bright people will almost always make sound decisions. Managers thus need to focus on getting their people to make rational and timely decisions, not on making these decisions for them. In the occasional case where a decision is of critical importance to the organization, they then need some simple mechanism to catch serious mistakes and oversights.

MANAGEMENT PERSPECTIVE

Managers' views of job responsibilities change dramatically as they move up the ladder. First-line managers and supervisors generally expect their superiors to clear up interdepartmental confusion by precisely specifying each manager's job. They see job overlaps as wasteful and confusing and cannot understand why the boss doesn't resolve this mess with a simple directive. As they progress to more senior positions, technical executives recognize, however, that they cannot precisely structure their subordinate managers' jobs. With rapidly changing technology, all formal organizations quickly become out of date. Senior managers must expect and encourage their subordinates to adjust their behavior to accommodate to changing situations.

Defined goals and responsibilities help provide a working management framework. The managers, however, must learn to adjust these roles in unanticipated situations. Only in this way can the management team keep pace with the rapid changes in their working environment.

TRANSPARENT MANAGEMENT

Transparent managers pass instructions from superior to subordinate without assuming responsibility. When, for example, their employees ask why a decision was made, they tell them that senior management has so directed. They may have an opinion on why the decision was made, but they make it clear that they are not responsible.

Although this is not the normal management attitude, senior managers often force their subordinates to behave this way. When managers are not involved in decisions that have an impact on their departments, they have trouble understanding them. Since most decisions involve many complex trade-offs, managers who have not been involved can't explain their logic to their people. Rather than blaming these decisions on "those idiots upstairs," it would be wiser to admit they didn't understand the issues and promise to find out. This is hard to do.

Blaming their superiors harms the subordinate managers far more than their superiors. For by acting in this way, they demonstrate to their employees that they are not part of the management team, they do not represent senior management, and they are powerless to protect the employees' interests. Since motivated professionals need the help and support of an effective manager, transparent managers quickly lose the respect of their people. This severely limits their value to the organization.

BUILDING THE MANAGEMENT TEAM

Welding a group of ambitious, contentious, and aggressive managers into a cooperative and effective team is not easy. The first step is to respect the views of the team. When a decision affects their department, the team should be involved from the outset. Their views should be carefully weighed, even when it is known in advance that they are opposed. Any disagreement should be openly discussed, all the issues considered, and the key alternatives evaluated before a decision is made. Open debate enables managers to understand the issues and explain the conclusions to their employees.

Another advantage of involving team members in decision making is that it enables the managers to recognize new issues when they are raised by their people. If the issues were not considered during the decision making, the managers can reopen the discussion to ensure a more complete evaluation. It is surprising how often the professionals will see problems that their managers had not considered. Such reassessments can cause changes in the plans and produce better final results. By ensuring that all affected managers are part of the decision making, the organization can better utilize the knowledge and creativity of its people.

True Participation

Although it is important to have all the top managers sit in on all key decision meetings, this alone will not build an effective management team. True participation requires active involvement, and the environment must encourage debate and contention. When everyone agrees, even experienced and capable managers are reluctant to object. It takes enormous self-confidence to voice the lone counteropinion, but speaking up is the necessary first step in preventing serious mistakes. If senior managers truly want to understand their managers' views, they must provide an environment where everyone feels comfortable raising questions and voicing disagreements.

The final step in management team-building is to encourage management team members to work together. One senior manager did this effectively when he learned that his previously approved department budget had to be cut by $800,000. The division plan was being completed, and an error had been found in the departmental totals. The plan was too expensive and all departments had to make cuts to bring it into balance. Since the senior manager's budget cut was only about 3%, he was tempted to arbitrarily reduce everybody's budget by the same percentage. His people had worked hard to put together the plan, however, so he was reluctant to be arbitrary.

He called his top managers together, explained the situation, and emphasized the futility of an appeal. He was willing to make an arbitrary cut but wanted to see if his managers had better ideas. In the ensuing discussion, they each proposed cuts in other departments' budgets but none from their own. The senior manager finally concluded that he would have to make the cut himself, but offered to leave them for an hour to see if they could work out a better answer. None of them knew what the senior manager would cut, so they spent the next hour reassessing their priorities. They finally concluded that one major project should be completely eliminated and two others delayed, with the rest of the plan left as before. After they explained why they had decided on this new plan, the senior manager agreed with their proposal.

When the management team works together openly and honestly, it invariably produces the best results. These are generally the most capable and best informed people in the organization. They, as a group, are best able to balance technical and business issues and decide on sound plans of action. When they understand the decisions, believe they are right, and can defend them to their people, the professionals will know that their needs have been considered and are most likely to work energetically on implementation.

NOTES

1. Paul R. Lawrence and Jay W. Lorsch, "Organization and Environment: Managing Differentiation and Integration," Graduate School of Business Administration, Harvard University, Boston, 1967, p. 73.

2. Alfred P. Sloan, Jr., *My Years with General Motors* (Garden City, NY: Doubleday, 1964).

PART

6

The Organization

19

Integration and Disintegration

The primary reason for establishing an organization structure is to allocate work. If one individual could do the entire job alone, no structure would be needed; but with two or more people, things become more complicated. To describe the kinds of problems that arise, Jay Galbraith uses the example of carpenters working on the interlocking faces of a joint. One carpenter can easily decide what to do when the parts don't fit. When two carpenters are involved, however, they must first decide how to divide the work between them, then identify the problem, and finally figure out what to do.[1]

No one likes to fix someone else's mistakes. Team efforts thus invariably raise questions of blame. The most fundamental decisions involve how the work should be divided up, how to relate these pieces, what needs to be changed to correct problems, and who should do it. Debates over these issues can become intense both because the workers each believe they did their jobs properly and because they don't want to be blamed for someone else's mistakes. Often, in fact, the individual team members have done their jobs properly and the problems are not with their work but with the relationships among their individual products.

When two professionals work closely together, they can usually resolve their mutual problems quickly and informally. They probably both understand the entire job, and they are generally on good enough personal terms to compromise their individual needs to achieve a better overall result. In larger groups, informal coordination can still work as long as everyone shares a common goal and understands the work of the entire team. As job size increases, however, a point is reached where the work must be divided among several teams. This now changes the situation completely. These separate teams no longer share the common bond of membership, and they are less able to settle their differences without management's help.

An example of team relationships is a military project to design a secure voice communications system. The electronics team was charged with designing the circuits, and the mechanical engineering group was to devise a packaging structure that would withstand rugged army field conditions. Although these two teams shared the same general objectives, they did not work cooperatively together. The electronics group was preoccupied with circuit design problems and couldn't be bothered with power and space considerations. The mechanical engineers had to know the size and weight of the power supplies before they could start their work. The situation was further complicated by the tight schedule and the need to order specially fabricated structural members early enough to meet the manufacturing schedule. The transformers were critical to this design, and they could not be specified until the circuit power requirements were known. This in turn could not be accurately estimated until the circuit designs were completed.

Relations between these two groups deteriorated until the department manager decided to combine the two into a single group with one project leader. The leader of the electronics group was given this job, and he quickly realized that the mechanical engineers had a real problem. They could not possibly finish their work on time unless the electronics engineers made a reasonably accurate estimate of power consumption. The project leader knew the circuit designs weren't done, but he ordered a complete power study and then added a contingency to take care of changes. Although some later adjustments were needed, this estimate was close enough to permit the mechanical engineers to start work. The project was then finished close to its original schedule.

In many organizational conflicts each team is often completely correct in its own narrow terms. The electronics engineers really did not know the power needs of the military project, and they were understandably reluctant to make an inaccurate guess. On the other hand, the mechanical team had to start the design so that the long lead-time parts could be ordered. Making the leader of the electronics group manager of the total project and having him balance these conflicting views turned out to be an effective way to resolve the impasse.

PROJECT MANAGEMENT

Lawrence and Lorsch have studied 10 corporations in three different industries to determine the importance of the project management function to corporate success.[2] They found a close correlation between the effectiveness of the project management system and corporate profit growth. They also found that the most effective groups used a formal management process to couple the working elements of each project into an orderly and efficient whole.

The design of a new device, such as a telephone handset, illustrates some of the problems of project management. Starting with the requirements phase, the development team first addresses the problems customers have reported with prior units and any information that can be obtained on the features they would find most desirable. The characteristics of the leading competitive instruments are also examined, and price and manufacturing volume targets are established. Next, the design phase starts with work in such areas as electronics, acoustics, packaging, styling, and safety. As the design progresses, serviceability must be considered, as should manufacturing costs and production tooling. The final development steps include market planning, pricing, production scheduling, and service planning.

Even such a seemingly simple device requires the involvement of many different specialists at almost every development phase. One way to manage all these different efforts would be to assemble everybody into one large team. This strategy would minimize coordination problems, but it would introduce practical problems of recruiting. Few manufacturing experts would be needed before the design was completed. Similarly, the marketing people would only be busy at the beginning when the requirements were being established and near the end during sales planning. Since every project requires a constantly changing mix of talents, full self-sufficiency would require the perpetual recruiting of needed skills. If project managers were saddled with this chore, they would have little time left for anything else.

The common answer to this problem is to use specialized support departments to provide needed skills to all the projects. A market research group, for example, can help every project with customer preference data and market introduction planning. Styling, cost estimating, manufacturing engineering, forecasting, and pricing are also commonly handled in this way. Typically, project managers have a core team with the talents needed for the major technical work, and they obtain support from these specialist groups for everything else.

SUPPORT PROBLEMS

Specialist support departments thus play an essential part in any technical organization, but they are also subject to various problems. As they grow larger, for example, support groups frequently lose touch with their end users and forget that their real purpose is to help the project teams. As soon as these specialists begin to think of their specialty as an end in itself, they become much harder for the project people to deal with.

Large staffs are also popular targets for budget cutting. Since they are generally unpopular with the project groups, they invariably have trouble defending their plans. As a result, the larger a support staff becomes, the more likely it is to be understaffed and overloaded. At this point, it is often possible to divide it into several smaller staffs that can each still be large enough to smooth project work loads and retain a critical mass of technical skills. The smaller groups can then be assigned to the major development departments so that a single specialized staff will be dedicated to serve each group. This permits the organization to have many of the benefits of a project structure and much of the efficiency of specialized staffs.

The reorganization of the data processing department in a large development laboratory some years ago illustrates the reasons for breaking up large support groups. The computers were run very efficiently, but everybody complained about the shortage of computer time. Terminal response was so slow that weekly meetings were needed to allocate the limited number of sign-ons that could be serviced. Since inadequate computing was now blamed for almost every problem in the laboratory, the manager launched a study which found that much of the work load could be handled by smaller computers managed by each of the line projects. With this change, the development people were happier, the coordination meetings were eliminated, and the development managers could be held responsible for their projects' performance. Although the separate departmental computing facilities weren't run as efficiently as before, response time was much better, and overall departmental efficiency was significantly improved. Such problems provided the incentive for many groups to adopt distributed computing systems. This solution has often been seen as a way to get rid of a large and unresponsive data processing staff.

THE ELEMENTS OF STRUCTURE

British management expert Edward P. Hawthorne explains that the balance between specialized support groups and dedicated project teams presents a fundamental organizational conflict.[3] The projects must remain flexible and respond to changing market and technology opportunities. They are thus a highly disruptive influence in the otherwise stable administrative and support structure. The specialized support groups conversely seek to maintain a stable and predictable working environment. They thus resist the periodic and disruptive crash efforts common to challenging projects.

Every organizational arrangement has advantages and disadvantages, and it is rare to have a pure structure. Some dedicated project effort is always required, and certain specialties must be handled by dedicated support groups. At one extreme, large teams can be nearly self-sufficient. This, however, introduces the question of the maximum practical size of a working group. Pelz and Andrews found in their studies that the largest teams performed best, but they did not examine groups larger than 10 to 15 engineers and scientists.[4] Since each team is directed by a single manager, it is generally unwise to have teams much larger than this. To provide proper guidance and support, managers must devote a reasonable amount of time to each individual in their groups, and with too many people, this is not possible.

As soon as the project team gets larger than one manager can handle, it must be split, and responsibilities divided. The four common structural approaches to this problem are as follows:[5]

1. *Subject Discipline.* Project managers are grouped according to their areas of specialization, such as hardware engineering, software engineering, or heat transfer; and project coordination is a staff responsibility.

2. *Stage Phase.* The organization's departments each handle one project phase, such as requirements, design, test, or manufacture and release; and project responsibility moves from one department to the next as the work progresses. In the interest of continuity, it is common to move the manager and some of the key people along with the project at each transition.

3. *Product Type.* Each group focuses on a specific product set, such as radios, televisions, or stereos. Members of the television group, for example, would move relatively freely from one television project to another in response to staffing needs. This arrangement is generally used for relatively small and short-term projects, with department managers acting as project leaders for all their projects at the same time.

4. *Project Type.* Each group is entirely dedicated to a specific project, such as the development of a computer program or of an aircraft engine. Department heads are the project managers, and all members of their respective departments are dedicated to the same project.

MATRIX STRUCTURES

The Stage Phase approach is often set up in what is called a matrix structure. In a matrix, the project manager has a core team, and representatives from the required support groups are assigned full time to this team when they are needed. Although this does not give the project leader direct line-management control over all project participants, it does provide a degree of team membership and project responsibility for the support groups.

Matrix structures have proven very successful and are widely used by such organizations as Microsoft and Boeing.[6,7] Often the principal engineering people are directly assigned to the project manager, with all other staffs provided on a matrix basis. Full matrix staffing with only a small project-management staff can work as long as the support departments truly serve in a support role and as long as the project manager is given clear and unquestioned decision authority.

One example of a matrix structure that did not work illustrates some of the potential problems. In the early days of the 370 computer system development, IBM established a headquarters group of project managers with the laboratory engineering groups providing matrixlike support. The project managers had funding control, but the engineering managers had most of the development staff reporting directly to them. The reason this arrangement did not work was that the engineering managers had previously been the project managers and were used to running entire projects. The project managers principally had marketing backgrounds and did not know how to run projects. Perhaps most important, IBM management did not respect the project managers' technical judgment. Thus, when it came time to make basic system choices, management reviewed the project managers' decisions in detail and generally backed the development managers on major disputes. As a result, the matrixlike structure was abandoned within a year.

SPECIALIST DEPARTMENTS

Regardless of the way the organization is arranged, there will always be problems in the way the work is divided among the project teams and the supporting departments. Some of the advantages of using specialist support groups are the following:

- Specialists are best managed in a department where they can work with their peers and be guided by technically competent managers. It is hard, for example, for research chemists to do competent work without a suitably equipped laboratory, a knowledgeable manager, and association with other professionals who understand their work.

- Most specialists are needed on any given project only for a brief period, and when one group needs more help, another will often need less. A support department can smooth the distribution of work loads more efficiently than any one project could possibly do for itself.

- When a project gets into trouble, the support specialists are better able to blow the whistle. This invariably causes friction with line management, but it also increases the visibility of controversial issues and improves the quality of project decisions.

- Special tools and support processes are expensive. For example, usability test laboratories are expensive, so it would not be feasible to provide one for every software project.

The advantages of specialist departments are compelling, but there are also good reasons for directly assigning as many of the specialists as possible to the project teams:

- If they have all the resources under their control, project managers have no need to get agreement from the support-group managers. They can thus make decisions faster.

- Support groups make convenient scapegoats when a project gets in trouble. It is easier to measure project managers' performance when they control all the resources they need.

- Comprehensive project responsibility provides one of the best training grounds for future technical leaders.

- A close-knit project team develops the esprit de corps needed to produce superior results.

Although there are no simple answers, it is generally best to retain scarce specialized skills in support departments. Once this talent becomes more widely available, however, the need for specialist groups should be reconsidered. In most cases it is wise to split large support groups and divide their skills among projects or groups of projects. The key exceptions are such business control functions as pricing, accounting, cost estimating, and market forecasting, which are often kept in separately managed staffs to ensure better financial control. Research, advanced technology, and specialized tool support should also be protected. If not, the projects will soon divert their resources to meet the next crisis. Other than these limited exceptions, if there is any serious doubt, it is wisest to assign the responsibilities and the resources directly to the project manager and matrix the rest.

DEFINING SUPPORT

It is easy to get confused about the definition of product support. The key is to define your products with great care. An example of this support-definition issue was IBM's 1968 decision to price software separately from hardware. Even though this actually made software a product, the software developers were still seen as a hardware-support function. The problem was that every IBM machine needed programming support and the programming department had become the bottleneck for every product announcement and delivery. By 1969, this group had grown to nearly 4000 software professionals in 15 laboratories and 6 countries.

While it made sense to break the programming group into smaller pieces, the company unfortunately disbanded the entire operation. They allocated all the programming work to the hardware projects, retaining only a central coordination staff. While this gave the hardware managers considerable independence, it left no common programming resource. Since programming had been the only link between many of the different IBM systems, it had become the principal advocate of a compatible IBM product line. Without their pressure to retain compatibility, IBM subsequently introduced several incompatible machines just as the Digital Equipment Corporation was introducing its compatible line of low-end computers. The lack of a compatible IBM family was soon a serious marketing problem.

The longer-range problem was that this reorganization was made just a few years before the IBM PC program was launched. As a result, the hardware managers all had to obtain their own programming support. Since the new PC product group had no programming staff of its own and there was no central group to draw on, they had to go to an outside supplier. The message from this case is to define support groups with a clear understanding of the longer-range strategic direction of the key product technologies.

PROJECT INTEGRATION

Although there is no best way to divide the work among the line project organizations and the specialist support groups, there is compelling evidence that some form of project control structure is important. Badawy, for example, cites data from companies such as Shell Oil, Dow Corning, and TRW to show that matrixlike integration structures can be highly successful.[8]

The purpose of integration is to coordinate the many parts of the project into an effective final result. Another, and perhaps more important, purpose is to provide each project with a general business focus. In any large organization, the senior executives personally set the business direction and establish overall objectives. Producing the products that generate revenue and profit, however, is the role of members of such functions as development, sales, manufacturing, and service. These people are responsible for delivering products and services to paying customers. Although they all work in support of the company's overall aims, they are each constrained by their functional focus. A sales team, for example, is most concerned with getting a big order, while a manufacturing team must emphasize product quality and cost. These are all vital efforts, but they all have a functional bias. An integrator is then needed to relate them to overall corporate needs. In short, the job of integrators is to run their projects as if they were company presidents.

THE INTEGRATOR'S ROLE

Integrators thus have three overriding concerns: customer satisfaction, profit, and competitive superiority. Their primary objective is to satisfy customers' needs in a technically superior and profitable way. This requires that they understand customer and competitive pressures and appreciate both the technical and financial aspects of their projects.

Projects soon build a momentum of their own. But first the direction must be set. The initial decisions should establish quality goals, financial objectives, and schedule targets. Senior management generally delegates the authority to make these decisions to the integrators, empowering them to set the project direction and resolve functional disputes. As official project champions, the integrators are responsible for deciding what to do and seeing that it gets done.

Integrators are also responsible for project control. They ensure that the project objectives will meet business needs, and they obtain the resources to do the work. They conduct project reviews, manage the control staff, and track progress. To help with these tasks, they may have line responsibility for such pivotal functions as planning, architecture, standards, or system test.

The integrators must also have the full backing of senior management. Lawrence and Lorsch cite an example where the lack of a properly supported integration responsibility caused damaging contention between one company's production and engineering departments.

> The informal integrators were unable to achieve effective collaboration, at least in part because their roles were not clearly defined. Therefore, their integrative attempts were often seen as inappropriate infringements on the domains of other departments.[9]

THE IBM FS SYSTEM

Although an integration function can provide the oversight to ensure that projects are properly run, integration alone will not ensure success. Starting in 1969, IBM launched a major development effort for the FS (future systems) project to replace the 360 and 370 systems. These systems were to use a radical new system architecture for essentially high-level-language machines, and they were to be optimized for communications and real-time applications. At one point, more than half of the development resources of IBM's four major development laboratories were devoted to the FS project and many millions of dollars were spent.

Designed to provide many advanced functions, the FS system was ultimately killed because it could not provide competitive performance on the COBOL applications that were then IBM's bread-and-butter business. Incompatibility and conversion problems from the installed 360 and 370 systems ultimately caused the marketing organization to reject these new systems. In spite of the skills of the project manager/integrator, the FS project failed because suitable COBOL performance was simply not feasible with this architecture and the circuit technology available at the time.

FS was an early omen and a partial contributor to IBM's later difficulties. It was the last attempt of the large-systems architects to address the centralized-systems problems of previous generations. The FS strategy was to treat computing power as cheap and to design systems to directly serve distributed users. While this grand concept was ahead of its time and was essentially sound, it was in many ways a casualty of the traditional thinking of the IBM contention system. The FS system project tied up a large proportion of IBM's system development talent for nearly four years. The company was thus ill prepared to respond to Digital Equipment's VAX/VMS systems or to the growth of distributed systems and powerful workstations. FS was a marvelous concept, but it was one of the rocks upon which IBM's great ship foundered.

MANAGING INTEGRATION

With proper oversight and management support many different integration structures can be effective. Informal committees can provide a coordination focus, while at the other extreme, entire organizations may be required. Intel, for example, reported having 25 strategic business segments, and a loose structure of coordination committees to make operational decisions. Robert Noyce, one of Intel's founders, said that "workers may have several bosses depending on the problem at hand. Instead of staff specialists for purchasing, quality control and so on, Intel had several dozen committees or councils that made decisions and enforced standards in specialized fields."[10]

The matrix structure, as used at Dow Corning, was more formal. For each of its 10 major business areas, Dow Corning established a business manager who held profit responsibility and reported to a senior corporate executive. Each business manager operated through a business board whose members were drawn from the various specialist cost centers that housed the working professionals. Through these boards, the business managers had both the authority and the control over the resources needed to meet their project goals.[11]

Boeing also used a matrixlike structure for the development of its large commercial jet aircraft. The 777, for example, was such a massive project that a special program manager was given responsibility for all 777 manufacturing and development. He ran the program through a number of project managers and a hierarchy of design-build teams (DBT).[12] Ultimately, a total of nearly 250 DBTs were assigned to cover all aspects of aircraft design and manufacture. For example, a wing DBT would have subordinate DBTs dealing with the outboard flaps, the inboard flaps, the spar, and so on. The DBTs were staffed with experts from engineering, manufacturing, suppliers, and even customers to ensure that all potential issues were identified and resolved in a timely manner. Computerized design and project control systems helped to identify design issues and conflicts and to track project status. Final project integration and control was provided through the weekly megameeting where all the chief project engineers would gather with the program manager every Thursday to review issues, make decisions, or set direction.

Projects have typically been broken into largely autonomous phases for requirements, development, and manufacturing. The accelerating pace of technology, however, has now made this approach obsolete. Most organizations stress cycle time, which is the time from the start of product development to final availability of manufactured products. To reduce cycle time, organizations generally resort to multidiscipline teams involving all relevant groups. This ensures maximum overlap of the time-critical activities and greatly reduces cycle time. Such multidiscipline teams are generally managed in a matrix structure.

INTEGRATION RESPONSIBILITY

There are many ways to break a project into separate implementable parts. The principal issue is to ensure that these parts can be put back together again. This is the job of integration, and there is no standard way to do it. Sometimes entire departments are devoted to coordination and control, but in other cases integration can be done with no formality at all. With small projects or relatively stable technologies, informal integration is often adequate. More formality is generally needed as projects become larger, involve more disciplines, or encounter rapid technical change. There are no universal guidelines, but the integration system is so critical it should be designed with great care.

One way to determine whether an organization has integration problems is to ask the following questions of each key project:

- Who is responsible for meeting the customer's needs?

- Who is answerable for profitability?

- Who is accountable for superiority in the competitive marketplace?

- Who owns product quality?

If no one can be clearly identified with each of these responsibilities, an integration problem undoubtedly exists. When no one has been specifically assigned such roles, the senior manager over all the project elements becomes the de facto integrator. Since most large projects span engineering, manufacturing, marketing, and service, few companies have such a common manager below the company president. While company presidents would undoubtedly make good integrators, few can afford to dedicate the time required.

STRUCTURAL PARALYSIS

Every structure has advantages and disadvantages. As organizations become larger, the integration problems become more severe. Now many different projects must contend for the same scarce resources. One way to allocate resources is to appoint special staff oversight groups to identify and resolve interproject issues. These staffs further encumber organization structure, reduce efficiency, and require management themselves. If not properly controlled, they will grow until the cost and complexity of the organization can itself become a problem.

Thomas Blackburn draws an interesting parallel between organizations and large biological systems.[13] He points out that the tropical rainforest develops a larger and more complex structure as it grows, and this structure requires a progressively larger share of the ecosystem's total reserves of energy. As growth progresses, this "overhead" gradually reduces net system productivity until the energy consumed by the structure equals the total capacity of the system; net productivity then reaches zero, and growth stops.

The structure of large technical organizations can follow a similar cycle. When projects become very large, they require many teams of technical people who don't individually understand the total project, know the other teams working on the job, or appreciate many of the projectwide problems. Informal relationships no longer suffice, and more formal coordination methods are needed.

The various practical coordination methods all use staffs of one kind or another to monitor and direct the technical professionals. The working engineers and scientists, however, typically know their technical assignments quite well, and they begin to resent this increasing outside interference. As the number and size of these staffs grows, the professionals' resentment increases along with it, and this both reduces their initiative and makes them less willing to voluntarily adjust their work to meet the changing needs of the rest of the organization. The increasing friction between the teams then requires more management involvement and more staffs to help identify and resolve the resulting issues. At some point, as in the tropical rainforest, further structure is added solely to support and control the rest of the structure.

There is no single universal answer that resolves all these issues. Advancing technology and accelerating competition dictate increasing use of interdisciplinary teams. Even so, as projects become larger, they require more formally structured mechanisms for integration and control.

NOTES

1. Jay R. Galbraith, *Organization Design,* (Reading, MA: Addison-Wesley, 1977), p. 443.

2. Paul R. Lawrence and Jay W. Lorsch, "New Management Job: The Integrator," *Harvard Business Review,* November-December 1967, p. 142.

3. Edward P. Hawthorne, *The Management of Technology* (Maidenhead, England: McGraw-Hill, 1978), p. 102.

4. Donald C. Pelz and Frank M. Andrews: *Scientists in Organizations: Productive Climates for Research and Development* (New York: Wiley, 1966), p. 52.

5. Hawthorne, *Management of Technology,* p. 104.

6. Karl Sabbagh, *21st-Century Jet* (New York: Scribner, 1996).

7. G. Pascal Zachary, *Showstopper!* (New York: The Free Press, 1994).

8. M.K. Badawy, *Developing Managerial Skills in Engineers and Scientists: Succeeding as a Technical Manager* (New York: International Thompson Organization, Van Nostrand Reinhold, 1982), p. 217.

9. Lawrence and Lorsch, "New Management Job."

10. Steve Lohr cites this quote by Robert Noyce in his January 4, 1981, article in *New York Times,* "Overhauling America's Business Management," sec. 6, p. 42.

11. William C. Cogan, "How the Multi-Dimensional Structure Works at Dow Coming," *Harvard Business Review on Management* (New York: Harper & Row, 1975).

12. Karl Sabbagh, *21st-Century Jet* (New York: Scribner, 1996), ch. 4.

13. Thomas R. Blackburn, "Information and the Ecology of Scholars," *Science,* September 1973, p. 1141.

20

Managing Size

As organizations grow, their increasing complexity inhibits initiative and reduces the overall effectiveness of the individual professionals. Hage and Aiken have described several ways this can happen, as summarized in the following paragraphs.

With increasing size, many of the skilled professionals become grouped into specialized departments. The more uniform technical environment is less stimulating. Large organizations often centralize decision making, which further reduces communication, submerges conflict, and inhibits innovation.

The rules, procedures, and guidelines necessary in large organizations reduce individual initiative by constraining people within narrowly defined jobs. Workers in such large, and often impersonal, environments, instinctively feel that anything not explicitly in their job definition must belong to somebody else. They thus feel less responsible for resolving the problems they encounter.

With the growing size of the organization, the number of management levels inexorably increases as well. This adds to the communication problems, buries new ideas, conceals problems, and consequently inhibits change.

The high-volume focus of many large manufacturing and development organizations necessarily emphasizes predictability as a way to minimize production disruptions. Predictability also increases resistance to change.

Very large organizations properly use productivity as a management measure, but this leads to an emphasis on perfecting known methods and avoiding new and unproven ideas. This in turn reduces the organization's willingness to take the risks that necessarily accompany innovation.[1]

THE PROBLEMS OF SIZE

Since top management in large organizations cannot deal with very many of their people in person, they must rely on their management team for much of their communication. If communication is not handled properly, they can run into the kinds of problems that Eric faced when he took over a large department. He came to work promptly at 7:30 every morning and was annoyed by the large number of employees who came straggling in at 9:00 A.M. or even later. His annoyance increased when he realized that some of his senior managers were equally tardy. He brought this issue up at his weekly staff meeting, but his managers did not think the problem was very important. They argued that they worked long hours and were entitled to come in a bit later to compensate. The prior department head had also been in the habit of arriving late, and the managers didn't see where it had caused any problems. Eric did not mind occasional lateness, but he believed that sloppy attendance habits tend to get out of hand and that some working-hours discipline is necessary. After a heated discussion, he lost his temper and insisted that the managers get to work by the regular 8:00 A.M. starting time and make sure their people did so as well. To make sure this was done, he had the laboratory security guards count the late arrivals every day. The punctuality problem was soon resolved.

While there is no question that tardiness is undesirable, it is an issue that should be handled by first-line managers. Although Eric's concern was proper, he should not have lost his temper and given a direct order. By doing so, he relieved his managers of their responsibility for punctuality. They could now tell their people to come to work on time because the boss said so. Although this transparent behavior solved the direct punctuality problem, it made Eric appear to be a bureaucratic administrator and damaged his long-term effectiveness.

In well-run organizations very few people straggle in late. When they are busy and challenged by their work, punctuality is not a problem. In an organization with serious attendance problems, the first-level management is typically not properly supervising their people and keeping them busy. Some employees then start to slack off, lose interest in their jobs, and become attendance problems. When an employee exhibits such behavior, the manager should find out if this loss of job interest is due to poor supervision or if the employee has other and possibly deeper problems that need attention. If Eric had taken the time to explain his concerns and convince his managers of the symbolic importance of their personal punctuality, they would have been better able to manage their people. This would then not be enforcing a directive from the boss, but doing something they personally believed in.

INDIRECT COMMUNICATION

Whenever senior managers communicate through the management team, there is always a chance of misunderstanding. Not only do problems arise when their subordinate managers disagree in their interpretations of senior management's meaning, but there is often real confusion about what senior management wants. Unless senior managers make a very special effort, their pronouncements will generally be confusing, and frequently their people will be reluctant to ask for clarification. A simple request will be greeted by debate about its meaning, with several people offering opinions. Soon some of these opinions will take on the character of established fact. Rumors often start with people trying to logically deduce what the boss had in mind, but they are often based on no more than the people's individual hopes and fears. This is especially true in "closed" organizations with autocratic managers.

One of the greatest problems in large organizations is thus the propensity to misunderstand senior management. The larger the organization, the more senior managers' desires will be modified by the chain of command. If senior managers show concern, middle management will amplify it, and when the senior managers become angry, the reactions of people at lower levels may approach panic. When top managers' suggestions are amplified by each management level, there is a great risk that the working-level people will spend a large part of their time responding to their casual questions and not devoting themselves to the truly essential work of the organization.

Although frequently amplified, senior managers' instructions can also be attenuated. When they don't know precisely what senior managers want, rather than make a mistake subordinate managers will often hold back, waiting for clarification. Experienced professionals know that they are likely to get into trouble when they blindly follow some remote manager's instructions, so they generally follow only the simpler actions that they agree with. If real work is required, however, they stop and wait for further developments. Unless the manager follows up, the professionals have so much to do that they will soon forget about the remote manager's instructions, and nothing will end up being done.

SPAN OF CONTROL

Beyond a few dozen professionals, a controlling management style is no longer practical. Although this limit depends to some degree on the manager and the kind of work being done, everyone has some limit beyond which he or she can no longer personally make all the decisions. If managers try to exceed this point, they must work long hours and acquire a growing staff to track progress and enforce instructions. Even then, they will likely be a serious bottleneck.

When organization size approaches about 100 people, senior managers must rely on the management team to deal directly with the technical professionals. That team now becomes the conduit through which executives learn about problems and by which they issue goals and directions. As the organization grows, senior managers become too busy to handle many of the decisions that must be made, and they must increasingly delegate responsibilities to their subordinates. Instead of supervising work, they must become more concerned with their managers' goals, performance, and style.

The first step from direct personal control is difficult for most technical managers. Up to this point, their technical knowledge has been their prime talent and the basis for much of their success. Beyond the first level, however, managers must guide their subordinate managers and depend more on leadership ability than on technical skill.

INDIRECT MANAGEMENT

Managers' leadership styles must change as they move up the organization ladder. First-level managers, for example, work directly with the engineers and scientists and are intimate with each of their work assignments and how well they are being handled. They suggest new ways to attack the most difficult problems and they praise individual achievements. They also know who needs help and who can proceed effectively on their own.

At the next level, second-line managers should focus on how well the first-line managers are handling their people. They are now more concerned that goals be clear and challenging, and they have less time to focus on the direct technical work. Second-line managers may give a few specific instructions, but it is up to first-level managers to see that they are carried out. This difference is fundamental, because the first-level managers must thoroughly understand what the second-level managers want in order to properly direct their people. These second-level managers are doing what is called indirect management: they are managing through other managers—that is, managing by delegation.

MANAGEMENT COMMUNICATION

Indirect management can cause severe problems in advanced technical work, where most of the jobs involve complex questions that cannot be anticipated. At each step of a project, new knowledge is gained and new circumstances arise that must be considered before proceeding. When senior managers are unwilling to delegate this technical decision making, the first-level managers can't take action on their own. Since the first-line managers often have the most current technical knowledge, this style not only causes unacceptable delays and confusion, but it can also result in poorer decisions.

The most successful management style is for the senior managers to focus on ensuring good first-line management understanding of what is wanted and why. When conditions change, the line managers can then make timely decisions themselves without running to upper management for new instructions. The need for communication becomes progressively more important with each successive management level. The higher managers advance in their organizations, the further removed they are from technical issues, and the more effort they must devote to translating their broader business goals into directions the technical professionals can understand.

When technical professionals do not truly appreciate the manager's goals, serious problems can ensue. An example of the problems of management communication came up during the original design of the RCA Spectra 70 computer series in the early 1960s. General David Sarnoff had called for compatibility with the IBM 360 machines, but his people did not fully appreciate his intentions.[2,3] As a result, the finished machines had a few "improvements" over the IBM designs, and each of these differences required modifications in the customer's 360 programs before they could run on the new RCA systems. It was thus more difficult for IBM customers to get their programs to run, so the machines were much harder to sell. As a result, these machines were not the success they could have been if Sarnoff's objective of full compatibility had been achieved.

Although fully compatible designs were a technical challenge, they were far from impossible. The RCA engineers could have made their machines fully compatible if they had realized this was the company's objective. Since they did not truly understand Sarnoff's priorities, however, they followed their natural instincts to produce an improved design. Designers have their own views on what makes a better machine, and they are always tempted to make an instruction a little more elegant, to improve the I/O and channel commands, or to make any of the hundreds of changes that are always possible when redesigning a complex system. Any single change destroys full compatibility, however, and although the Spectra 70's "architectural improvements" may have been technically better, they cost RCA the business success Sarnoff had envisioned. It was not until Gene Amdahl produced his fully IBM-compatible machines a decade later that the full implications of Sarnoff's concept were demonstrated.

INDIRECT LEADERSHIP

When Napoleon was asked how he made his army cross the Alps to defeat Italy, he replied: "One does not *make* a French army cross the Alps; one *leads* it across.[4] This, of course, is the key to indirect management: to lead rather than direct. When managers of large organizations know what they want done, they must convince their people of the importance of their goals before they can expect to get a great deal accomplished.

Even when managers know what they want done, however, it often takes a great deal of effort to convince their followers that they are right. Tom, the manager of a large development group, did not understand this. His group was developing a new programming system, and he knew from experience that performance was undoubtedly going to be a problem. Simulation models had previously been used very successfully to predict programming systems' performance, so he told the development manager to set up a simulation group. Tom followed up to make sure the simulation group was properly staffed with competent people. He then felt reassured that the performance issue would be properly handled and turned his attention to other matters.

When this new programming system was ready for test, about a year and a half later, its performance was unacceptable. The simulation model had been built as Tom had directed, but the system designers had not bothered to use it. Tom had correctly foreseen the problem and had even known how to solve it, but he had failed to convince the design managers that the model would be useful to them. As a result, they did not use it to analyze the performance implications of their designs and thus did not have any idea how bad performance would be.

When senior managers want to get something complex done, they must convince their subordinate managers of its importance. If they don't and they are unable to stay personally in touch with the work, their subordinate managers are not likely to do what they want. When senior managers do convince them, however, subordinate managers can properly direct their people, track their progress, and take timely corrective action when things go wrong.

LEADERSHIP PRIORITIES

When dealing with a specific issue, senior managers' actions are usually fairly clear-cut, but when they try to set some new direction, they will almost always be misunderstood. They should stick to goals and objectives and focus more on what, when, why, and who and progressively less on how.

The case of a vice president shows how effective this can be. In reviewing the results of a customer survey, he became concerned about some of the problems with his company's products. The project manager agreed to do something about them, but he did not have any specific plans. When he was pressed, however, he promised to look into the problems in the next week or so. The vice president still did not feel he was taking the problems seriously enough, so he insisted that the project manager produce an action plan and bring it back to him for review within one week. He didn't tell him which problems to address or how to solve them, but he did insist on immediate and aggressive action. The project manager put his people right to work, and a week later, they had a suitably responsive plan.

NOTES

1. Jeffrey Pfeffer, *Organizations and Organization Theory* (Marshfield, MA: Pitman, 1982), cites Hage and Aiken on p. 272.

2. In a private conversation General David Sarnoff is reported to have complained that the Spectra 70 engineers did not have the same kind of standards discipline as the early radio and television engineers, so that they had not been able to make a truly IBM compatible series of computers.

3. Katharine Fishman, *The Computer Establishment* (New York: Harper & Row, 1981), p. 182.

4. Arnold Brown and Edith Weiner, *Supermanaging* (New York: McGraw-Hill, 1984), p. 189.

CHAPTER

21

Power and Politics

ower is the ability to cause action, while politics is the art of obtaining power. Power and politics are important management concerns because they form the basis for dealings between managers. When a manager needs another's help, he or she must figure out some way to convince the other manager to lend support. Occasionally, the manager's job will be to provide support and he or she will have planned to provide it and will have the needed resources available. More usually, however, at least some of these conditions will be a problem. Official departmental missions rarely anticipate all such issues in advance, and few organizations have sufficient resources to do their own jobs, let alone provide unplanned support for someone else. Most organizations are thus reluctant to take on additional work, and managers must either use the power of their positions to force compliance or apply their political talents to getting the help they need.

THE NATURE OF POWER

Power can be measured only in relative terms. Managers generally hold significant power only over the people in their own organizations. Staff directors or project managers, however, can have broader powers if they enjoy the confidence and support of some more senior manager. As long as they are believed to speak for this senior manager, they can reflect some of his or her power in their actions.

This, in fact, is one of the most interesting aspects of power. As long as it is successfully used, power holders will appear more powerful, and they can thus act with increasing assurance. In the case of reflected power, however, if staff managers overstep their license and are not supported by senior management, their power base will quickly disappear. The reason is that other managers will realize their perceptions of this manager's power were exaggerated. Staff heads can thus wield immense power as long as they are careful not to overstep the limits of their senior executive's support.

HOW POWER AFFECTS THE USER

Based on his research David Kipnis suggests that the successful exercise of power "strengthens the power-holder's belief that he or she controls the other person."[1] In fact, when people successfully use strong or coercive tactics, they see themselves as more powerful and the person they control as less so. In an experiment, Kipnis measured the performance of 200 business students whom he had act as managers of a small manufacturing operation. Some were told to behave as highly authoritarian managers and to give their "employees" no latitude in their work. The rest were instructed to behave democratically and to involve their people in the working decisions.

The specific work was a simple parts assembly in which performance could be easily measured. Kipnis found that all the employees produced roughly equivalent results regardless of the manager's style but that the managers' evaluations of their people were radically different.

> [The] authoritarian leaders routinely complained that their employees were not motivated to work hard. They also evaluated their employees' work less favorably than democratic leaders did. That is, the authoritarians rated their workers as less suitable for promotion and downplayed their skills and talents.

This is counter to almost every traditional view of management. The common conception is that people's performance is affected by managers' style and that managers' opinions of them are based on their performance. Kipnis's work implies that the primary determinant of job ratings is the manager's own behavior and that his or her style, at least for very simple tasks, does not affect workers' output. Considered another way, managers' use of their power over their people determines how well the managers evaluate their people, almost regardless of the people's performance. An authoritarian management style thus not only demotivates people, but it also actually damages them. This is because managers' opinions of their employees determine their opportunities for advancement. When managers' authoritarian behavior reduces this opinion, individuals' prospects for advancement are reduced, possibly for the rest of their working careers.

At the lowest working levels, there are often fairly objective performance measures, but for more senior managers, this suggests that ratings be based not so much on their groups' objective performance as on the managers' ability to identify and develop their best people.

AUTHORITY

Legitimate power is the authority officially given managers by the organization. They obtain it when they assume their jobs, and they lose it just as quickly. This is often hard for people to accept, for once they have held powerful jobs, they somehow begin to feel they have become powerful people. A senior manager from a small regional office was promoted to headquarters. He had grown accustomed to being the top man with a corner office and comfortable upholstered furniture. He belonged to the best clubs, the local papers reported his activities, and he was frequently recognized at social occasions. On moving to the headquarters staff, he was given a small office on an inside aisle and shared a secretary with two other staff members. Even though his position was now more important in the corporate hierarchy, he had lost his power of office and the feeling of superiority that went with it.

Legitimate power carries great weight. It includes the authority to hire and fire, set salaries, and make job assignments. Without managerial backing, people cannot be promoted, and managers are the prime source of nominations for management development opportunities. Although these formal powers are rarely expressed, they are well understood and underlie all managers' dealings with their people. No threats or even hints of threats are needed because the professionals intuitively know that their manager is the single most important person in their working lives.

BLIND OBEDIENCE

An interesting characteristic of legitimate power was demonstrated by management expert Harold Leavitt some years ago.[2] A series of experiments were conducted with paid volunteers to demonstrate the degree to which people will blindly accept orders from a legitimate power figure.

> [The subjects] were asked to help as "teachers" in a teaching experiment designed to test the effects of punishment on learning. They were given an electric shocking device and told to push the shock button every time the "learner" in the next room gave a wrong an-

swer. They were also told to increase the intensity of shock with each wrong answer, if necessary, up to a point on the shock machine scale marked with danger warnings. The "learner" in the next room was actually part of the experimental team. His job was to groan and on occasion scream in pain as the shock got stronger. He would, in late stages of the experiment, beg to be released and complain that he was suffering from a heart ailment.

Leavitt goes on to say that

the results came as a surprise both to the researchers themselves and to many other presumably sophisticated observers. They had forecast that very few subjects would push the shock buttons all the way. In fact, about 50 percent (and somewhere around that figure seems to hold up for many kinds of subjects) followed orders to the hilt, even while thinking that they were inflicting very severe electric shocks on a screaming middle-aged man with heart disease.

The authority of position is thus very powerful, and it seems to stem more from the badge of office than from the manager's ability to hire, fire, and promote. The simple fact that managers have been put in charge somehow makes what they say right, regardless of their employees' previous values and beliefs. Senior managers thus have an enormous responsibility for the way subordinate managers behave. This aspect of management behavior may at least partially explain the unethical behavior of professionals in the Watergate and Iran Contra affairs or even the inhuman behavior of American soldiers in the My Lai massacre of Vietnamese villagers or soldiers involved in "ethnic cleansing" in Bosnia.

THE USE AND ABUSE OF POWER

The phenomenon of blind obedience probably explains Lord Acton's famous observation that "power tends to corrupt; absolute power corrupts absolutely."[3] Evidence is compelling that petty powers are even more corrupting than major ones. Rosabeth Moss Kanter cites a study of U.S. Air Force officers which showed that those with the lowest status and the least advancement potential were most authoritarian in their dealings with subordinates.[4]

The way people abuse their minor powers can be quite frightening, as Professor Zimbardo of the Stanford University psychology department showed.[5] He advertised in the local newspaper for volunteers to participate in a "prison" experiment. Early one Saturday the "prisoners" were picked up, "booked," and enclosed in a wallboard "prison" in the basement of the Stanford University psychology building. Some of the volunteers were randomly selected to act as guards and the rest were treated as inmates. Zimbardo reports that in only a few hours the "guards" started to act like real guards and the "prisoners" behaved like typical prisoners. By the end of the first day some of the guards had physically and psychologically abused some of their charges, and by the end of the second day two of the prisoners had to be released for severe psychiatric problems. In only four days of the planned 10-day experiment "Warden" Zimbardo stopped the experiment because, as he said, he was "afraid of his own behavior as well as that of the others."

Kipnis points out that when people impose their will on others, they are more likely to do so again.[6] This is because the successful use of power reinforces the power holder's self-confidence and undermines that of the person being controlled. Further, those managers who have the least actual leverage are most likely to resort to threats and coercion. This tactic, however, is often counterproductive because the power behind a threat is the fear of punishment, and the minute the punishment is applied, the power is gone. People with little power thus tend to diminish it through misuse, while the more powerful gradually increase their strength by using it effectively.

People's attitudes also adapt very quickly to their power position. Lieberman studied a large number of factory workers and found that the attitudes of foremen were quite different from those of the regular workers. Further, when employees were promoted to foreman, they soon behaved just like the other foremen.[7] When Lieberman later resurveyed the same organizations, some of the foremen had been demoted and they had rapidly reassumed the traditional attitudes of the other workers.

THE POWER OF INFORMATION

Pfeffer has used the example of computer programmers to demonstrate how knowledge can provide an important source of leverage.[8] To use most programs, manuals are generally needed, but as important as these materials are, the most frequent complaint about application programs is lack of adequate documentation. As Pfeffer points out, this "inadequate documentation makes those involved in developing the system quite powerful." The programmers hold power based on their unique knowledge, and this power is reduced the minute they produce complete and readable manuals.

Considering the work involved, is it any wonder that programmers often fail to document their work?

Leavitt studied the flow of information in organizations and showed that control over the sources of information also provides considerable leverage.[9] He arranged test subjects so they could communicate only in prescribed ways. In one case one subject was placed at the hub of the communication network, so that everyone had to work through him, but in a second case everyone was given equal access. After running a number of tests, Leavitt found that those who had control over the flow of information were invariably seen by the rest as powerful figures; everyone else felt relatively powerless.

Managers are often the primary source of information for their employees. They give assignments and evaluate performance. They are the conduit for personnel policies and salary information, and they are the contact with the organization's management team. Thus the employees must learn from their manager about changes in work plans, their own personal working situation, or modifications in the organization structure. In short, managers, in addition to their legitimate power, also have great power over the information their people receive.

HANDLING POWER RELATIONSHIPS

The fundamental purpose of organizations is to handle complexity. After all, if the issues were simple, we would not need an organization to handle them. We thus set up organizations to handle more complex issues than we could handle alone. The logic for using an organization is thus to bring "order" to the work by structuring it into tasks that can be parceled out among organizational elements. In essence, then, we handle complexity by devising an orderly structure to break big complex jobs into less complex smaller jobs.

Organizations by their nature thus depend on order and structure to be effective. As one might expect, the problems of maintaining a rational and orderly structure become more difficult as organizations grow larger. This is not because large organizations are somehow bad but because the work they do is generally vastly more complex.

Other forces are at work, however. Physicists speak of entropy, the disorder of a system. Maximum entropy is the condition of maximum disorder. A physical law states that natural systems tend toward increasing entropy, or disorder, and that it takes energy to reduce the entropy of a physical system. Similarly, organizations naturally tend toward disorder and it takes energy to establish and maintain order.

The Forces of Disorganization

One can consider organized and structured systems as rational. Thus, rational behavior tends to maintain order and structure while irrational behavior leads toward chaos. Here, of course, we need to define rational behavior as objective decision making based on logical and thorough analysis of available facts. This definition implies, for example, that the apparent order and structure of an authoritarian management system may actually be irrational if it does not objectively make sound decisions. The reason is that authoritarians tend to oversimplify complex issues. While executives are often tempted to misuse their power by insisting on impossible commitments, this ultimately leads to chaotic behavior. A rejection of rationality merely defers analysis of the task's inherent problems, thus making matters worse.

Handling Power

A common cause of irrational behavior in organizations is the difficulty many people have dealing with the exercise of power. This problem can best be understood in terms of transactional analysis.[10] In simplest terms, human interactions are viewed as transactions between people who behave as children, parents, or adults. When children are submissive or rebellious in relating to a power figure, they are not being rational. They are essentially acting out their insecurities and inhibitions. Parents, in contrast, assert authority, either because they know better or because they feel their authority is threatened. Parents tend to dehumanize the other party through a lack of respect, trust, or consideration. Adults deal rationally with issues and respectfully with people. They seek facts and can accept complex situations as beyond their full comprehension. Both parents and children seek approbation while adults are willing to be anonymous achievers.

In handling power relationships, the objective is to deal as adult to adult. The following example is typical of the way many project schedules are established.

> *An executive directs his software group to complete its project in six months. The program is needed to support a new hardware product and delay would be costly. When the software manager says that the schedule is exceedingly aggressive, the executive replies that if the manager won't do it, he'll get someone who will.*

This executive is exhibiting parental behavior. He is insisting on a simple answer to a complex problem. The inevitable result is a crisis-driven project that is in trouble from the start and will probably never recover.

The next example shows typical child behavior:

When the manager tells an engineer to finish his program and get it into test this week, the engineer does as he is told. He does not speak up, even though he has not fully tested the program and knows it likely has several remaining defects.

Here, the engineer is acting like a child. The manager-parent has spoken and his word is law. Even though the engineer knows of potential problems, he obediently does what he is told. The inevitable result is that defects will be found in test and they will take longer to diagnose and fix than they would have if the engineer had properly tested the program in the first place.

An example of adult to adult behavior is:

The executive has a critical requirement for a new product feature. He explains the issue to his program manager and the need for an aggressive schedule. The programming manager tells him that this is a tighter schedule than they have previously achieved but that she would like a few days to review the problem with her team to see what they could do.

This behavior is deemed adult to adult because both the manager and the executive understand the issues and are rationally seeking the best alternative course of action. Such behavior cannot make impossible jobs possible, but it can produce the most effective overall result. If the requirement is truly impossible, adult behavior will most likely identify the problems at the earliest point when there are more recovery alternatives.

FOSTERING ADULT BEHAVIOR

When you, as a manager, sense that your subordinate is exhibiting childish behavior, you can take several steps:

1. Acknowledge the subordinate's concerns and demonstrate that you respect his or her views and opinions.

2. Explain that you seek the best solution to the problem and need his or her help in getting facts and developing a plan.

3. Outline the problem and ask for help in solving it.

The strategy is to defuse the implicit threat of your authority and explicitly state your need for the subordinate's help. It is essential to start by focusing on the subordinate's concerns before moving to the problem. Remember that until you do, you are talking to a child.

When you as an engineer or a manager sense that a superior is exhibiting parental behavior, there are several steps you can take:

1. Explain that you understand the superior's needs and are motivated to address them.

2. Make it clear that you understand and accept the superior's authority and seek to meet the objectives as expeditiously and effectively as you can.

3. Point out that the requested action is a substantial challenge and that you will need time to review the options and develop a plan.

4. Discuss the time needs for the planned actions and explore any questions you might have about the assignment before you leave the meeting.

This strategy will likely lead to more adult behavior. Remember to start by demonstrating that you understand the problem and that you accept the superior's authority. Until you do this, you are dealing with a "parent" who will not likely listen to rational discussion.

Transactional analysis provides a powerful framework for bringing rationality to management-employee behavior. Almost everybody is capable of child, parent, or adult behavior and either party in a transaction can initiate movement toward rationality. While you may not always be successful, you will be surprised at how often a rational approach will defuse a potential power conflict.

THE DISTRIBUTION OF POWER

The way power is distributed in organizations has a profound effect on the way people behave. A typical university, for example, generally has two authorities: A faculty senate sets basic policy and approves major decisions, and an administration operates the university. Senate debates can be long and acrimonious, and committees are frequently convened to explore the facts and develop a consensus. In corporations, control is typically vested in chief executives, who act under the general guidance of a board of directors. These chief executives personally hold all the official power and delegate it as they choose through the organization structure.

Where universities have vested significant decision authority in the senate, these forums have the advantage of widely distributing power. This ensures the involvement of many people in the decision process and provides ample opportunity for discussion and contention. Decisions are often made slowly and laboriously, but this wide involvement provides a broader base of support and a more fertile environment for creative ideas. Conversely, in most corporations, the pace is generally too hectic to permit extensive committee debates. The decision process must be geared for competitive reaction and rapid technological change. Although this centralized authority structure can generally react very quickly, it can also stifle creativity.

POWER AND POLITICAL BEHAVIOR

The level of political activity also depends on the way power is distributed in the organization. If each member of the management team has a comparable power base, issues will be widely debated, and the most controversial decisions will be completely aired. While this result is generally desirable, relatively wide and even power distribution can also result in extensive debates and an apparent lack of direction. When power is centralized in a strong leader, however, there is little room for political maneuver, contention is suppressed, and the focus is on the facts to help the power holder make decisions. The leadership style and level of political activity in most organizations fluctuates between these extremes.

Political behavior is often seen by management as indirect and underhanded, and their natural reaction is to attempt to stamp it out. This can be done by simply strengthening central control and making most members of the organization relatively powerless. Although this reduces contention and submerges natural conflicts, Pfeffer notes that it only "provides the appearance of rationality and satisfies social expectations concerning order."[11] Unfortunately, the resulting neatness merely papers over the inherent conflicts in the organization without resolving them. As Pfeffer adds: "Most organizations operate under the guise of rationality with some elements of power and politics thrown in, and thereby manage to obtain the worst of both worlds."[12] Conflict and contention are natural in complex organizations, and they must be dealt with openly. Honest political behavior is a natural and healthy part of this process.

Dishonest Political Behavior

Powerful people can act directly, while the powerless must either submit to them or resort to political activity. Politics provides the powerless a way to enhance their power so they can have more influence. Although political action is often seen as manipulative and vaguely dishonest, it is perfectly appropriate for people to privately accumulate evidence to buttress their views and to seek supportive allies.

Unfortunately, highly political situations can also lead to unprincipled behavior. People develop strong loyalties and tend to see issues through the parochial perspectives of their own specialties. Sometimes they become so convinced of their position that they will make up those supporting facts that they "know" will be found in time. In presentations they will stress the points that support their own views and suppress the opposing ones. This can generally be rationalized, but it is dishonest to misrepresent facts or suppress those that are pertinent to the other side.

Another political action is managers' attempts to privately convince allies to join their causes. This again is perfectly appropriate as long as it is not carried to the point of final decision. Any attempt to have the final decision made without involving all the contending parties is dishonest politics and usually results in poorer decisions and a deterioration in the level of honesty and trust in the organization.

Cliques and Coalitions

When individuals band together to increase their power base, they form a political grouping that is called a clique. Cliques generally persist for long periods, and as Tushman says, they form the basic building blocks of political organizations.[13] Several cliques banding together to effect a decision become a coalition, which is generally disbanded after the immediate objective is achieved.

The establishment of an engineering quality program demonstrates how this works. A corporate headquarters had issued a directive that every new product was to have higher quality than its predecessor. This policy was broadly accepted in principle, but the engineers did not agree on how to implement this directive. The Service Department unilaterally tried to impose its own plan, but Development would not go along. Something had to be done, however, so the head of the technical staff decided to run a workshop to see if they could work out a development answer. He invited representatives from each of the major development organizations, but they were unable to reach agreement. His staff, however, now understood the issues well enough to make a specific proposal. When this was completed, he met separately with the leaders of the three largest development groups to obtain their agreement, and after negotiating some changes they all accepted the proposal.

With this basic agreement, the staff head circulated his proposal to the other development groups. Each was given 30 days to respond with a position or specific examples of any problems. These managers had limited resources to do this added work, so only a few raised new issues. The issues were quickly addressed, and then these groups also fell into line. With this base of agreement across the entire development organization, the Quality staff, the Service Department, and the other staffs all quickly agreed.

The political debates required to build a coalition can take a lot of time, but they can also produce very good decisions. As each faction builds the case to support its own position, it obtains more data and can make progressively more informed judgments. When sufficient time is allowed to hear all the positions, most groups will typically back the most logical and best supported story. This is also likely to be the soundest position for the overall organization. This process only works, however, when all concerned groups are actively involved and the process is open and public.

Committees and Task Forces

The members of a properly formed coalition should be well informed and thoroughly convinced on the issues. Until this point is reached, there is always the risk that some members will change their minds when an opposing faction tries to win them over. One way to obtain informed conviction is to use committees or task forces to study the issues and make recommendations. When the most knowledgeable people from each group are involved in the task force, they can usually win over their home departments to their final conclusions. Although an informed and aggressive task force membership is invariably hard to manage, it generally produces the most creative and enduring results. There is ample evidence to show that such heterogeneous groups of outspoken professionals produce far better work than uniform, well-behaved ones.[14]

Task forces, however, have limitations, as Lippitt and Mackenzie discovered by studying the performance of faculty committees at the University of Kansas.[15] They discovered that such groups were most effective when used to gain broad acceptance of an already defined decision. Although the larger groups were the hardest to control, they found that those task forces with members taken from all the involved factions were also the most likely to achieve a broad consensus. Even when some groups had little to contribute, their representation both kept them informed and helped to gain their allegiance.

One of the major risks of task forces and committees is their propensity to compromise. This may be politically desirable, but it rarely produces a superior technical result. A good principle to follow, therefore, is to use large task groups to achieve a political consensus on managerial, procedural, and strategic issues. These questions rarely have a single best answer, so the objective is to get all the concerned groups to agree with the final recommendation. When the issues are largely technical, however, smaller expert groups should explicitly focus on the technical points in question with the objective of finding a truly superior solution.

Co-opting

Occasionally, one opposing group ends up not agreeing with the final conclusion. Although this may not always be a problem, sometimes it is important to gain their allegiance. Co-opting is a way to do this. It is done by having an influential member of the opposition take an important role in the new effort. When people see the issues from this different vantage point, they invariably end up contributing to the program's success. Some years ago, when IBM introduced the new PL/1 programming language, the FORTRAN user community vigorously opposed it. This was because they felt that IBM's FORTRAN support would be reduced. Lois Frampton, chairperson of the FORTRAN users group at the time, energetically championed her constituency's interests. Her vigorous opposition, however, also demonstrated her managerial talents and made her a logical choice to head the new PL/1 user committee. Once she was convinced that this new direction made long-term technical sense, she took the job and made important contributions to early user acceptance of the PL/1 programming language.

THE BUREAUCRACY

The behavior of bureaucracies demonstrates the political behavior of powerless people. The role of the bureaucracy is to handle such routine tasks as issuing pay checks, heating the buildings, and running the cafeteria. Although these details are all essential, the senior managers can't take the time to attend to them. Each one is thus reduced to a set of rules and procedures and given to an administrative function to handle.

As Hague and Aiken point out, the routine nature of bureaucratic work eliminates uncertainty, reduces complexity, and requires less skill. This ends up making such workers fairly easy to replace and thus relatively powerless.[16] According to Kanter such powerless people become rules-minded by "invoking organization rules and insisting on careful adherence to them."[17]

An extreme example of this occurred in Russia before the breakup of the USSR. A political delegation from several eastern European countries was visiting a museum in Moscow. On arrival, they all checked their hats and coats. When time came to leave, one of the diplomats could not find his hat check. Even though there was only one hat left and all the visitors assured her that this was the owner, the hat check lady refused to release the hat without the check stub. Finally, the museum director was called and he could only obtain release of the hat by drawing up an official-looking contract that was signed by all the parties.

Although line management can generally win any single battle with the bureaucracy, each struggle takes a lot of effort, and few managers have the time or inclination to engage in such battles very often. The case of the programmer from a company's New York office shows the kind of effort that is generally required. On Friday afternoon he was told to be at a meeting in California on Monday morning. After his manager approved the trip, he went to the cashier, but the office was closed. At the finance department he learned that the cash was locked up and nothing could be done until Monday. His manager then called the chief accountant, who refused to help. By now the manager was irate, so he appealed to progressively more senior financial managers until he reached the finance vice president, who had to be called out of a meeting. The VP was annoyed at the interruption but agreed to fix the problem. The cash was then available within 15 minutes.

The bureaucracy has a valid role in enforcing the rules and preventing recurrent problems. The accumulation of such constraints, however, becomes a kind of organizational scar tissue that builds up in response to problems. The bureaucrats are then cast in the role of defenders against the professionals, who are the cause of all the trouble. Although all bureaucrats are not necessarily obstructionists, their focus on procedures naturally opposes them to anything new or different. This causes frequent contention with the line organization, which is busy doing its best to produce innovative results.

In large technical organizations this natural conflict is weighted against the professionals because the many bureaucrats quickly learn that by banding together in cliques and coalitions they can increase their leverage. Unless steps are taken to maintain a reasonable balance of power, the rules will continue to accumulate until the engineers and scientists dissipate much of their energy fighting an increasingly powerful and highly autocratic bureaucracy.

Managing the Bureaucracy

One way to counter a powerful bureaucracy was demonstrated by a university museum director. He urged the faculty and students to complain freely about bureaucratic rules and to suggest ways for improvement. Since the director acted on these complaints, the bureaucrats soon learned to treat the faculty and students as customers instead of adversaries.

The most effective way to manage bureaucratic behavior is through a focus on the service nature of the work. One approach is to require such groups to identify their users and to establish measures of the quality and responsiveness of their service. This, of course, requires that you look carefully at who they define as their users.

The reason to look closely at such groups is best illustrated by the example of an IBM quality report. George had recently been given responsibility for a quality group and the quality staff manager came to him to approve the group's standard monthly report. George asked what it was used for, and the staff manager responded that all the laboratories needed it. Since the report was due out shortly, George signed off but took a copy to review. While it contained volumes of numbers, he could not see how a laboratory or product manager would use it. Over the next month, he asked several managers what they did with it and found they had staffs who reviewed the report every month to find and correct problems and inaccuracies. They did not, however, use the report to help them run the laboratories or projects. The next month, when he got the report to approve, George insisted on one change. That was to insert the statement that henceforth, this report would be issued quarterly. His people argued that they couldn't issue it only quarterly, but George assured them that if the complaints were too severe, they could return to the monthly report. After issuing two quarterly reports with no complaints, George then insisted on another change. He inserted the statement that this would be the last report. Since no complaints were received from any of the laboratories or headquarters, they stopped the report and reduced the size of several staffs.

Bureaucracies foster bureaucracies and they can generate so much pseudo-work that they seem very busy. The key is to see if any one who designs, develops, manufactures, markets, or services products needs the staff to help them do their jobs. If no one does, get rid of the staff.

NOTES

1. David Kipnis, "The View from the Top," *Psychology Today*, December 1984, pp. 30–34.

2. Harold J. Leavitt, *Managerial Psychology*, 4th ed. (Chicago: University of Chicago Press, 1978), p. 141.

3. Bergen Evans, *Dictionary of Quotations* (New York: Bonanza Books, 1968), p. 547: 15.

4. Rosabeth Moss Kanter, *Men and Women of the Corporation* (New York: Harper & Row and Basic Books, 1977), p. 189.

5. Thomas J. Peters and Robert H. Waterman, Jr., *In Search of Excellence: Lessons from America's Best-Run Corporations* (New York: Harper & Row, 1982), p. 79.

6. Kipnis, "The View from the Top," p. 32.

7. Jeffrey Pfeffer, *Organizations and Organization Theory* (Marshfield, MA: Pitman, 1982), p. 74.

8. Ibid., p. 113.

9. Ibid., p. 130.

10. Thomas A. Harris, *I'm OK—You're OK, A Practical Guide to Transactional Analysis* (New York: Harper & Row, 1969).

11. Jeffrey Pfeffer, *Organizations and Organization Theory* (Marshfield, MA: Pitman, 1982), p. 88.

12. Ibid., p. 344.

13. Michael L. Tushman and William L. Moore, *Readings in the Management of Innovation* (Marshfield, MA: Pitman, 1982), p. 243.

14. Ibid., p. 90.

15. Ibid., p. 173.

16. Pfeffer, *Organizations*, p. 272.

17. Kanter, *Men and Women*, p. 192.

PART

7

Managing Change

22

Structural Change

O rganizations are typically designed to fight the last war. Since they need to solve current, known problems, they tend to defer the vaguer concerns of the future. Moreover, many of the most important problems are hard to identify. A vested interest in the status quo makes many managers reluctant to admit that things are not working as they should. Although it is generally wise to follow the credo, "If it ain't broke, don't fix it," managers should recognize that every organizational structure is a trade-off between conflicting pressures. When this balance changes, the organization should change as well.

LEADERSHIP PROBLEMS

Henry Mintzberg suggests that the four basic kinds of organizational behavior are determined by their leadership situation: the Autocracy, the Political Arena, the Closed System, and the Meritocracy.[1] In the Autocracy, the leader is the driving force and is typically the organization's only important power figure. Autocracies behave much like a palace court, where power is measured in distance from the throne, and autocratic leaders think of themselves as embodying the organization. They typically feel no need for such details as job descriptions, operating plans, or formal procedures. What they say goes; but often that is all that goes.

Since autocrats rarely groom successors, their departure forces the organization into Mintzberg's second phase, the Political Arena. The organization is highly vulnerable in this period, with no coherent leadership and with power widely dispersed. Without direction from the top, few organizations can revise their strategies. Thus the Political Arena coalesces around the departed leader's goals and is, in effect, run by his or her ghost. Structure petrifies around an outdated strategy and is dangerously exposed to change in the marketplace or technology.

Organizations that survive the Political Arena become either Closed Systems or Meritocracies. In the Closed System, the bureaucracy takes charge, and its nominal leader is concerned with maintaining the status quo. The focus is on administrative management through cost controls, documented plans, and formal procedures. The growing formality inhibits innovation and exposes the organization to competitive or technological surprise. Once fully entrenched, the leadership is immutable, except by external force.

If the technocrats beat the bureaucrats in the power struggle of the Political Arena, it will be succeeded by the Meritocracy, a structure in which the engineers and scientists are in charge. This organization is typically better informed and less exposed to technological surprise; the professionals' natural aversion to procedures generally protects it from becoming bureaucratic. Because financial controls are often neglected, however, the greatest danger is the technologist's tendency to believe that all problems have technical answers. Focusing on laboratory and plant, the organization can lose touch with the marketplace.

Symptoms of an Autocracy

Even though autocratic behavior is most obvious at the corporate level, it can also occur in individual departments with equally severe consequences. Some of the symptoms of an overbearing autocrat are the following:

- The leader is the sole spokesperson for the organization and appears to be the only source of ideas. The boss makes decisions in private, with no open disagreement and little prior discussion even with the organization members who are most involved.

- The leader has a low opinion of his or her subordinates, does not promote from within, and has not groomed a successor.

- The leader has a small circle of intimates who share in the leader's private thoughts and plans. These cronies, however, are not viewed as potential successors, and they rarely hold official power.

- The organization has no formal plans, procedures, or job descriptions.

- There is little or no delegation of authority.

- No reward and recognition programs exist.

- Creativity is limited, except by the leader.

There is an enormous difference between a dynamic and forceful leader and an autocrat. Leaders typically believe in themselves and are not afraid to defend their convictions. Most leaders are good salespersons and enjoy converting people to their cause. Autocrats, conversely, lack confidence. Insecure managers appear highly autocratic simply because they are unwilling to risk the give and take of personal interaction. They quietly, even secretively, prepare their positions before announcing their final conclusions. The lack of advance notice leaves the troops unprepared to ask questions or disagree, so they feel compelled to silently follow orders.

This was the case with a small department of experienced engineers. The manager was technically competent and spent most of his time working out design problems behind his closed office door. Every few days he would call in one of his people, ask for his work status, and give him his next assignment. Although his engineers viewed him as a tyrant, the manager was actually terrified of them and dreaded their infrequent encounters. He soon asked to be relieved of his management responsibilities so that he could return to the technical work that he really enjoyed.

It takes a great deal of self-confidence for managers to deal honestly and openly with their employees. Some managers feel so humiliated when their subordinates prove them wrong that they retreat behind the shield of authority. This attitude is self-destructive, however, for managers must interact freely with their followers if they are to lead them. The autocratic style develops over many years, and it is rarely possible to change it. Even when others convince the autocrat of the need for change, such behaviors are often so deeply rooted in the autocrat's personality that self-improvement is extremely difficult.

Other Leadership Problems

Not much can be done about the problems of the Political Arena or the Closed System until the lack of effective leadership is addressed. At the corporate level these changes must be initiated from the outside, but at the department level, these characteristics can be identified and changed rather quickly. Although there are no general guidelines, the most common solution is to find and install an energetic new leader.

The Meritocracy can operate quite effectively under a form of consensus management. But the consensus structure often faces serious problems, as shown by the following symptoms:

1. Deeply engrossed in technology, the organization pays less and less attention to customers and competition.

2. Cost controls, productivity measurements, and profit management receive little or no emphasis.

3. A blind focus on product narrows management's view, leaving no vision or time for the process, tools, and personnel-development actions needed for long-term improvement.

The problems of the Meritocracy can be addressed in several ways, depending on their severity:

1. Add some strong marketing and financial people to the management teams of laboratories and manufacturing plants.

2. Give high priority to management development to ensure that future general managers have been exposed to several facets of the business.

3. Emphasize market awareness, including the purchase and use of competitive products, customer surveys, management participation in customer executive briefings, and short temporary assignments of key technical people with the marketing organization.

THE AGING ORGANIZATION

Much like people, organizations exhibit problems of youth and old age. John Aplin and Richard Cosier point out that organizations can be divided into either creative or maintenance types.[2] Creative organizations grow rapidly, are highly innovative, and undergo perpetual change. Organizations in the maintenance phase are more stable, have more formalized plans and procedures, and emphasize cost management. The key words in the maintenance period are productivity and control.

Since creative leaders rarely pay much attention to formal plans, the technical professionals often complain about the lack of long-term direction. Management typically knows exactly where it is going but has not bothered to tell its people. Rapid growth also produces a young, self-confident management team who made it on their own and see little need to formally develop new managers. Since the incessant demand for talent generally outstrips any internal supply, formal development programs rarely seem worthwhile. The constant infusion of new blood, however, does help to keep the organization intellectually stimulated and technologically aware.

The creative organization provides an exciting environment, but it also has serious drawbacks. Since management's emphasis is largely on tactical reaction, rapid management turnover often means problems are swept under the rug rather than solved. Management continuity is insufficient to make two- or three-year changes, so longer-term problems accumulate. Finally, creative organizations have not yet been humbled by serious failures, so there are no seasoned "old salts" from prior disasters to temper the optimism of this brash young organization.

The creative phase is self-limiting, its success inevitably leading to a maintenance phase. The initial burst of success cannot be long sustained, and growing organizational size demands more discipline and control. The maintenance organization addresses these problems with a formal structure, organization charts, job descriptions, and a healthy emphasis on employee benefits and management development. Growing numbers of good people are now available for internal promotion, and stability brings formal long-term plans, product procedures, cost controls, and improved profitability.

Although the transition from the creative to the maintenance phase is natural, it is also traumatic. The enthusiasm of the early days is replaced by painstaking attention to the problems of success. Slower growth means less opportunity for advancement, and workers now worry about their careers and resent the loss of the earlier excitement and challenge. The growing bureaucracy produces a more structured organization with a new emphasis on efficiency and measurement. If this reaction swings too far, it can stifle innovation in a web of financial and business controls.

Addressing Creative-Phase Problems

The trick to sustaining the huge productivity of the creative phase is to adjust to its problems while not diminishing its pace and excitement. The leader should lean into the wind and personally stress areas that are commonly ignored, such as management development, financial control, project coordination, formal planning, process improvement, and quality goals. The growing number of seasoned hands should be nurtured and heeded as a source of advice and council.

Addressing Maintenance-Phase Problems

In the maintenance phase, too, managers should act as a balancing force. But now, they need to shift focus to the marketplace and technical awareness. The prime threat in this phase is the propensity to focus on internal problems. To avoid technical or competitive surprise, managers should challenge their people to demonstrate the technological superiority and competitive leadership of their planned products.

In any large organization many projects properly belong in the maintenance phase, while a few need insulation from tight control. Multimode structures are difficult, however, because one product typically dominates management's thinking. When this product moves from its creative phase to its maintenance phase, everything else tends to move with it. Better planning and improved financial control seem logical at any time, so more procedures and controls are applied to everyone—even those that are still in the creative phases.

One answer is to isolate the creative parts of such organizations so they can have a more suitably tailored management system. This is the principle behind the skunk works described in Chapter 15. IBM set up the Independent Business Unit (IBU) with responsibility for introducing the first IBM personal computer. The IBU was free to use rules and procedures appropriate to a new business venture rather than being bound by the constraints applied to the other divisions. The vehicle used to speed decision making was approval by a corporate executive review board. This flexibility resulted in several innovations, including the first development and manufacture of a major IBM machine largely through subcontractors. Marketing was also done through independent retail stores, even though IBM had a large and highly skilled field sales force. Although several of the innovations were strongly opposed by the various staffs and operating units, the personal computer IBU used the executive review board to bypass their objections. As is typical of creative organizations, the tactics were a great success but, as noted previously, the PC was a long-term disaster for IBM.

Management Priorities

The essential difference between managing the creative phase and managing the maintenance phase is a matter of priorities. In the creative phase, the thrust must be on innovation, and building the base for sustained growth. Success will bring a host of new problems, but many will be irrelevant until this base has been established.

In the creative organization, the first priority must be to see if there is a profit to be made from the new product or service. Once it is likely that the proposed innovation will succeed, then it is possible to plan with more certainty. Until the key technical and market issues have been identified and partially resolved, however, it would be pointless to develop detailed plans. In principle, the creative phase strives to prove technical and business feasibility while the maintenance phase concentrates on running an established business.

Organizational Tenure

The stability of the maintenance organization often means that many technical groups remain largely unchanged for long periods. Working together for an extended time leads to complacency and intellectual stagnation. Pelz and Andrews classify groups as old if they have worked together for more than four to five years; in a study they found that the performance of such groups generally declined.[3] The few older teams in the study that maintained an attitude of friendly internal competition remained effective, while all the others performed poorly. The optimum age fell between one and five years, groups younger than a year lacked the internal cohesion to be fully effective.

Katz and Allen reached similar conclusions from their study of 50 project teams.[4] They determined each team's performance by asking several managers their opinions and then averaging the responses. Correlating performance with team age, they found an increase for the first 1.5 years, a flat period up to about 5 years, and then a decline. The decline was so pronounced, in fact, that the difference in performance between the 1.5 and 5-plus year groups was over 20%. Of the 10 teams with superior performance, none had worked together for more than 5 years.

A key reason for the performance decline of the older teams was what Katz and Allen call the "Not Invented Here" syndrome. This syndrome, they found, caused older groups to have minimal internal communication, not to seek external technical contacts, and to quickly reject those outside ideas that did reach them. Katz and Allen concluded that this attitude is most likely to develop in groups that have worked together in one field for so long that they have become the local experts. Their status as experts, coupled with their limited outside technical exposure, leads them to believe they have a monopoly on innovation in their field. This further limits their curiosity and creativity.

Organizations that have the good fortune to be on the crest of a new technological wave, as were IBM, Intel, and Microsoft, are generally blessed with rapid growth and high profits for many years. The temptation to believe that their success is due to their unique technical or business brilliance reinforces the Not Invented Here attitude and makes them increasingly vulnerable. No organization has a monopoly on brilliance, and it is only a matter of time until disaster befalls those who assume they do.

Addressing the Problems of Tenure   When a laboratory or manufacturing plant has the same organizational structure for five years or more, many of its groups will stagnate. A working-level reorganization is called for. In many reorganizations, management and executive assignments are reshuffled, while functional teams are left pretty much intact. Such rearrangements may be useful in reorienting priorities and responsibilities, but they don't freshen the stagnant pool. The technical groups need new challenges and associations.

When John was put in charge of a major development laboratory, its administration and support groups had been largely unchanged for more than 10 years. The direct development teams were complaining ever more loudly about the entrenched and rigid bureaucracy, and there were seven levels of management between the director's office and the working engineers. John decided to restructure the working level completely. The laboratory's development managers were grouped into several committees to examine each administrative and support department to see if it could be eliminated without causing specific problems for the project.

Several failed this stringent test and were subsequently eliminated. The remaining functions were then logically grouped together under second- and third-level managers to produce an entirely new departmental structure. The reorganization affected almost every administrative and support group in the laboratory and almost completely disrupted the established bureaucracy. Two levels of management were eliminated, and nearly 200 of the first-level managers were reassigned. Most of the excess managers and professionals were given direct development jobs, thus improving the efficiency of the total organization while increasing the size of the direct development work force. Surprisingly, the demoted managers were generally happier in their new assignments. Smart people know when they are in a stagnant position and will appreciate a reassignment.

NOTES

1. Henry Mintzberg, *Power in and Around Organizations* (Englewood Cliffs, NJ: Prentice-Hall, 1983), p. 314.

2. John C. Aplin and Richard A. Cosier, "Managing Creative and Maintenance Organizations," *Business Quarterly,* Spring 1980, p. 56.

3. Donald C. Pelz and Frank M. Andrews, *Scientists in Organizations: Productive Climates for Research and Development* (New York: Wiley, 1966), p. 259.

4. Ralph Katz and Thomas J. Allen, "Investigating the Not Invented Here (NIH) Syndrome: A Look at the Performance, Tenure, and Communication Patterns of 50 R and D Project Groups," *R&D Management (UK),* vol. 12, no. 1 (1982), p. 7.

23

The Change Process

Although a reorganization can change the work people are supposed to do, it often has little effect on the way they do it. Instituting challenging productivity or quality programs or adapting to technological change calls for a much more complex change process. Simplistic directives from management often elicit resistance if not open hostility. Being creatures of habit, most people must be convinced of the need to change before they will willingly comply. Management's job is to lead and direct this change process.

RESISTANCE TO CHANGE

It is human nature to want to improve things; thus people should embrace change, but, paradoxically, they almost universally resist it. Douglas Sherwin explains why: "Change is great when you are its agent; it is only bad when you are its object."[1] Edgar Huse further notes that change is often seen as a personal threat by those involved unless they have participated in its planning.[2]

Paul Lawrence describes the case where an identical change was introduced to several factory groups whose productivity was closely matched.[3] One group was merely told to make the change. Offered no explanation, they resisted all management's efforts during the entire test period, and their output dropped by a full third. The other two groups were involved in the change planning from the outset, and despite an initial small drop in productivity, rapidly recovered and ultimately reached a higher performance level than before.

Lawrence suggests that resistance to change should be treated as a symptom rather than a problem. Focusing on overcoming the resistance of their employees, whom they view as obstructionists, causes management to increase its pressure to conform. This increases resistance further, and as positions become entrenched, the change becomes harder to implement than before. Lawrence found that this vicious cycle can be broken by concentrating on the reasons for resistance and dealing with them one at a time.

Every change involves unknowns, and people are reluctant to take risks and face the unknown. Their involvement in the planning, however, allows them to understand the change, to see why it should be made, and to learn what to expect. This reduces the unknowns and helps overcome resistance. Another way to overcome resistance is to show people how the change can help them, presenting it as an opportunity instead of a threat. With this outlook, coupled with the opportunity to participate in planning and to make suggestions, many employees will start to act as change agents instead of objects. Since resistance to a change is proportional to its magnitude, resistance can be reduced by breaking a large change into smaller steps. Each step is then easier to sell and to implement and total resistance is reduced.

UNFREEZING

When the change process is well thought out and properly structured, it generally starts with a phase of "unfreezing" attitudes. Unfreezing is a way to break the organization out of its current constraints. Its purpose is to overcome resistance.[4] An extreme example of unfreezing is brainwashing, which overcomes resistance by destroying the will to resist through physical and psychological torture. A less brutal unfreezing process is used on new military recruits. Isolated in boot camps, they are dominated by demanding drill masters, who put them through grueling exercises, rugged obstacle courses, and forced marches. The survivors become a proud and cohesive fighting unit.[5]

Obviously, unfreezing large technical organizations requires less direct methods. There is, however, still a need to overcome resistance. When management issues a directive to make a change, people often resent the implication that they need to be told and are inclined to resist. But if management waits for grass-roots acceptance, it is likely that nothing will happen, at least not for a very long time.

The working engineers and scientists are rarely the source of the most resistance. Being closer to the problems, they generally understand what needs to be done better than their managers, but unless their immediate managers support and encourage them, professionals cannot institute significant changes by themselves. In fact it is their immediate supervisors, first- and second-level management, who generally present the greatest resistance to change. When these managers are convinced that the change will help to get the job done, they will encourage their people, who will then welcome change as an opportunity.

It also helps to set forth an ideal. Executive statements of purpose or benchmarks of success can provide an image of what is wanted. Coupling this ideal with education programs, pilot demonstrations, or expert consultation helps members of the organization grasp the need for change and better prepares them to support it.

One of the most successful change programs is Alcoholics Anonymous. AA has found that until alcoholics are so unhappy with their own situations that they come for help, any effort to offer assistance will be fruitless. For more typical organizational problems Leavitt suggests that managers can help to accelerate recognition of the need to change in three ways.[6] (1) make the problems more obvious; (2) simply point them out (paradoxically, this often causes the people to blame the problem on their managers); (3) wait for the employees to come to them for help and respond by describing the change as a potential solution to these newly recognized concerns.

PLANNING THE CHANGE

Once the frozen situation has thawed, the people are unhappy with the status quo and ready for improvement. The vacuum must now be filled with a plan of action and early implementation steps. If action is not taken promptly, people will become disgruntled now that they better understand the unsatisfactory conditions. Management should thus select a change agent and a staff at once to lead the change process. Some points to consider in making this selection are the following:

- Agents should be enthusiastic about leading the change process. Irwin and Langham point out that "enthusiasm can be contagious and people tend to perform better in an optimistic environment than in a won't-work environment."[7]

- Agents must be both technically and politically capable of understanding the problems and ensuring that proposed solutions will be effective.

- Agents need the respect of the people they are to deal with.

- Agents must have management's confidence and support or they will not act with the assurance needed to win wide cooperation and acceptance.

It is wise to pick as a change agent someone who has strong views on the subject. Gerald Salancik cites the example of Pitney-Bowes's president, who, in a feedback meeting with a group of his employees, was interrupted by a young woman who asked what the company was doing to improve opportunities for female employees. She said that "80 percent of the customer account jobs were going to women and only 13 percent of the management positions."[8] Seeing this challenge as an opportunity, the president promptly removed the woman from her current assignment and put her in charge of a special task force to study the role of women in the firm.

Participative Planning

Once the change agent has been selected, planning for change must begin. Planning starts by identifying the people who will be affected by the change and making sure they are at least partially involved in the process. When a great many people are involved, working groups should be established with representatives from each constituency. While the representatives' obvious task is to participate in planning, their less obvious but more important job is to ensure that all the members of their groups are kept informed about the planning work. The planning teams then consider ways to implement the change, anticipate problems, and find ways to address them. Keeping this process open and visible and addressing all concerns thoughtfully will minimize resistance.

IMPLEMENTING THE CHANGE

The rate of change is a factor in its success. Some changes can be accomplished with lightning speed, but others require a great deal of patience. Purely technical changes rarely affect working habits and can generally be implemented quickly. When people's behavior is directly involved, however, the pace must be more deliberate. A more gradual pace gives them time to understand the change, to accept it, and to adapt to its effects on them. Since the time needed to adapt depends on the magnitude of the change, an attempt to move too quickly will increase resistance and delay progress.

One of the most important considerations in any change process is continuing evidence of progress. Changes are often started with great fanfare, but then nothing is heard for a long time. Having been convinced that change is needed, the people start to worry that something has gone wrong. As Irwin and Langham point out, "An expression of progress dispels fears, ensures confidence, encourages the doubters to join the team, provides the background for further achievement."[9] Progress can be demonstrated by dividing the total program into small and manageable stages and publicizing each one as it is completed.

REFREEZING

The purpose of refreezing is to make the change permanent. One of the most discouraging experiences a manager can have is to encounter a problem that he or she has already solved. Unfortunately, this can happen every time a change is made incompletely. When initially implemented, most changes get plenty of attention, but after the original impetus, priorities change and organizations tend to revert to their prior habits. An example of what can happen is the introduction of design and code inspections in IBM's programming development laboratories.[10] For the initial introduction, education programs were established and all programmers were trained in the ways to perform inspections, the procedures to follow, and the people who should participate. Some years later, the effectiveness of inspections had seriously deteriorated. Most of the courses had been dropped, and, although the inspection formalities were still being observed, the programmers had taken shortcuts with the process. Reducing the discipline of the inspections had significantly damaged their effectiveness. When the problem was identified, several laboratories had to launch their inspection programs all over again.

Some practices are so obviously helpful that they remain in place once introduced. A good scheduling discipline, for example, is such a fundamental part of technical work that professionals who have worked on well-run projects find it hard to operate any other way. Once fully established, therefore, such practices generally stay in place with little management attention. But first it often takes a great deal of time to convince professionals of their benefits and persuade them to incorporate them in their permanent working methods.

The reasons that the inspection process did not stick at IBM are instructive. First, software inspections are done early in the software process and they take a great deal of time. After inspections have been in force for some time, their initial benefits can easily be forgotten. If, as in IBM's case, there is no overall quality measurement and analysis program to continually demonstrate inspection effectiveness, the inspections will soon be viewed as a luxury. Under the inevitable time pressures, eliminating the inspections can erroneously be seen as a way to shorten product schedules.

Ample evidence exists, however, that eliminating inspections lengthens development schedules and reduces product quality.[11] The IBM inspection experience is an example of a refreezing problem. Some of the ways to address these problems are:

1. Keep in place the management team that originally instituted the change. They will be sensitive to erosion and make sure the change is retained. Unfortunately, in most technical organizations management tenure is not predictable.

2. Modify the organization's procedures to incorporate the change as part of the bureaucratic process. This solution is more practical for administrative tasks, such as planning and estimating, where compliance can be ensured by relatively straightforward rules and guidelines, than for more complex technical processes.

3. Use the measurement system to foster new methods through awards or special bonuses. Pay incentives can be very effective but must necessarily be based on simple objective measures. This can be a serious drawback, however, for few complex technical tasks can be captured by one measure, and people who are paid accordingly will tend to ignore all other considerations to maximize the one most important parameter. If financial incentives are to be used, they should first be tried experimentally and should always include an element of management judgment. Note also the cautions in Chapter 9 on rewards.

4. For complex situations, establish a dedicated staff with the responsibility for monitoring the changed process and alerting management when it starts to deteriorate. This can be a responsibility of the quality assurance staffs.

5. Educate. When the objective is to change the working methods of the professional people, education is probably the most effective refreezing mechanism. As long as the course materials are well presented and the courses permanently retained, education programs will provide continuous support for the change process.

Several of these techniques can be used in combination, but education should be part of any professional refreezing program. Knowledgeable professionals are the strongest force for improvement, and a sound education program will motivate them to use the best known practices and methods.

SETTING GOALS

Pfeffer cites a number of studies that demonstrate the importance of goals in the change process.[12] When people understand and accept a goal and believe they can meet it, they will generally work very hard to do so. The case of a programming manager who recently attended a quality course shows how effective a shared goal can be. The manager discussed with the programmers what he had been taught, and together they decided on the goal of delivering their next program version with no defects. This was a challenging objective because their project was to develop improvements to a sort program used by several thousand customers. In spite of all their efforts, previous similar products had always contained several hundred defects. After much study, they decided that exhaustive testing was possible. They found, however, that nearly 10 times the normal number of test cases and several more weeks of testing would be required. Senior management supported their goal, so the schedule was extended and the testing was done as planned. After installation and a full year of use, not a single program defect was found!

The quality program worked because the programmers had a clear and measurable goal. They knew exactly what they were trying to do and why it was important. They also believed they could do it. It is essential that goals be reasonably close to the professionals' ability to perform. When there is no hope of meeting a target, each day's work reinforces the existing doubts and builds feelings of inevitable failure and discouragement.

Set goals carefully, however, for when goals require too dramatic a change, people have trouble knowing how to start. This is the time to break change into small and realistic increments, with subgoals for each. As progress is made and a new step is reached, the bar is raised to a new level that is nearer to the final objective. Each step thus demonstrates continued progress and increases the motivation to continue striving for improvement.

The immediacy of the goal is also important. A distant objective rarely motivates current action. There are so many short-term crises that a long-term objective is often deferred until it too becomes a current crisis. Unfortunately, a hectic environment easily leads to makeshift solutions with no sustained progress. Here again, it helps to divide a long-term program into shorter steps with their own goals and measurements. Employees then face a sequence of immediate goals that directly relate to the daily work.

Although professionals may understand a goal and agree that it is desirable, they may have no idea how to meet it. Managers can damage motivation by pressing plans too aggressively. An example would be a corporate goal to improve productivity by 10 times in 10 years. The goal may be laudable and even feasible, yet the engineers may not be able to conceive of how to achieve it. The goal thus seems unreasonable and is likely to be demotivating. If, however, the long-range goal is stated in more immediate terms, say 25% productivity improvement this year, it will seem more achievable. Even though a 25% annual improvement achieves the same result in 10 years, the shorter-term goal seems more realistic and thus provides more motivation. Managers are often tempted to arbitrarily cut cost targets or tighten schedules in the mistaken belief that doing so will motivate people to try harder. Often, however, this discourages them by making a difficult job seem impossible.

Although managers should set overall direction, people should define their own goals with measurable steps and detailed plans. When they cannot see how to do this, managers should discuss the problems with them and seek ways to remove constraints or simplify the job. When managers work this way, their people are more likely to accept aggressive goals and strive to meet them.

THE PROCESS IMPROVEMENT CYCLE

One way to accomplish the objective of having short-term goals and a long-term strategy is to view change as a cyclic process. The Software Engineering Institute has formalized the improvement process in what SEI calls the IDEAL^{SM} change model. IDEAL stands for Initiating, Diagnosing, Establishing, Acting, and Leveraging. As shown in Figure 23.1, the change process is continuous. The key steps in the IDEAL framework are:

Initiating.   The organization's management team sponsors the improvement process and establishes an environment receptive to improvement. The team also forms an improvement group with appropriate resources and defined responsibilities.

Diagnosing.   The leader of the improvement effort launches an organizational assessment as described in Chapter 24. The assessors identify the key problems in the organization and recommend improvement actions to the management team.

Establishing.   The management team sets the priorities and assigns resources to implement the improvement actions defined in the previous phases.

Acting.   Following management's priorities, the improvement action teams execute the improvement plans and the management team tracks and monitors their work.

Leveraging.   At the conclusion of each improvement cycle, the improvement teams review their work to determine what worked best, see what changes are needed, and what they recommend for future improvement teams. The management team then initiates the next improvement cycle.

---

^{SM} IDEAL is a service mark of Carnegie Mellon University.

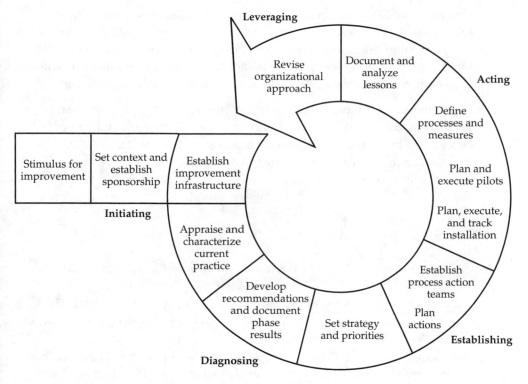

Figure 23.1   The IDEAL Model

By following the IDEAL framework, organizations can maintain their focus on long-term improvement while continuing to address short-term goals.

The Process Staff

Process improvement involves many issues and requires participants who have special knowledge and skill. In its work supporting software process improvement, the SEI has found that organizational improvement is slow and often ineffective unless management assigns dedicated professionals to assist in the work. Software Engineering Process Groups (SEPG) have thus been formed in many organizations.[13] These groups should be staffed with knowledgeable professionals and should have about 2 to 4 full-time people for every 100 software professionals in the organization.[14] Some of the caveats on the staffing and use of process groups are as follows:

- Keep the SEPG small. The many people needed for action teams and working groups should be drawn from the line projects, while SEPG staff should serve as specialists, facilitators, or team leaders.

- Dedicate the SEPG to process change rather than saddling them with miscellaneous support tasks. It is often tempting to assign the SEPG responsibility for monitoring technology, handling training, or any of the many other miscellaneous tasks that arise in technical organizations, but this will soon occupy all their time, leaving little or none for process improvement.

- Hold project managers responsible for implementing process change. Effective change alters the way the project members work and can only be induced by project management. SEPG staff can advise, assist, track, and support but cannot actually install a change. That is the responsibility of the line project managers.

NOTES

1. Douglas S. Sherwin, "Strategy for Winning Employee Commitment," *Harvard Business Review on Management* (New York: Harper & Row, 1975).

2. Edgar F. Huse, *Organization Development and Change* (St. Paul, MN: West, 1975).

3. Paul R. Lawrence, "How to Deal with Resistance to Change," *Harvard Business Review,* January-February 1969, p. 4.

4. Hersey and Blanchard discuss this subject, starting on page 289, in their book *Management of Organizational Behavior: Utilizing Human Resources,* 3rd ed. (Englewood Cliffs, NJ: Prentice-Hall, 1977).

5. Ibid., p. 293.

6. Harold J. Leavitt, *Managerial Psychology,* 4th ed. (Chicago: University of Chicago Press, 1978), p. 165.

7. Patrick H. Irwin and Frank W. Langham, Jr., "The Change Seekers," *Harvard Business Review,* January-February 1966, p. 75.

8. Michael L. Tushman and William L. Moore, *Readings in the Management of Innovation* (Marshfield, MA: Pitman, 1982), p. 217.

9. Irwin and Langham, "The Change Seekers."

10. Design and code inspections were introduced by Mike Fagan of IBM in 1976 and have proven to be the most effective quality improvement technique in software development. The original article on inspections was in the *IBM System Journal,* vol. 15, no. 3 (1976).

11. Watts S. Humphrey, *Managing the Software Process* (Reading, MA: Addison-Wesley, 1989), Ch. 10.

12. Jeffrey Pfeffer, *Organizations and Organization Theory* (Marshfield, MA: Pitman, 1982), p. 51.

13. Priscilla Fowler and Stan Rifkin, "Software Engineering Process Group Guide," CMU/SEI-90-TR-24, Software Engineering Institute, Carnegie Mellon University, Pittsburgh, 1990.

14. Watts S. Humphrey, *Managing the Software Process* (Reading, MA: Addison-Wesley, 1989), p. 295.

24

Technical Assessment

U nfreezing a technical organization is particularly difficult for three reasons. First, the technical professionals and working-level managers are so busy they are reluctant to look for anything else to do. Second, operational inefficiencies seem so entrenched that people cannot conceive of fixing them. Finally, senior management is often unaware of the problems the technical workers must overcome to do their jobs more efficiently. Organizations thus often continue using progressively more outdated methods while their people work under severe constraints. This situation generally continues until some external event forces a change.

FINDING PROBLEMS

Dale Zand, a professor at NYU's School of Business, objects to managers who say that "I don't want to hear your problems, I want to hear your solutions."[1] In Zand's view, a major source of long-term failure is management's unwillingness to systematically search for problems. Many managers operate in crisis-management mode, concentrating on problems and solutions rather than thinking. They put out the latest fire, but rarely uncover the smoldering hidden embers of the organization's basic problems. In modern technology, problems are often symptoms of deeper ills. Managers who do not occasionally step back to think about these problems and to assess their organizations will be, according to Harold Leavitt's metaphor, "buffeted by the waves instead of making on-course headway through the waves."[2]

LOOKING INSTEAD OF REACTING

The objective of assessment in the change process is to systematically identify the deepest problems in the organization. Peter Drucker says that to be
a successful manager you should start out by asking yourself, "What are
the few things I can do…that would make a difference? If you do this, you
have a chance, if you don't do it, you have no chance."[3]

One of the best ways to do assessments is to ask the professionals in the
organization what they think is wrong and what should be done about it.
They generally know the problems very well and can be an enormously
valuable source of information. When approached in the right way, the engineers and scientists will invariably have many good ideas and be willing
to suggest some practical improvement steps. As John Gardner has said,
one way to ensure an attitude of continuous improvement "is for the organization to encourage its internal critics."[4]

SELF-ASSESSMENT

Gardner also made the perceptive point that "most ailing organizations
have developed a functional blindness to their own defects. They are not
suffering because they can't solve their problems, but because they won't
see their problems."[5] It is surprising how often the people in a large organization will be well aware of the key problems but do nothing whatever
about them. They may have a vested interest in the status quo, or they may
not think the problems are really very important, or they assume the problems can't be changed anyway. When people see problems only one at a
time, each problem seems fairly trivial, and it is hard to grasp their combined impact. Force of habit also causes a blindness to the possibility of
change. A structured assessment is often needed to break this impasse.

"There is always room for improvement," Dr. Arthur Anderson, a retired IBM vice president, used to say. He believed that every complex technical organization was necessarily out of date. Its structure, methods, and
even its people could never change fast enough to keep up with the rapid
pace of modern technology. Andersen addressed this problem by having his
management team periodically assess their own operations, identify their
key strengths and weaknesses, and then establish improvement plans.

A self-assessment takes a great deal of work, for it must involve the key
managers and examine all the organization's principal operations. The objective is to find and remove the major constraints on creativity, productivity, or
quality. At the outset many managers will object that they know their operations and that such a study would be a waste of time. Experience has shown,

however, that the people who object the loudest generally learn the most, and they then often become the strongest supporters of the assessment process.

The most difficult single step in doing an assessment is to actually get it started. Most managers will agree in principle with the idea but never find a convenient time to start. It is tempting to wait until the current crisis blows over, but we can safely predict another will follow right behind it. To really get an assessment started, therefore, the manager must make a plan, assign the right people, and set a firm starting date.

Assessment Guidelines

The first guideline for ensuring that assessment will be effective is to have the entire management team agree with the objectives and plan for the study. Next, the assessors should be technically knowledgeable and sufficiently independent to be objective. The process should be open and public, and everyone affected should know in advance what is going on and why. Otherwise they will likely be confused, concerned, and reluctant to speak out. Finally, management must agree to address the problems the assessment identifies.

Taking these steps and presenting the conclusions and the resulting action plans openly will lead to improvement in the attitudes of all the people involved. People like to be asked their opinions, and as long as some action is taken, they will think more constructively about further improvements. The positive attitude can be maintained and enhanced by taking action to address the identified problems and by following up the first assessment with another about 18 months later. If enough time is allowed for progress to be made on the prior problems, a second study will reinforce the improvement process.

THE SOFTWARE ENGINEERING INSTITUTE ASSESSMENTS

In the early 1980s, the U.S. Department of Defense became very concerned about the quality of the software work their contractors were delivering. The quality of the products was frequently so bad that major rework was required; contracts were generally late and seriously over budget. In one Air Force study, 17 major contracts averaged a total of 75% late. One 4-year contract was completed in 7 years.

In 1984, the Software Engineering Institute (SEI) was formed at the Carnegie Mellon University to address this problem.[6] In 1986, SEI launched a project to help the U.S. Air Force identify the software contractors most likely to deliver the highest quality products.[7]

The experience SEI gained from this project, coupled with earlier work at IBM, resulted in a framework and a procedure for assessing software organizations to determine their capability.[8,9] In principle, the method is to establish criteria for a competent software process and then to assess the software organizations to determine to what degree they met these criteria.

A key part of this method, a software process Capability Maturity Model (CMM)[SM], was developed by SEI to provide criteria for evaluating the quality of software processes.[10] An assessment method was also developed to guide organizations in evaluating the quality of their organization's software process.[11] Maturity models are discussed in the next chapter.

The Assessment Process

The first step in an assessment process is to obtain management agreement to do the assessment. This is probably the most important step in the entire method but is one often given inadequate attention. If the senior manager is not fully convinced of the need for an assessment and if the management team is not committed to making the resulting changes, there is no point in starting. Once the senior manager is convinced, it is not difficult to convince the rest of the management team.

Once everyone has agreed to the assessment and the importance of process improvement, an assessment team can be selected and preparation work begun for the assessment itself. The most important criteria for the assessment team are that they be knowledgeable in the key processes to be assessed and that at least some of them have prior assessment experience and training. The entire team can then be trained and preparation for the on-site period can start.

After training, the principal preparatory work is to select sample projects to study in detail and to identify the engineering participants to interview. It is essential that the assessment team talk to working engineers to find out what they do. They should concentrate on how specific projects were handled rather than what the procedures say or what the engineers intend to do in the future.

The assessment team should work by consensus and take the time to thoroughly review and discuss the relevant aspects of the organization's process. After completing the interviews and fact gathering, the team should agree on preliminary findings and review them with the organization's participants. It is next important to review these findings with the project managers to clear up any problems and misunderstandings. Finally, the

[SM] Capability Maturity Model and CMM are service marks of the Carnegie Mellon University.

assessment team presents its results to senior management in a large meeting attended by all participants. The presentation should make it clear to management and the participating technical professionals that their views and concerns were the most important single part of the assessment process.

The Assessment Questionnaire

SEI has developed an extensive software process assessment method and an assessor training program.[12] The assessment support materials include a detailed questionnaire that is based on the CMM model of the software process.[13] When they use trained assessors, organizations generally have very positive results. The key consideration in the SEI method is to recognize that the CMM model and questionnaire are merely aids and that the real assessment results come from the information gained and the attitude changes caused by the assessment interviews.

A common mistake of inexperienced or untrained assessors is to view the assessment process as data gathering. In one organization, before they had been trained by the SEI, a headquarters assessment group obtained an early copy of the SEI questionnaire. Rather than doing on-site assessments and interviews, however, they merely sent out questionnaires to several laboratories with instructions to complete a questionnaire form and return it. The results were then tallied and reported to corporate headquarters. The laboratories were so incensed with this approach they refused to participate with this headquarters assessment group on any process improvement work for almost five years.

An assessment is not a fact-gathering exercise. Generally, the engineers and managers know pretty well everything the assessment will find. The assessment objective should be to launch a process improvement program. The assessment then enrolls a large number of the organization's key people in the improvement process. The assessment team asks their views on the key issues and then presents them to senior management in a clear and compelling way. Typically, the assessment ends with a highly motivated group that is prepared to launch an improvement program. As one engineer said at the end of an assessment, "This is the best thing the company has ever done."

Confidentiality

Confidentiality is a crucial prerequisite for an effective assessment. Since the process is founded on trust, it must be done *for* the local people and not *to* them. The people most intimately involved should be the first to hear the results, and any reports should be designed to support and not to embarrass them. There may be differences in priorities, but the basic principle is that the local managers and professionals are as eager to improve their operations as are the senior managers or headquarters staffs. The assessment is merely an organized way to help them.

If the assessment is seen as a headquarters' attempt to expose problems, all doors will quickly close, and cooperation will cease. Although audits can be valuable in certain circumstances, their results are typically presented to corporate management and call for a public response. The result is often a defensive attitude, with endless debates over procedural details. For relatively standardized operations, audits can be useful, but they are of little value in improving professional attitudes or working methods.

Some steps that can be taken to assure confidentiality are the following:

1. Apply confidentiality at every organizational level. That is, treat problems as anonymous (although positive results can be credited to the person or team responsible).

2. At each reporting stage, combine lower level findings so that no specific project, team, or individual can be identified with a problem. Team data go to the team, project data to the project, and lab data to the lab. No reports should be made above the laboratory or plant level unless made by the local management team itself.

In spite of the need for confidentiality, it is necessary to make reports to higher management. After senior management has been exposed to and understands process improvement and the assessment process, open reporting is not usually a problem. At the outset, however, an average of all the results should be shown, with no one project or location identified. Describing many of the positive steps each group is taking will show senior management what is being done while it will protect local management's interests.

Avoid using a rating system, which invariably causes trouble, since some group will always come out on the bottom and management will insist on knowing who it is. Each laboratory or plant will, however, want to know how it compared with everyone else, which leads to a last bit of advice:

3. Preserve projects' anonymity by delaying such reports until a reasonable number of projects have been reviewed, and then the local projects can be compared to this larger, unidentified sample.

These cautions apply to reports by independent assessment groups. Line management of the assessed groups, however, is always free to report their results. In fact, after senior management becomes more familiar with the assessment process and its importance in improving organizational performance, periodic reports of assessment results and improvement status can demonstrate local management's interest in and emphasis on improvement.

Assessment Considerations

Almost any approach to assessment will work as long as it is professionally done and line management publicly supports it. Although few people will commit to action plans before they understand the problems, local management must have a positive attitude toward improvement before they will accept ownership of the recommendations. Without such an attitude they will not solve the identified problems and the study will be a waste of time.

Because word will quickly spread of any weaknesses or blunders, the first assessment in an organization is the most sensitive. Careful planning is necessary and a few rehearsals are often desirable. There also is considerable pressure from higher management for a summary of the problems and actions to be taken. Any leak of a critical finding, however, will invariably generate requests for executive presentations, action plans, and checkpoints. Local management will then know that the study was the source of these requests and conclude that it really was an audit.

Each assessment must be the property of the line organization. If they want to report the results to their management, the assessment team should support them. It is wise, however, to delay such reports until the managers have formulated action plans. Since senior management would rather hear of solutions than problems, a short delay is rarely a problem. If the action plan will take a long time to prepare, an earlier status report should be issued. The report should name a date for the improvement action plan.

Finally, significant organizational improvement takes a lot of work. Unless local management is truly dedicated to the task, little will actually happen. Most managers will responsibly react to their key problems once they have been identified, but some managers are so hypnotized by their current project demands that they are either unwilling or unable to make the effort. In these cases no further progress can be made until senior management takes steps to change their priorities.

CONTINUOUS ASSESSMENTS

As organizations gain experience with assessments, they should adjust the processes to keep pace with their needs. The first assessment of any laboratory or plant is generally a learning experience for everyone involved. It is also the point at which the organization being studied is most receptive. The organization's members have accepted the fact that they have problems and have agreed to an assessment; they thus are open-minded and relatively uncritical of the process. At subsequent reviews, however, the assessment team needs to be progressively more disciplined with their process, or they will lose credibility. Some of the key considerations at this point are the following:

1. When changing an area's rating from the prior study, base the change on specific identified differences. Management has often worked hard to make improvements and their efforts should be recognized; otherwise the assessment appears superficial.

2. If the state of the technology has improved and the organization is downgraded in some area because these new methods were not adopted, identify the omitted techniques and explain why they should be used.

3. Let project managers explain poor performance. When several projects are reviewed in an organization, the results are generally averaged for the presentation to senior location management. If some of these projects are different from those in a prior assessment, the organization rating may look worse even though the original projects may have actually improved. If this is the case it should be carefully explained at the beginning of the management review. Doing this, however, without appearing overly critical of the new project is extremely difficult. One answer is to have the manager of the new project actually make the explanation. This not only preserves the principle of confidentiality, but it also permits that project manager to explain in a positive way something that will ultimately become obvious to the other projects.

Even with the best planned assessment program, some groups will have difficulty improving. This is not because they don't want to improve but because they face some stumbling block they cannot surmount. Most projects are under intense schedule and resource pressure and have trouble devoting attention to the agreed-upon improvement programs. This often means that despite their commitment, action plans don't get done. One answer is to occasionally use the assessment specialists as a consulting team to work with the projects on specific improvement plans. If done properly, this provides graphic evidence of the new methods' value and convinces the project members to work in these new ways, even under crisis conditions.

Leaders of the assessment process must be trained and experienced assessors. Inexperienced assessors often view the assessment as a measurement rather than a change program. They thus concentrate on finding the facts about the organization's process rather than focusing on the critical views and concerns of the participants.

Another common problem with untrained and inexperienced assessors is that they are easily swayed by pressure from local management. For example, one organization was so anxious to get a positive assessment report that the local management leaned heavily on the assessment team. They thus gave a far more favorable report than was warranted. Somewhat later, when the organization was evaluated by a U.S. government agency as part of a software acquisition, the government's unfavorable evaluation results prevented them from getting the contract. Because of the earlier favorable assessment, management had not given adequate priority to process improvement and their organization thus did not meet the government's capability requirements. Incomplete or inaccurate assessment reports will not, in the long term, help any organization.

IMPROVEMENT RESULTS

Since 1987 the SEI and teams it has trained have assessed many hundreds of software organizations. The results of this work have been truly astounding. For example, in one study of 13 assessed organizations, the following results were found:[14]

Yearly cost of improvement	$245,000
Years engaged in improvement	3.5
Cost per software engineer	$1,375
Productivity gain per year	35%
Yearly reduction in time to market	19%
Yearly reduction in post-release defects	39%
Business return per dollar invested	5.0

While these average improvements were impressive, perhaps the most important result is the change in the attitude of the engineers and their managers. As pointed out by numerous studies, the engineers gain a strong feeling of participation and ownership from the assessment process. As the organization works on improvement and as its performance improves, the engineers gain pride in their achievements.

NOTES

1. Dale Zand made these comments at a Peter Drucker conference in New York City on April 22, 1982.

2. Harold J. Leavitt, *Managerial Psychology*, 4th ed. (Chicago: University of Chicago Press, 1978), p. 306.

3. John J. Tarrant, *Drucker: The Man Who Invented the Corporate Society* (New York: Warner Books, 1976), p. 111.

4. John Gardner, "Renewal of Organizations," 20th Annual Meeting of the Board of Trustees, Midwest Research Institute, Kansas City, MO, May 3, 1965.

5. Ibid.

6. Neil S. Eastman, "Report of Findings and Recommendations—Software Engineering Institute Study Panel," Document D-49, Institute for Defense Analysis, Alexandria, VA, December 1983.

7. Watts S. Humphrey and William L. Sweet, "A Method for Assessing the Software Engineering Capability of Contractors," SEI Technical Report SEI-87-TR-23, Software Engineering Institute, Carnegie Mellon University, Pittsburgh, September 1987.

8. Ron A. Radice, John T. Harding, Paul E. Munnis, and Richard W. Phillips, "A Programming Process Study," *IBM Systems Journal*, vol. 24, no. 2 (1985), p. 91.

9. Watts S. Humphrey, *Managing the Software Process* (Reading, MA: Addison-Wesley, 1989).

10. Mark C. Paulk et al., *The Capability Maturity Model: Guidelines for Improving the Software Process* (Reading, MA: Addison-Wesley, 1995).

11. Watts S. Humphrey, *Managing the Software Process*, pp. 17–52.

12. S. Masters and C. Bothwell, "CMM Appraisal Framework, Version 1.0," CMU/SEI-95-TR-001, 1995.

13. Mark C. Paulk et al., *The Capability Maturity Model: Guidelines for Improving the Software Process*.

14. J. Herbsleb, A. Carleton, J. Rozum, J. Siegel, and D. Zubrow, "Benefits of CMM-Based Software Process," CMU/SEI-94-TR-13, 1994.

Strategies for Managing Change

CHAPTER 25

Organizational
Maturity

S uperior technical organizations combine many elements into a single effective whole. Capable and skilled members are trained and motivated and they are assigned to jobs that fit their abilities. Their management has a vision of the future and provides the leadership to inspire. This, however, is not enough. As organizations produce increasingly sophisticated products, their management problems become more complex. There are many examples of capable teams who have failed. Often these failures are not caused by a lack of creativity or technical skill but by an insufficiently disciplined implementation. As the scale and complexity of technical projects increase, organizations increasingly need to establish orderly and effective ways to manage their work. This is the principal reason to address organizational process improvement.

URGENCY VERSUS IMPORTANCE

There are so many aspects to effective management that it is impossible to address them all at once. The problem is that fast-paced organizations often generate issues faster than managers can resolve them. When choosing which important issue to address, managers generally end up doing those things that must be done immediately and deferring the others. Crisis-driven managers, however, are reacting and not leading. There will always be a next crisis, and managers who let the current crises control their schedules rarely learn to resolve problems *before* they become crises. Like any bad habit, crisis management continues until it is forcibly stopped.

Surprisingly, taking charge of priorities turns out to be easier than one might expect. While the crises must be addressed, most are not as dire as they first appeared. A surprising number, in fact, can be delegated to subordinates. An example was a policy crisis in a large international company. A senior manager in the European division called corporate headquarters for advice. A customer had asked for an exception to a long-standing policy and the manager expected trouble if he refused. Corporate staff reviewed the matter and was equally concerned. The corporate legal department then recommended a thorough study.

Before starting the study, the staff head called Europe to check on the problem's status. After some checking, they found that a copy of the original request had been routinely routed to an administration clerk who had handled it according to established procedures. He had sent a letter informing the customer that their request was counter to established policy and was refused. The customer had accepted this answer and appeared perfectly satisfied to continue doing business as usual. The crisis evaporated.

There will always be crises, real and imagined, and, unless managers make a concerted effort, crises will take all of their time. To meet their long-range improvement objectives, managers must distinguish what is truly important from what currently seems most urgent. Then they must make the time to do what is truly important. This and the next chapters deal with means for improving organizations. The objective should be to build your organization so it can anticipate and prevent crises rather than merely react to them.

ORGANIZATIONAL IMPROVEMENT

Effective improvement programs involve many elements. As noted in Chapters 23 and 24, the success of any improvement program is determined by the management team's conviction that improvement is important and by their commitment to accomplish it. Without this commitment, nothing will happen. With it, everything becomes possible.

Once process improvement has high priority, the next step is deciding where to start. In fact, once managers decide what to do first, the remaining issues become much more straightforward, like making plans, getting resources, and assigning responsibilities. The key is to treat the improvement job just like any other project: break it into manageable tasks and assign responsibility for each task. Then set completion goals and track each major task to completion.

THE ORIGINS OF CAPABILITY MATURITY MODELS

Capability Maturity Models (CMM)[SM] were invented to address the problem of setting short-term improvement goals. CMMs provide a framework for thinking about and analyzing the change process and they help establish interim plans and checkpoints. While CMM concepts have a long history, the Software Engineering Institute has refined them into a generally applicable improvement process.

In 1986 the U.S. Air Force asked the SEI to develop a way to evaluate software contractors to see which would likely produce the best results. With the MITRE Corporation, they formed a study group. Initially this study considered the differences between successful and unsuccessful software contractors. This led to a deeper study of the characteristics of successful software organizations. The obvious next step was to devise a method to identify software organizations that had these successful characteristics.

The study group hence developed a family of questions to distinguish effective practices from ineffective ones. Since the study group had a great deal of software development and contracting experience, they quickly assembled over 100 questions that would help to distinguish successful from unsuccessful contractors. The idea was to identify organizations that had used effective practices on prior contracts. It was felt that these contractors would be most likely to use these effective practices on future contracts.

While this was a useful way to evaluate a single bidder, the critical need was for a way to compare several bidders. Comparison was especially difficult because the evaluation procedure had to be usable by both contract and systems experts in the Air Force. While these people could be expected to have some knowledge of software, they would not necessarily be software experts. They could not, for example, be expected to evaluate and judge the relative importance of over 100 different items in a large questionnaire.

MATURITY LEVELS

The solution was to rank the questions in some order. Borrowing the name and general concept from Phil Crosby, the group decided to call this ranking a maturity model.[1] Rather than using Crosby's framework, however, the CMM levels were designed to progressively build a quality improvement system much along the lines pioneered by quality experts J.M. Juran and W.E. Deming.[2,3]

[SM] Capability Maturity Model and CMM are service marks of Carnegie Mellon University.

A total of five maturity levels were selected, with Level 1, the Initial Level, at the bottom. Each of the 100-odd questions was then assigned to one of the levels. Every organization would fall at the lowest level unless they met the criteria for Level 2. These required that the organization have effective project management practices, routinely make estimates and plans, manage commitments, and have effective quality assurance groups. If organizations could satisfy the criteria implied by a level of the questionnaire, they would be considered to be operating at or above that level.

Following this approach, the group completed the initial five-level CMM with a questionnaire and a technical report to help acquisition groups evaluate software organizations.[4] From this beginning, a family of assessment and evaluation methods was developed that has been adopted by many U.S. government agencies as a standard for evaluating bidders on software-intensive contracts.[5]

INDUSTRIAL ADOPTION

Because of the government's planned use of this evaluation method and because of growing industrial concern about the performance of their software groups, major U.S. government contractors started evaluating themselves using the CMM and the SEI assessment method. Their intent was both to improve their software capability and to better compete for government contracts.

From this beginning, an international software process improvement effort has developed. Many organizations have reported substantial progress in improving the performance of their software groups. As noted in Chapter 23, these efforts have paid an average five times return on investment and produced substantial productivity and quality improvements.[6] Largely as a result of these successes, a movement was started to develop maturity models for other fields. Examples of other CMMs that are being developed or proposed are systems engineering, software acquisition, integrated product development, people management, system security, and data management.[7]

WHAT IS A CMM?

A CMM is a framework that characterizes a process improvement path. It describes the key activities and practices for each level and establishes the goals the process must meet at each level. For example, a CMM Level 2 requirement is that projects be planned and their performance tracked against this plan. There are also other Level 2 criteria as well as criteria for Levels 3, 4, and 5.

Suzanne Garcia and others at the SEI have defined the characteristics of CMMs that might apply to any technical discipline. In summary, the levels are:[8]

Level 1 organizations typically do not provide a stable environment for developing and maintaining products. Overcommitment is common and cost and schedule targets are frequently exceeded by large factors. While Level 1 organizations frequently develop working products, their successes depend on the heroic efforts of project teams rather than on the inherent capability of their organizations. You might say that Level 1 organizations succeed in spite of their processes.

Level 2 organizations typically meet their schedule commitments, although their costs are not as well controlled. They have policies for managing projects and established procedures to implement these policies. Projects are planned and operated against defined commitments and all commitments are based on plans developed from estimates. The estimates, in turn, are developed using historical data on previously completed projects. All projects track their costs and schedules and procedures are established for requirements development, subcontract management, quality control, and configuration management.

Level 3 organizations provide stable and repeatable cost, schedule, and quality performance. They consistently meet costs and frequently deliver ahead of schedule. They have defined standard processes for developing and maintaining products. Resources are dedicated to developing, maintaining, and improving the organization's processes and an organization-wide training program provides the staff with the knowledge and skills to perform their assigned roles.

Level 4 organizations operate within predictable quantitative performance limits. They generally meet or exceed defined quality goals. These organizations have established process measurements and quantitative quality goals for both their products and their processes. Productivity and quality are measured and an organization-wide process database is used to collect and analyze process data.

Level 5 organizations continuously strive to improve their process capability, thereby steadily improving project performance. They consistently provide world-class quality at steadily improving productivity. Product cycle time is measured and controlled and improvement goals are established and tracked. These organizations regularly identify their weaknesses and work to prevent their defects. Their objective is continuous process improvement.

CMM STRUCTURE

CMMs generally have five levels, with various key process areas (KPAs) defined for each level. The software CMM framework shown in Figure 25.1 has six KPAs at Level 2.[9] For each KPA, goals are defined and activities given as examples of how to satisfy each goal. For each activity, various practices are described as more refined examples of how the activity might be performed.

Common features are also identified as indicators of how thoroughly each activity has been institutionalized. Examples are the organization's commitment and ability to perform the activity. Measurements and verification steps are suggested to determine whether the work is consistently performed and whether it meets the goals.

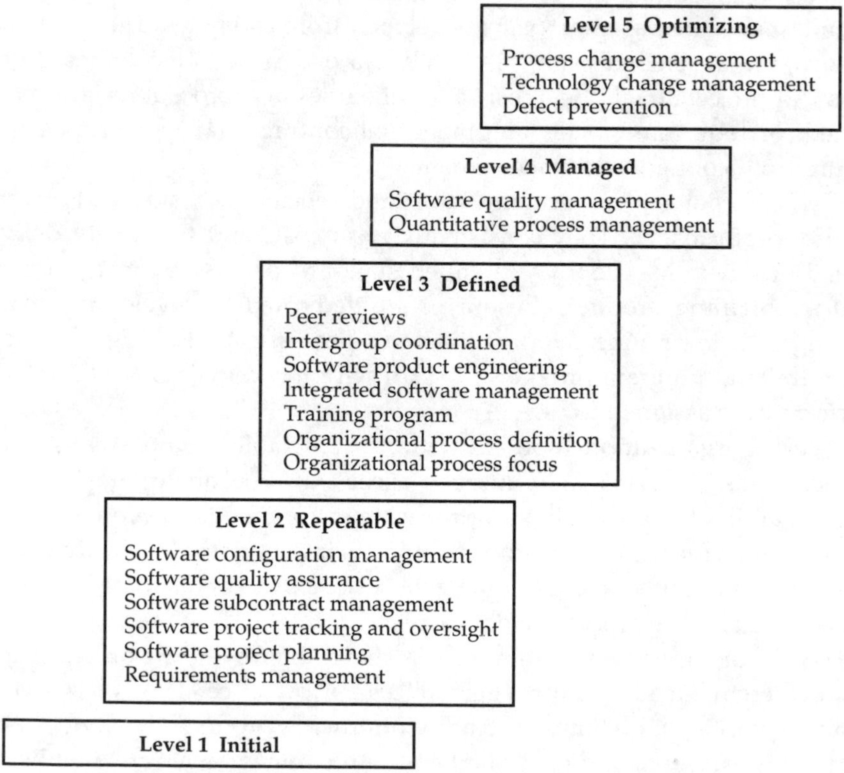

Level 5 Optimizing

Process change management
Technology change management
Defect prevention

Level 4 Managed

Software quality management
Quantitative process management

Level 3 Defined

Peer reviews
Intergroup coordination
Software product engineering
Integrated software management
Training program
Organizational process definition
Organizational process focus

Level 2 Repeatable

Software configuration management
Software quality assurance
Software subcontract management
Software project tracking and oversight
Software project planning
Requirements management

Level 1 Initial

Figure 25.1   The Software Capability Maturity Model

SOFTWARE PROCESS IMPROVEMENT

The principal objective of the software CMM is to guide organizations in improving their performance. While U.S. government procurement provided the original impetus for CMM development, it was recognized that customer demand would provide the strongest possible motivation for supplier process improvement. This was particularly important in software because the vast majority of all software organizations were found to be at Level 1. The pervasiveness of Level 1 behavior, in fact, originally motivated the U.S. Department of Defense to establish the SEI.[10] Although it was important to pick the best supplier for each contract, the government was much more interested in improving the capability of all its suppliers.

WHY MATURITY MODELS WORK

As noted in Chapter 24, the CMM and the SEI software assessment process have proven to be very effective in helping organizations improve their software capability. A principal reason that CMMs are so helpful is that they provide a common language for organizational problems and a vision of what the organization could be like in the future. CMMs help organizations evaluate themselves and they assist in setting improvement priorities. CMMs also provide improvement goals and guidelines rather than merely prescriptions.

Communication

A principal problem in technical organizations is the inability of the technical professionals to communicate with their managers and executives. The professionals see the organization from the bottom and are most concerned with operational problems. The executives, on the other hand, see the organization as an entity. They think in terms of products, financial measures, and productivity. This lack of a common framework often results in a communication breakdown. When executives do not understand the working-level problems, product quality and responsiveness suffer. When the technical people do not understand management's priorities, they are confused and less likely to be fully productive. They may even work on the wrong problems.

In one example of the communication power of the CMM, Girish Seshagiri, the CEO of Advanced Information Services, heard about the software CMM at a management meeting. He bought a book on the subject and gave copies to every member of his technical staff.[11] This provided a common terminology for discussing organization problems and agreeing on improvement priorities. In the next few months, all members of the 35-person technical staff submitted dozens of improvement suggestions. The next year, for the first time in seven years, the organization met its business plan.

A Vision of the Future

As discussed in Chapter 22, part of the unfreezing process is providing a vision of the improved organization. For software engineering, the software CMM provides such a vision. It characterizes the properties of capable organizations and it shows how such processes can actually work. As highly mature organizations publicize their process improvement results, this will help to make this improvement vision more explicit.[12–15]

Defining Process Strengths and Weaknesses

A principal objective of the assessment process described in Chapter 23 is to determine the organization's current status and key problems. The CMM helps to do this by providing a measurement yardstick. The assessment team can then determine which CMM goals the organization's process meets. Besides suggesting the organization's level of maturity, this identifies the organization's strengths and weaknesses.

The assessment capability has proven so useful that a small industry has developed to provide software process assessments on a commercial basis. Many software assessors who have been trained by SEI now conduct client assessments for a fee. This has relieved organizations of the need to train their own assessors and it has developed a pool of independent professionals to help organizations with their improvement programs.

The software CMM also provides a way to characterize the state of software practice.[16] Organizations thus have a tool for measuring where their processes stand in relation to other organizations' processes and to compare their improvement progress with their competitors'.

CMMs can also be used as guides for the improvement work itself. When properly developed, they contain benchmark practices that organizations can use as models. Showing improvement teams what practices others have found effective provides them a guideline on which to build their own improvement programs.

SETTING IMPROVEMENT PRIORITIES

A principal problem with process improvement is setting priorities. Organizations generally have trouble when they try to make too many improvements at once. When companies first decide to apply for the Malcolm Baldrige National Quality Award, for example, they often try to meet every one of the dozens of evaluation criteria at the same time.[17] While each of these criteria makes sense, they do not all make sense at the same time. Improvements have prerequisites and some will not be effective until others are in place and working efficiently. It is thus impractical and expensive to try to make too many improvements at once.

Every improvement costs money, so establishing priorities is a business necessity. Moreover, few improvements yield immediate benefits. Since it takes time for people to learn new procedures, the expense will be immediate but the benefits will accrue slowly. Until an organization has made a preliminary process definition, for example, a process measurement program would make little sense. This is because the measurements cannot be fully specified until the processes are defined. When organizations launch crash improvement programs without thinking through their priorities and prerequisites, they incur the improvement expenses with few of the benefits.

Another reason to thoughtfully set priorities is the need for demonstrable results. If, after launching an improvement program, people can't see noticeable benefits, they will not view the improvement program as helpful. It is then only a matter of time before they discontinue the program. By following a well-structured CMM, improvements can be planned in an order that is most likely to generate early and visible benefits.

The Improvement Context

Since most technical organizations have complex processes, improvement programs can only address a small portion of the activities at any one time. Most of the organization must continue working as before. This does not mean that the areas that are not initially addressed are not important, just that other areas need to be addressed first.

For example, in the software CMM, measurement is not an improvement focus until Level 4. This does not mean that the organization should stop or defer all its measurement work until it starts working on Level 4 issues. It merely means that the measurement program should not be a principal focus of improvement attention in organizations at lower maturity levels. If measurement work is currently being done, and if it otherwise makes sense to continue it, the organization should do so. For example, cost and schedule performance should be measured for projects even at Level 1 and inspection data are needed at Level 3. In the software CMM, for example, design methods, inspections, training, and a host of other activities are not addressed in moving from Level 1 to Level 2. If currently performed, however, these activities should be maintained.

CMM Goals

Most technical organizations have many more activities than can possibly be described in reasonably sized models. CMMs must thus be high-level descriptions of very complex real processes. A CMM should thus be viewed as a guideline and its goals considered as the key criteria. Other model elements, like activities and practices, should be viewed as examples and not prescriptions.

No maturity model can anticipate future technology developments and processes change far faster than any model can possibly evolve. As organizational maturity advances beyond Level 2, the technical professionals will have many clever ideas on how to address these new issues. The key again is to focus on principles and goals but to give the technical professionals considerable flexibility in how they address these goals.

USING CMMs

Several CMMs have been developed and more can be expected. CMMs have proven so helpful that every process-improvement program should use one if it can. If a CMM is not available for their type of work, managers have three choices: develop a CMM, abstract the useful parts of an existing CMM, or make the improvements without a CMM.

Developing a CMM is not a simple undertaking. It not only takes a great deal of work, but it requires considerable administrative support. To be widely useful, the model must represent the best available knowledge about the process and its application domain. This requires the involvement of key members of the potential user community. The resulting CMM will then encapsulate the best known practices from the entire community and is most likely to be accepted by both technical personnel and managers.

If there is no CMM for the organization's type of work and if the managers decide not to develop one, they can still take advantage of CMM principles. They should get and read copies of the available CMMs and take advantage of the improvement principles they embody. While they may not develop a complete framework of their own, they should examine the goals of their key process areas and see which can be adapted to their work. Then they can use these goals as guides to help improve their processes so they meet their organization's needs.

NOTES

1. Philip B. Crosby, *Quality is Free, The Art of Making Quality Certain* (New York: Mentor, New American Library, 1979).

2. W. Edwards Deming, *Out of the Crisis.* (Cambridge, MA: MIT Center for Advanced Engineering Study, 1982).

3. J.M. Juran and Frank M. Gryna, *Juran's Quality Control Handbook*, 4th ed. (New York: McGraw-Hill, 1988).

4. Watts S. Humphrey and William M. Sweet, "A Method for Assessing the Software Engineering Capability of Contractors," SEI Technical Report CMU/SEI-87-TR-23, Software Engineering Institute, Carnegie Mellon University, Pittsburgh, 1987. (SEI and CMU/SEI reports are from the Software Engineering Institute.)

5. This method is described in "Software Capability Evaluation Version 2.0 Method Description," SEI Technical report CMU/SEI-94-TR-6, June 1994.

6. J. Herbsleb, A. Carleton, J. Rozum, J. Siegel, and D. Zubrow, "Benefits of CMM-Based Software Process Improvement," CMU/SEI-94-TR-13, 1994.

7. Two of the efforts that have been published, at least in draft form, are the People CMM (CMU/SEI-95-MM-02, September 1995) and the draft Software Acquisition Capability Maturity Model, by Jack Ferguson et al., SEI, February 21, 1996.

8. This material is paraphrased from a draft SEI Technical Report on the Principles of CMMs by Suzanne Garcia.

9. Mark C. Paulk et al., *The Capability Maturity Model: Guidelines for Improving the Software Process* (Reading, MA: Addison-Wesley, 1995).

10. Neil S. Eastman, "Report on Findings and Recommendations—Software Engineering Institute Study Panel," Institute for Defense Analysis, Document D-49, Alexandria, VA, December 1985.

11. Watts S. Humphrey, *Managing the Software Process* (Reading, MA: Addison-Wesley, 1989), ch. 1.

12. Watts S. Humphrey, T.R. Snyder, and R.R. Willis, "Software Process Improvement at Hughes Aircraft," *IEEE Software,* July 1991, pp. 11–23.

13. Will Hayes and Dave Zubrow, "Moving On Up: Data and Experience Doing CMM-Based Process Improvement," SEI Technical Report CMU/SEI-95-TR-008, August 1995.

14. Dennis R. Goldenson and James D. Herbsleb, "After the Appraisal: A Systematic Survey of Process Improvement, Its Benefits, and Factors That Influence Success," SEI Technical Report CMU/SEI-95-TR-009, 1995.

15. Tom Haley et al., "Raytheon Electronic Systems Experience in Software Process Improvement," SEI Technical Report CMU/SEI-95-TR-017, November 1995.

16. Dave Kitson and Steve Masters, "An Analysis of SEI Software Process Assessment Results 1987–1991," CMU/SEI-92-TR-24, 1992.

17. The criteria for the Malcolm Baldrige National Quality Award provide useful guidance for any improvement program. Copies can be obtained from the National Institute for Standards, U.S. Department of Commerce, Washington, DC.

The People-
Development
Strategy

S uperior organizations have clear and well-defined missions. They strive to meet aggressive goals, and they capitalize on their members' talents. This chapter and the next outline management strategies for improving organizations. In this chapter, we concentrate on the workforce-management issues of supporting, utilizing, and developing people and what you the manager can do to address them.

DEFINING THE ORGANIZATION

Before we talk about improving an organization, we need to agree on what we mean by the word *organization*. In general terms, an organization is a collection of people engaged in a joint activity. There is a management structure, an identified leader, and a legal entity that serves as the employer of record. As used in this and the following chapters, the organization is the group, team, or corporation that you the manager lead. It could be a two- or three-person team or a 5000-person corporation. Regardless of the size of your group, your role as a manager is to use the available skills and talents to best address your assigned responsibilities. The previous chapters have discussed many aspects of the manager's job and this chapter puts them in a framework that will help you to identify problems in your workforce-management activities and to address those problems.

THE MANAGEMENT TEAM

If your organization has more than about a dozen or so people, you will likely have managers or supervisors reporting to you. Your role is then to use these managers to help you manage the organization. The management team is then you plus all these managers and supervisors who report directly to you.

Your first improvement actions should be to examine this management team. Do these managers work together effectively? Do they get things done? Are they making constructive progress or are they merely reacting to events as they occur? The management team's job is to take the organization where you lead it, not merely to administer it as it drifts from one crisis to the next. They must understand your goals, behave professionally, and be effective managers. Are you confident they can do this?

You cannot build a superior organization without an effective management team. If your management team does not measure up, you must make some changes. To do this, consider the following questions. Are the right people properly assigned? Are they tired, cynical, or stale? Are they striving to do their current jobs as best they can, or are they more focused on their next promotions? While it is desirable to have ambitious managers, it is essential that your management team know that their next promotions depend almost entirely on how they perform in their current assignments.

Managers should also be role models for the people who report to them. Do they plan their work? Do they set personal goals? Do they track performance and meet commitments? If the managers do not have at least as mature a process as their people, improvement will be painfully slow or nonexistent.

To fully utilize your management team, ensure that they own your goals and have goals of their own. Have them participate in setting the organization's direction and make them part of the improvement process. Ensure that they understand and believe in your vision for the future.

EXAMINING YOURSELF

Finally, ask yourself if you are behaving like an effective leader. Are you properly using your subordinate managers' talents? Have you given them challenging jobs with defined roles? Do you set aggressive goals and track them to completion? Ensure that your management team's responsibilities are clearly defined and then insist that they handle them. Stay out of their way but stay involved. Don't second guess them or do their jobs for them, but ask probing questions and demand results.

Most important, think about your people and what you can do for them. Do you give priority to recruiting, selecting, motivating, training, and developing your people? How often do you recommend your people for promotion? Are you grooming your successor(s)?

Even if your organization is too small to have a management team, you should ask these questions of yourself. As Socrates said, "The unexamined life is not worth living."

VALUES

In thinking about workforce management, it is helpful to start by considering your values. The workforce-management system, in the final analysis, will reflect the management's values. Regardless of what you say or the programs you establish, the values of the management team will permeate every action they take.

Values are hard to fake. Regardless of your words, your beliefs will affect your actions. A major automobile company that had long been losing money spent months negotiating a union pay reduction program. On the day the pay reduction was announced, management also announced a new executive bonus plan. While the employees had been willing to sacrifice, they expected management to do so as well. The company chairman professed surprise at the employees' anger. He argued that the increased bonuses were needed to attract management talent. If he had thought about the employees' feelings, he would almost certainly have anticipated their reaction.

To be innovative, engineers need to be operating at Maslow's self-actualizing level. They can't do this if they are antagonized or insecure. This suggests that your values include respect for the rights of every individual. You thus need to recognize and honor each person's individuality. To capitalize on your employees' ideas, you also need to give them a stake in the organization's success.

Consider the kind of organizational culture that would foster the behavior you seek. Then determine the workforce-management values that will foster this culture. What do you believe is important in a superior organization? What is the right way to treat your people and how do you want them to treat you? Try to put yourself in the professionals' shoes and think what would be important to them.

THE PEOPLE–CAPABILITY MATURITY MODEL (P-CMM)

Organizations are not creative; only people can create. To build an innovative organization, you must therefore be effective in utilizing your people. Thus, the first step in improving your organization is to improve the way your organization deals with its people. While this can be a daunting challenge, Bill Curtis and others have defined a People CMM (P-CMM) framework for this important task.[1] You can use the P-CMM framework to help you change and evolve your resource-management practices. In doing this, however, it is important to recognize that your personal priorities must change with the levels of the P-CMM. The next sections of this chapter outline these changes and suggest the strategic improvement priorities you should consider as you make these improvements.

Moving from P-CMM Level 1 to Level 2

Using the P-CMM, your first step should be to assess the people processes in your organization. Using an assessment process like those described in Chapter 23, you will get a picture of the people-management issues and be able to define the priorities for addressing them. Follow the IDEAL improvement model described in Chapter 23.[2]

Although you must still set and manage aggressive goals, the key concept of people management is to change the tone and attitude of the organization from a Level 1 focus on controlling and directing to a more mature attitude of supporting, enabling, and motivating. At Level 2, the need is to get management and the organization out of the way of its people so they can more effectively do the work they are capable of doing. The people must know and understand the organization's plans and strategies, and they need an avenue to tell management their concerns and problems. An effective recruiting and staffing program is also needed, as is a training program that supports the skills needed for accomplishing your mission.

At the Initial Level, or P-CMM Level 1, organizations lack basic people-management practices. To get to P-CMM Level 2, the management team must recognize that managing people is their responsibility. While the human resources department can administer the people-management programs, the line managers must own these programs and ensure they are effectively followed.

To get to Level 2, you need a fair and equitable compensation system and an effective communication program. You not only seek to communicate management's goals and objectives, you also need to provide explicit personal communication to each of your people. How are they doing and what do you think about their work? If you like what they are doing, tell them, and if you don't think they are performing properly, tell them and let them know why.

The principal P-CMM goals in moving to Level 2 are as follows:

- Foster an environment that supports the type of work you do.

- Provide the resources needed to do the work.

- Establish a two-way communication system that builds trust and shares information.

- Regularly discuss performance and provide guidance on improvement.

- Maintain an effective recruiting and orientation program.

- Manage performance problems.

- Recognize outstanding performance.

- Make suitable training available to all individuals.

- Provide a fair and equitable compensation system.

Moving from P-CMM Level 2 to Level 3

In moving from P-CMM Level 2 to Level 3, the focus turns to identifying and developing the core competencies required to meet the business needs. What skills are critical and where can you get them? Is the mix of talents and abilities right, and are your people thoroughly familiar with the latest tools and methods of their fields? Without a competitive workforce, it is hard for organizations to be superior, regardless of anything else they do.

Lest this be confusing, let me reemphasize a point made in Chapter 10: The key is to fully develop and capitalize on the talents you have rather than to seek geniuses from somewhere else. While you may wish to hire some people, the critical step is to assess the people you have and to establish programs to develop and utilize them to their fullest potential. Ensure that all employees have development plans tailored to their needs and aspirations. Also, seek out and develop the potential leaders you will need in the future.

Remember, for the organization to achieve its potential, you need to help every employee achieve his or her maximum potential. This will reveal a surprising array of latent talent. Also, by helping to develop the people, you will help them to help you. Surprisingly, when you have effective people-development programs, your people will improve and you will find it easier to hire talented people.

The principal P-CMM goals in moving to Level 3 are as follows:

- Understand and manage the core competencies needed to meet the organization's mission.

- Plan for and develop the people needed for the key organization positions.

- Build the future skills needed in each key technology and core competency.

- Support all the people in improving their skills and competencies.

- Support each individual's career development.

- Motivate individuals to improve their knowledge and skills.

Moving from P-CMM Level 3 to Level 4

In moving from P-CMM Level 3 to Level 4, the focus is on integrating the core competencies into business operations. You seek to match skills to jobs and to anticipate the competencies you will need in time to obtain or develop them.

Technical work often involves numbers of engineers and/or scientists working cooperatively on many interrelated aspects of complex jobs. Here, teams are needed and team performance becomes a key concern. This calls for a special management focus on the team styles and structures that best fit the organization's mission and culture. Team building then starts by providing teams with clear charters and granting them the authority to manage themselves. The objective is to develop, lead, guide, and empower effective teams.

At P-CMM Level 4, you also need to consider the effectiveness of the organization's workforce management. How effective are the various programs? How well do you develop and apply the talents you need, and how well do your teams perform? Establish measures for these items and track them to ensure you achieve the results you need for the organization, the teams, and the individuals.

At P-CMM Level 4, the key goals are:

- Establish a mentoring practice.

- Facilitate and support effective teamwork.

- Define, measure, and compensate team-based performance.

- Measure and track the development and performance of each of the organization's key competencies.

- Align individual, team, and unit goals with the organization's goals.

Moving from P-CMM Level 4 to Level 5

The move from P-CMM Level 4 to Level 5 stretches the entire organization. The focus is now on coaching and continuous improvement. At Level 5, the managers' roles are to act as coaches and to ensure that the professionals understand and improve their personal competencies. The managers must recognize excellence, know their people's strengths, and help them address their performance needs. The essence of coaching, however, is to motivate and to help each employee personally strive for excellence.

The focus at P-CMM Level 5 is on coaching, continuous improvement, and goal achievement. The key goals:

- Develop manager-coaches who measure and improve team performance.

- Evaluate and continuously improve the workforce-management practices.

THE EMPOWERED ORGANIZATION

As you build your workforce-management practices, you will both develop and empower your people. This enhances their performance and motivates continuous personal and organization improvement. Empowered individuals strive for excellence and seek to improve their personal performance. These are the kinds of people who seek opportunities for continuing education and who are willing to develop and apply the proven disciplines of their professions.[3]

NOTES

1. Bill Curtis, William E. Hefley, and Sally Miller, "People Capability Maturity Model," Software Engineering Institute Technical Report, CMU/SEI-95-MM-02, Carnegie Mellon University, Pittsburgh, September 1995.

2. Bob McFeeley, "IDEAL, A Users Guide for Software Process Improvement," Software Engineering Institute Technical Report, CMU/SEI-96-HB-001, Carnegie Mellon University, Pittsburgh, February 1996.

3. Guidelines for how to develop professional disciplines for software engineering are contained in *A Discipline for Software Engineering*, by Watts S. Humphrey (Reading, MA: Addison-Wesley, 1995). While this text applies specifically to software engineers, many of the concepts are applicable in other fields.

The Process-
Improvement
Strategy

ichael Maccoby of Harvard University has coined the term "tech-noservice" to describe the increasingly complex nature of many of today's high-technology businesses.[1] He cites examples of technical jobs that require extreme competence and a high degree of responsibility. Two of his examples are the nuclear near-disaster at Three Mile Island and the collapse of Mobil Oil's Ocean Ranger drilling platform, which cost 50 lives. In both cases, the people on the scene should have had the knowledge to understand the problems and the authority to take prompt action. As the subsequent investigations showed, however, those closest to the problems did not have the requisite ability or authority to handle the problems.

Fortunately, few of today's professionals face such life-threatening situations. Many, however, are currently involved in tasks requiring both technical competence and sound judgment. In these situations, management's traditional focus on end results is no longer adequate. Managers must be concerned with the processes by which the work is done.

For example, in integrated circuit design no one can tell with certainty whether the chip will work until it has been built. Since modern integrated circuit chips contain thousands or even millions of circuits, there are many opportunities for error. A design process that is merely good will likely contain many mistakes. Since any single mistake is generally irreparable, the chip layout and fabrication must be repeated. To save the many months of delay this normally entails, designers typically use disciplined design methods, standardized designs, comprehensive reviews, and extensive simulations.

With relatively simple technologies, each development step can be reasonably self-contained, and a good intuition is generally an adequate guide. With advanced processes, however, uncontrolled or ill-defined methods can cause expensive and even dangerous errors. Such errors are frequently undetectable until too late. Here, the manager must ensure that every process step is competently handled and that the combined results are adequately tested and verified. With each technological advance, it becomes progressively more important to insist that the job be done right the first time. This can only be done with a defined and disciplined process.

ENVIRONMENTAL DISCIPLINE

The purpose of process management is to provide the kind of disciplined environment needed for advanced technical work. For example, the proper conditions must be maintained in space-walking astronauts' sealed suits or they will simply not survive. Their orientation must be controlled, and special tools are needed to compensate for the lack of stability caused by weightlessness. Although these elements are all absolutely essential, none is directly related to the work the astronauts will do. Without this environment, however, they would be incapable of doing any job.

Many of today's newer technologies require a disciplined working environment. Genetic engineering, for example, involves the use of extremely pure materials and long sequences of complex reactions. High-energy physics, highly integrated circuits, and nuclear engineering also demand equally challenging environments. The list continues to grow. In high-technology manufacturing, for example, an uncontrolled temperature change, a drifting instrument calibration, or a fluctuation in raw-material mix will generally cause yield to drop. In high-volume processes, it is essential to correct such deviations before yield falls and costs escalate.

In intellectual processes like systems programming, many of the same principles apply. Here, an interface error, a lost test case, or an uncontrolled program library can delay detection and repair of defects, increase costs, and delay schedules. The methods of process management help control such problems by providing a precise and early understanding of what is wrong at a time when corrective action can be most effective.

THE POWER OF PROCESS MANAGEMENT

Some people object to the concept of process management because they incorrectly believe process discipline is only needed when the professionals are not sufficiently talented. With simpler technologies, some people could intuitively perform with the necessary skill and precision even without any formal structure and training. Unfortunately, no large organization can be entirely staffed with such talents, and even a small percentage of less gifted people will seriously damage any sophisticated but uncontrolled process. Further, many of the more sophisticated methods in modern technology simply cannot be performed by untrained and undisciplined professionals, regardless of their other talents.

An intuitive process is comfortable for the professionals because it allows them great freedom. Intuition, however, will work only within very tight constraints on skills and experience and then only when the organization is of moderate size and the technology is relatively simple. Even then, sustained advances in productivity or quality generally require an orderly process-management framework.

A statistically controlled and managed process provides a firm base for improvement. The people will more readily learn new methods and better retain this knowledge in the intellectual structure the defined process provides. Finally, a quantitative discipline also permits each professional to learn from the experiences of others.

THE NEED FOR PROCESS IMPROVEMENT

Even with very good people and in spite of management's best efforts to develop, improve, and use these people, organizations often fail to perform effectively. Generally, the reason is that their processes are poorly designed or inefficiently implemented. This chapter outlines a strategic approach to reviewing and improving the processes in your organization.

THE IMPROVEMENT ROAD MAP

Since the technologies of the future will almost certainly be more demanding than those of today, your organization must improve, at least in some respects. The need, then, is to define the improvements required and to lay out a road map to improvement.

As we discussed in Chapter 23, organizational changes must be gradual and they must start from where your organization currently is. Chapter 23 described how to do an assessment and how to use a CMM improvement framework as a guide.[2,3] In implementing the improvement actions, you will also likely find it helpful to follow the IDEAL improvement model described in Chapter 23.[4,5]

To keep the management team involved in process improvement, establish a steering committee. Have every management team member join this committee and ask each to personally own a part of the improvement strategy. Make it clear that their job is to obtain the staffing and to monitor the progress of the action programs. They are to provide the continuous management attention to ensure that the process-improvement work is vigorously pursued. By holding each line manager accountable for improvement results, you will ensure that they stay involved. This will also maintain a suitable priority on process improvement.

THE FOCUS ON PROCESS IMPROVEMENT

As your organization advances up the levels of a CMM improvement framework, your perspective as the organization's leader should change. For example, in moving from Level 1 to Level 2, your primary focus is on gaining control. Level 1 organizations are in perpetual crisis. Their work is unplanned and their people largely react to events.

When paralyzed by crises, projects continually miss their cost and schedule targets. Panic leads to mistakes and mistakes take time to fix. Even though there never seems to be time to do the work properly the first time, there is always time to fix it later. In Level 1, productivity and quality suffer and cost and schedule commitments are meaningless.

To break out of this panic-driven state, your organization needs sound practices and you must insist that they be followed. Efficiency will quickly improve and projects will start to meet their targets. The people will see better ways to do their jobs and organizational change will start to seem possible. As the benefits accrue, process improvement will be recognized as helpful and the people will be more willing to participate.

Unless you personally insist that sound project planning and management practices are established and followed, however, nothing will happen. For CMM Level 2, the principal process improvement goals are as follows:

- Define and manage project requirements.

- Only commit to estimated and planned work.

- Track the work against the plans.

- Insist that the work meet established quality standards.

- Maintain rigorous control over the products and product changes.

- Ensure that all your suppliers work to the same exacting standards.

Moving to Level 3

In moving from Level 2 to Level 3, the management focus turns to investment in process. Now is the time to understand which processes have worked and which have not. The principal investments are in codifying the organization's experiences in a defined process and then training people to use these processes in their work. By defining their most effective processes, your employees can capitalize on the knowledge and experience gained by everyone else in the organization.

The first steps in getting from Level 2 to Level 3 are thus to invest in process and training resources. The defined process records prior experience in a format the people can readily use. With a defined process, the people will anticipate problems and be more orderly and efficient in their work. The managers will learn to stop blaming people for problems and recognize that most problems are caused by defective processes.

If you are in the software business, establish a Software Engineering Process Group (SEPG).[6] The SEPG's job is to lay out the organization's processes and to gather the lessons from prior projects. These guidelines should be packaged in simple and easy-to-follow process formats.[7] If you are not in the software business, you should still establish a process group to perform SEPG-like functions.

Recognize, of course, that if you have several parallel process-improvement activities, you may want to have a common process group focus. There will be interdependencies among the improvement efforts for the software process and the engineering process. You should thus ensure that they at least work together, even if you decide to keep the process groups organizationally separate.

As the organization's leader, your job is to ensure that the required process-improvement investments are made and that an adequate number of the best people are assigned. Your principal improvement goals are now as follows:

- Establish a dedicated process-improvement activity.

- Establish a family of standard processes.

- Provide training in the common processes, tools, and methods.

- Tailor the standard processes to the needs of the projects.

- Track the projects' use of these processes.

- Provide means to coordinate the technical work across all the relevant project disciplines.

- Review product quality at every process stage.

Moving from Level 3 to Level 4

In moving from Level 3 to Level 4, your attention turns to process effectiveness and quantified process improvement goals. In establishing these goals, ask yourself what is most important. How do the leading competitors perform? What would a truly superior organization look like?

To be most useful, these answers must be specific. This takes data and measurement. A general objective to improve quality, for example, is meaningless. Quality goals without numbers are just talk. If you want people to act, you must use numbers. Define key organizational measures and establish goals for each. Allocate the goals to managers, to projects, and to teams. Then measure and track performance against these goals. Finally, make progress visible and celebrate each success. Continue emphasizing the importance of process improvement, and when each goal is reached, set more aggressive goals. This will keep the spotlight on process improvement.

As leader, your job at Level 4 is to ensure that clear and quantified goals are established, that they are related to important business objectives, and that they are directly coupled to the processes of your organization. Then you must regularly track progress against these goals. Some of the key process goals at this point are as follows:

- Establish measures for all the key processes.

- Use these measures to track and manage process quality.

- Establish goals for product quality.

- Track progress toward achieving these quality goals.

- Publicize and celebrate the improvement successes.

Moving from Level 4 to Level 5

In moving from Level 4 to Level 5, the focus turns to achieving superior business and technical performance. Look for benchmark organizations and send your people to compare your performance with theirs. Use benchmark candidates in your own company, in the same industry, and in other industries. Consider who might be best in each area and establish goals to equal or exceed them. Explicit quantified benchmarks will motivate a competitive drive to excel. When people can see a target they believe is important, they will strive mightily to reach it.

At Level 5, the leadership focus turns to achieving world-class performance. The principal Level 5 goals that will help you to achieve superior performance are as follows:

- Identify the causes of defects in process and product.

- Establish programs to eliminate defect causes.

- Identify the new technologies that apply to your business.

- Adopt appropriate technologies to your organization's processes.

MAKING IMPROVEMENTS

As you advance from level to level, your organization's capability will steadily improve. This requires, however, that you continue to perform each practice after you have introduced it. The best way to decide when to start addressing the next maturity level is to observe the way the people work. Once they have mastered all the practices at Level 3, for example, and these practices seem normal and natural, it is time to start working on the next maturity level. If, however, parts of the organization are still struggling with the Level 3 practices, take time to consolidate the Level 3 gains before moving on to Level 4.

The best improvement ideas will come from the working professionals. Since they understand the organization's problems, they will have many ideas on how to fix them. Seek their ideas and incorporate them in the processes. Demonstrate that everybody's ideas are welcome and that they will be used.

Once the people see that they can change the process, they will submit a flood of ideas. Most will be small and seemingly minor, but it is the details that make the difference between a convenient and efficient process and an annoying and error-prone one.

When a change is completed, it is time for a celebration. Let everybody know what was accomplished and make it a big deal. Ensure that there is plenty of praise to go around and make everybody co-author of the success. They should be proud to have had a part in the achievement, even if their roles were only minor. When everyone wins from process improvement, further improvement will become much easier.

NOTES

1. Michael Maccoby, "A New Way of Managing," *IEEE Spectrum*, June 1984, p. 69.

2. W.S. Humphrey, *Managing the Software Process* (Reading, MA: Addison-Wesley, 1989).

3. Mark C. Paulk et al., *The Capability Maturity Model: Guidelines for Improving the Software Process* (Reading, MA: Addison-Wesley, 1995)

4. Bob McFeeley, "IDEAL, A Users Guide for Software Process Improvement," Software Engineering Institute Technical Report, CMU/SEI-96-HB-001, Carnegie Mellon University, Pittsburgh, February 1996.

5. Bill Peterson provided a brief overview of the IDEAL model in *Software Process Improvement and Practice*, August 1995 and Charles R. Meyers, Jr., provided a somewhat more detailed description in the September 1995 issue.

6. P. Fowler and S. Rifkin, "Software Engineering Process Group Guide," Software Engineering Institute Technical Report, CMU/SEI-90-TR-24, Carnegie Mellon University, Pittsburgh, 1990.

7. Guidelines for how to develop simple and easy to use processes are contained in Chapter 13 of *A Discipline for Software Engineering*, by Watts S. Humphrey (Reading, MA: Addison-Wesley, 1995).

CHAPTER 28

Building for
the Future

As manager of a function, whether large or small, your responsibility is to provide superior products or services to customers. The customers may be external to your business or they may be internal. In any event, your principal focus must always be on meeting your customers' needs in a superior way. The people, technologies, and processes you employ are means to this end and you must constantly check to ensure that these priorities are clear to you and to your employees. Whenever some technology, process, or people issue takes top priority, make sure it is only temporary and that everyone recognizes that the mission is paramount and everything else is a means to this end. In this last chapter, we focus on your improvement responsibilities as manager of an organization.

CLARIFYING GOALS

The first step in a process-improvement program must be to clearly define your objectives. The purpose of the process, after all, is to do something, and if you don't clearly define what you are trying to do, you cannot define a good process to do it. Thus, at the outset, start by reviewing the objectives you are trying to achieve for the business.

Next, define success and agree on the long-term goals you will use to measure success. Ask your employees to help define these goals in terms that will provide them clear and meaningful guidance. Above all, don't define these goals in narrow mechanistic terms. Focus on your products and what your organization contributes to the overall business and to the society around you. What is your competitive uniqueness as an organization and what do you offer that no one else can? Identify your strengths and build on them. Also recognize your weaknesses and ensure that you have them under control.

DEFINING THE MISSION

Once you have clearly defined your goals, produce a mission statement. This will establish the context for the work. It answers the question: What are we trying to do? To be of most value, your mission should focus on both today and the future. This requires a vision of the future and a description of where you want your organization to be in five or ten years. While defining such a vision is not easy, you can't do it unless you try. The most important point to remember is that, unless you have a vision of the future, you cannot establish a strategy to get there.

In defining a vision, ask yourself, What will the future look like? What are you trying to achieve and how can you characterize it? You don't have to invent this vision all by yourself. Use the talented people in your organization. While none of them will have a crystal ball, they will have many good ideas. Challenge them to elaborate their views and to think in unconstrained ways.

VISUALIZING RADICAL CHANGE

The principal problem in establishing a future vision is breaking through current intellectual constraints. People can rarely imagine radical change. While it seems inconceivable that our familiar world could turn upside down, every so often it does. In 1985, for example, IBM's world was comfortably predictable. The company had grown at an annual rate of 10% or more for many years and no one could imagine that this growth would not continue. Within five years, however, IBM had the largest financial loss in corporate history. This once invulnerable corporation was struggling to survive.

Radical changes generally have clear omens. Later, the evidence seems obvious and you wonder why no one saw it. Often, in fact, the best-informed people have the most trouble seeing ahead. This is not because they don't have the imagination; it is a question of nerve. They just don't dare to describe a future that is radically different from what they know. They delude themselves that the evidence is wrong, and then they act on this delusion.

Radical changes, however, do happen. We often don't see them because we build ourselves safe and comfortable boxes. As long as we stay in these boxes, we cannot see even obvious trends. You, as the leader, must break these barriers and insist that your people look at the evidence. What would happen if current trends continued? What could change these trends and what are their limits? Ask your people to construct scenarios and to explore their logical consequences.

Next, consider your organization's future roles. What are the likely opportunities? Where could your organization fit in this new world? What will society need and what can you as an organization contribute? What uniqueness can you offer and what value will you bring to the new marketplace?

To build an innovative organization, you must ask these questions. You cannot settle for the comfortable view that the world will continue as it has. While your vision of the future may not be completely clear, it should provide useful guidance. Since the world will undoubtedly change, a strategy based on the present will almost certainly be wrong.

THE IBM HARDWARE BUSINESS

Another IBM example is instructive. As early as 1968, the trends facing the company were obvious:

1. The percentage of the customer data processing budget being spent on hardware had steadily declined from nearly 100% to below 50%.

2. Per dollar, the power of computing hardware was increasing at an exponential rate.

3. The size, complexity, and cost of programming support was growing exponentially.

4. While new computer applications were proposed in every field, programming was a universal bottleneck.

In retrospect, it seems clear from this evidence that computing hardware would soon be a low-profit commodity. That conclusion, however, was not even debated in IBM. The assumption was that rapid application growth would sop up all the available computing power. No one studied what would happen when the cost of the programming to run new applications dwarfed the cost of the machines themselves. The obvious conclusion was that the programming problem would become the dominant customer concern. IBM senior management, however, never seriously debated this issue. They thus missed the opportunity to establish a dominant position in the newly emerging software business and, ultimately, lost control of their hardware business as well. A lack of vision? Possibly. But certainly a lack of nerve.

THE THREE DIMENSIONS OF IMPROVEMENT

Organizational process improvement involves three thrusts: the technology, the work processes, and the people processes. It is important to recognize that superior performance in any technical field requires a proper balance of these three dimensions. While you may need to stress improvement in one area or the other at any point in time, you must maintain a strong posture in all three or your overall performance will suffer.

The Technology Dimension

The technologies pertinent to your business are largely determined by your mission. While maintaining a strong position in key technologies is critically important, I will touch only briefly on this subject here. That does not mean it isn't important. The subject is so vast and so specialized, however, that there is not much I could say that would be very helpful.

One general approach that I have found useful is to identify a few of the best technical people in the organization and have them form a technology council. Ask them to assess your organization's position in the technologies that are key to your mission and identify your important strengths and weaknesses. In doing so, have them consider such topics as resident skills, available consultants, training capability, laboratory and experimental facilities, suppliers, fabrication and pilot manufacturing capabilities, testing, trade secrets, and the patent portfolio. This can be an enormous undertaking, so have them lay out a strategy and a plan for developing a position and recognize that it will take some time. Also recognize that the technology will change as the assessment is being done, so this should be a continuing activity. Treat technology assessment as a high-priority activity, however, and monitor their progress at least once a month.

SETTING INTERMEDIATE GOALS

In improving your organization, the greatest challenge will be to make the first change. Once you have demonstrated that you can actually cause an organizational change, you will have achieved a key milestone. You will know what is involved and your people will realize that the process really can be improved.

Once you get started, all you have to do is to keep making steady progress. The most effective way to do this is define intermediate improvement steps and establish goals for each step. As long as your goals lead where you want to go, you just have to keep moving. A marvelous example of the way this works is an anecdote by war correspondent Eric Severeid about his World War II experiences. He described the enormous value of short-term, immediate goals:

> During World War II, I and several others had to parachute from a crippled army transport plane into the mountainous jungle on the Burma-India border. It was several weeks before an armed relief expedition could reach us, and then we began a painful, plodding march "out" to civilized India. We were faced by a 140-mile trek, over mountains, in August heat and monsoon rains. In the first hour of the march I rammed a boot nail deep into one foot; by evening I had bleeding blisters the size of a 50-cent piece on both feet. Could I hobble 140 miles? Could the others, some in worse shape than I, complete such a distance? We were convinced we could not. But we could hobble to that ridge, we could make the next friendly village for the night. And that, of course, was all we had to do.[1]

WHAT GETS TRACKED GETS DONE

Delegate as much of the detailed improvement work as you can, but personally track the critical items. At first, track progress every week until each key improvement action is staffed, planned, and capably led. Then move to monthly reviews. In these reviews, ensure that problems are identified and resolution responsibilities assigned. Ask for specific actions and crisp dates and establish a routine commitment tracking system.

As you delegate the improvement work, make sure your management team knows that process improvement is the line managers' job. While staff and support personnel can help, the project managers must make it happen.

Also remember that what you ask about gets done and what you don't ask about will likely be deferred. If, for example, you only ask about schedules, your people will believe that schedule is all you care about. They may grumble and grouse behind your back, but schedule will immediately become top priority, above quality, usability, customer satisfaction, and even cost. Thus, if you want your organization to maintain a balanced focus on all aspects of the improvement work, you must maintain this same balanced focus in the way you ask about their plans and projects.

JUST DO IT

One software organization started an improvement program with great fanfare. The director was an enthusiastic supporter and he ensured that all the right steps were taken. They started with an assessment and then began developing an improvement plan. Unfortunately they had no one who was experienced in making process improvements, but they put together the best team they could and got started on the plan.

While this was all very positive, the bad news was that the director was soon promoted and his replacement came from another location. The new man seemed very supportive and he asked many questions about the improvement plan. The improvement teams thus planned and revised and then replanned for a full year until this second director was also replaced. While it seems hard to believe, there were eventually five different directors in five years. When the sixth director arrived, she took one look at this analysis-paralysis and told the management team to stop planning and just do it!

While planning the improvement work is important, remember that excessive planning can be an excuse for inaction. When ideas seem theoretical or studies call for more studies, stop planning and start doing. The people will learn far more from making the improvements than they will from planning them. Press the managers to quickly complete the plan and move on to implementation.

Process improvement is a bit like riding a bicycle, skiing, or swimming. You can study it and talk about it for just so long. Until you start to do it, you will never learn how. By all means, study the problems and make plans, but set a time limit. Recognize that you can only learn so much by planning and studying, then you have to actually do it.

THE REWARDS OF LEADERSHIP

There are many ways to improve the performance of organizations, but they all involve better utilization of people. When they have the proper leadership and when they are properly trained, supported, and managed, professional people will often perform astounding feats. The key is their leadership.

The job of leading people has both obligations and opportunities. Among the opportunities is the chance to get ahead, be recognized as a superior manager, and earn a higher salary. It turns out, however, that these opportunities pale in significance compared with the thrill of leading a motivated group of professionals to accomplish a challenging goal. Being part of such an endeavor and having the opportunity to help people to produce at their very best is among the most rewarding experiences one can have.

The obligation that goes with this opportunity is to do your utmost to develop and support your people. I have written in these pages what I could glean from nearly 50 years of experience in managing technical professionals. There is, however, much left to learn. Every time I work with a new group, I learn something new. The principal obligation of leadership is to both lead your people and learn from them. Observe them and think about their needs. Constantly strive to improve the way you lead and concentrate on being more of a coach and leader than a manager.

The real thrill of leadership is discovering that you really need to do very little managing. When people are motivated and properly led, they will generally manage themselves. Your job is to manage yourself so you will be a truly superior leader.

NOTE

1. Eric Severeid, "The Best Advice I Ever Had," *Reader's Digest*, vol. 70, no. 420 (April 1957), p. 140.

Index

M8373-TN
15